Dark Sound

ex:centrics

Series Editors:
Greg Hainge and Paul Hegarty

Books in the Series:
Philippe Grandrieux: Sonic Cinema by Greg Hainge
Gallery Sound by Caleb Kelly
Scott Walker and the Song of the One-All-Alone by Scott Wilson
Dark Sound: Feminine Voices in Sonic Shadow by D Ferrett

Forthcoming:
Black Sun, Lunar Dreams: The Music of Coil by
Michael N. Goddard

Dark Sound

Feminine Voices in Sonic Shadow

D Ferrett

BLOOMSBURY ACADEMIC
NEW YORK • LONDON • OXFORD • NEW DELHI • SYDNEY

BLOOMSBURY ACADEMIC
Bloomsbury Publishing Inc
1385 Broadway, New York, NY 10018, USA
50 Bedford Square, London, WC1B 3DP, UK
29 Earlsfort Terrace, Dublin 2, Ireland

BLOOMSBURY, BLOOMSBURY ACADEMIC and the Diana logo
are trademarks of Bloomsbury Publishing Plc

First published in the United States of America 2020
This paperback edition published in 2021

Copyright © D Ferrett, 2020

For legal purposes the Acknowledgements on p. viii constitute an extension
of this copyright page.

Cover design: Louise Dugdale
Cover image © Bridget Hayden

All rights reserved. No part of this publication may be reproduced
or transmitted in any form or by any means, electronic or mechanical,
including photocopying, recording, or any information storage or retrieval
system, without prior permission in writing from the publishers.

Bloomsbury Publishing Inc does not have any control over, or responsibility
for, any third-party websites referred to or in this book. All internet addresses
given in this book were correct at the time of going to press. The author and
publisher regret any inconvenience caused if addresses have changed or sites
have ceased to exist, but can accept no responsibility for any such changes.

Library of Congress Cataloging-in-Publication Data
Names: Ferrett, D, author.
Title: Dark sound : feminine voices in sonic shadow / D Ferrett.
Description: New York : Bloomsbury Academic, 2020. | Includes
bibliographical references and index. | Summary: "This book examines the
concept of 'dark sound', a strand of contemporary music that links the ideas of
death, desire and violence with women's and gender studies"–
Provided by publisher.
Identifiers: LCCN 2019050932 | ISBN 9781501325809 (hardback) | ISBN
9781501325816 (pdf) | ISBN 9781501325830 (epub)
Subjects: LCSH: Music by women composers–20th century–History and
criticism. | Women in music. | Sex role in music. | Desire in music. |
Death in music. | Violence in music.
Classification: LCC ML82 .F49 2020 | DDC 781.5/9–dc23
LC record available at https://lccn.loc.gov/2019050932

ISBN:	HB:	978-1-5013-2580-9
	PB:	978-1-5013-2579-3
	ePDF:	978-1-5013-2581-6
	eBook:	978-1-5013-2583-0

Series: ex:centrics

Typeset by Integra Software Services Pvt. Ltd.

To find out more about our authors and books visit www.bloomsbury.com
and sign up for our newsletters.

This book is dedicated to Val, Antti and Sunny

CONTENTS

Acknowledgements viii

Introduction: Cosmologies of dark feminine soundings 1

1 Rewiring love-sick text and listening for the presence of the dark lady 31

2 At the frozen borderline of a music lover's discourse: The dark white voice 53

3 Open to the demonic: A sonic articulation of desire 83

4 The black hole song of unsounding mothers 107

5 Becoming-shadow thing: Chelsea Wolfe's heavy mourning dirge in dark times 145

6 Abject virtuosa, darkened virtuosity: Diamanda Galás and swarms of power 177

Conclusion: Of the refrain – Is the future dark? 205

Notes 220
References 225
Index 241

ACKNOWLEDGEMENTS

My sincerest thanks to the editors of the ex:centrics series Greg Hainge and Paul Hegarty who were incredibly generous with their support, feedback and ideas. I am particularly indebted to Greg Hainge who offered invaluable time and guidance. I am grateful also to Bloomsbury, to Leah Babb-Rosenfeld and Amy Martin for their help, to the copyeditor Rachael Harrison, and to the anonymous peer reviewers that provided thoughtful feedback on my original proposal.

Thanks must also go to the wonderful artist and musician Bridget Hayden who gave the book its cover.

I am grateful to the students who have, over the years, invested in the dark sound module, making extraordinary music and having the kinds of breakthroughs I had hoped for when writing it. It is a great privilege to teach and work with such brilliant musicians and in this regard, I would particularly like to thank Simona Jareckaite and Lois French. My deep gratitude also to all the academics, musicians and artists who participated in the 'Dark Sound: Destructive Pop Symposium' held at the Academy of Music and Theatre Arts, Falmouth University in 2015 and to colleagues based at AMATA for their support at crucial moments during the writing of this book. I am indebted to Helen Searle for her advice and guidance during the early stages of this book. My sincerest gratitude to the friends and academics who have encouraged and guided my work across the years and these include Peter Mills, Barbara Engh, Marcel Swiboda, Nicholas Chare, Sheila Whiteley, Shara Rambarran, Andrea Petch, Tom Attah, John Lynch, Johnny Halton, Leo Arvan and Erwan Durand.

ACKNOWLEDGEMENTS

In truth, this book began many years ago in performances and rehearsal rooms amongst artists and musicians too numerous to name and who formed the Leeds music and art scene. I must acknowledge these artists, that city and all the musicians I performed, rehearsed, recorded, danced, travelled and lugged equipment with. Of the dancers and the music lovers, Andy Moore and Veronique Bourcier had the best record collection and the best moves. Of the musicians, Vincent Lee and Chloe Jarvis provided me with the most blissful, funny, wild and beautifully dark times of my life.

I would like to thank friends who offered support and words of encouragement. My deepest and heartfelt gratitude to Benjamin Hannavy Cousen and Sharon Palmer Adcock.

To my mum, brothers, sister-in-law, nephew and niece, thank you for for all your love and the wonderful outdoor respites from writing.

Finally, this book would not exist were it not for the support of Antti Sakari Saario whose faith and love kept me going.

Introduction

Cosmologies of dark feminine soundings

In the beginning God created heaven and earth. Now the earth was a formless void, there was a darkness over the deep, with a divine wind sweeping over the waters. God said, 'Let there be light,' and there was light. God saw that light was good, and God divided the light from darkness. God called light 'day', and darkness he called 'night'.
(GEN. 1.1-5)

In the first book of Genesis, God's voice is memorialized as the creator of heaven and earth. His first speech act is to create light, and then, on seeing light as good, he distinguishes light from darkness and names them day and night. This distinction establishes the temporality by which the first day of creation is measured. It is only by the end of the third day's work that God himself explicitly mentions temporality in the form of day and night as indications of 'festivals, days and years', which he follows by making the two great lights of the sun and the moon set 'in the vault of heaven to shine on the earth, to govern the day and the night and to divide light from darkness' (Gen. 1.14-18). Before time, before day and night, the image of formless 'darkness over the deep' is accompanied by sounds implicitly caught up in the divine wind sweeping over waters. By the end of the fifth and sixth day, a veritable orchestra of sound occupies both day and night as the world begins to teem with birds, fish, cattle, wild animals. This imaginary acoustic image of creatures is the 'great animal orchestra of sounds' discussed in Bernie Krause's understanding of 'biophony' (Krause, 2012: 82–105). In the 1980s, Krause went on a recording field trip to the Masai Mara, Kenya, to capture soundscapes of the natural environment (which he would later analyse as spectrograms). During recording, Krause hears not cacophony or chaos, but creation in a 'highly orchestrated acoustic arrangement of insects, spotted hyenas, eagle-owls, African wood-owls, elephants, tree hyrax, distant lions, and several knots of tree frogs and toads', noting that each creature occupies various frequency ranges across a sense of temporal duration, producing a sublime score that would bring Krause closer than he'd ever been to the revelation of God's existence (Krause 2012: 84). By listening to and evoking the choruses and soloists of this vivid soundscape, Krause's description conjures an audio phantasmagoria of the Garden of Eden and the very first explosions of life soundings on earth in a dynamic arrangement of *glissandos*, choruses, solos, melodies, harmonies, rhythms, pitches and timbres, across dawn, dusk, day and night, composed by an unseen composer and heard by the first human audience on earth, Adam and Eve.

According to the Judeo-Christian Bible, God makes man in his own image and takes from him a rib that he shapes and uses to make woman as man's companion and helper. Despite the narratival progression of the story of the beginning of the world, indicative of a linear time logic that propels from the beginning of all things and towards a future (albeit one based on the eventual revelation of an apocalyptic end signalled by trumpeting angels), the focus of my attention reverts backwards to the timeless void before God spoke His primordial word, to the scene of darkness before creation. This darkness conjures a fantasy that I consider to be the very essence of potential, since it imagines a moment before the beginning of the world, before measured temporality and before the gender binary in which woman is figured as secondary to man in a hierarchal chain of all beings on earth: this is the darkness of the unknown, the not yet specified, the not yet imagined. In effect, the primordial fluid darkness is the degree zero of the void and the epitome of the unknown in advance of the narratives of creation and destruction. Far from being silent, it is from out of this darkness that dark sound emerges. The term 'dark sound' is not, strictly speaking, charged with the same force that the concept of darkness is loaded with in this creation narrative, although it is undoubtedly related to it. Dark sound is articulated here in relation to the principles of creation and destruction, the meaningful ideological distinctions between light and dark, understandings of time and space, and, as I shall argue, to the darkening of 'Woman', darkened from the beginning of the world onwards. Dark sound as a concept has two primary use values in this book, it speaks of at least two things at once. Firstly, dark sound conceptualizes what I propose is the cultural and historical darkening of Woman and the feminine, and the emergence of that darkening within sound and music as well as the discourses that ascribe meaning and value to sound and music in a wider cultural context. Secondly, and contrary to the confines and strictures implied by the first use value, the concept speaks to a potential for *something else*, an as yet unspecified way of being and knowing that can be imagined, explored and created in music and sound, so that, in feminist terms, dark sound offers a femphonosophy: feminist thought and wisdom that may be derived from sound and music. Moreover, this book seeks to offer a dark femphonosophy; a way of questioning and thinking about feminism through dark sound, because it is darkness that simultaneously speaks to that which can be learnt about the darkening of Woman and that which can liberate possibilities to move beyond restricted understandings of both the dark and Woman. The two values of dark sound intertwine, conjoined rather than opposed in music discourse and in the music practice of the artists featured within this book. To begin, however, I'd like to return to the beginning, or rather to the time just after the beginning of the world.

Eve's fall

Very early on in the story of creation and the Garden of Eden, a third darkness occurs that is neither the primordial darkness, nor the darkness of night, but the darkness of the Fall: this is the first metaphorical moral darkening of humankind. Having been warned on pain of death by God not to touch or eat from the tree of the knowledge of good and evil, Eve, persuaded by the serpent and enticed by the wisdom offered by the fruit of this tree, ate an apple from it and gave some to her husband, Adam, who also ate some. Thus, both failed the test of free will and God expelled them from paradise forever. The notion of 'the Fall' attributes the motion of falling to sin and punishment, for which Woman is made principally responsible. She is punished by God who curses her with the intense pain of childbirth and condemns her to suffer yearning for her husband, whom God authorizes to dominate her. In this narrative, curiosity, susceptibility to persuasion, the exercise of free will, transgression of God's word, the apparent acquisition of the knowledge of good and evil, and the inevitability of death all characterize a 'fall' principally gendered feminine as a result of Eve's actions. The narrative of her original sin precipitates a fall into a metaphorical dark that is the genesis moment of all humanity's pain, power, guilt, shame, hardship and punishment: in effect, the 'dark side' of life. From then on, Eve's fall implicitly legitimizes misogynistic discourses which attempt to essentialize the darkness of women and their predisposition to the temptations of evil. God punishes Eve for her transgression of His Word and so she must yield to her Husband's word: obey. If this is a story of the beginning of creation, it is also the beginning of a suspicion and hatred of women because it is Woman who has initiated the transgression of God's word via her speaking voice: a voice *with words*. After all, Eve's communication with both the serpent and Adam brings about the fall of mankind from paradise and enshrines a painful distance between God and Man until death, when, ideally, Father and son are reunited in heaven. In other words, the first woman on earth instigated the necessity of mankind's arduous journey back to the Almighty, because she was tempted, curious and because she spoke (a similar curiosity drove Alice down the rabbit hole to a wonderland of eating and drinking). After that, male voices and their communication with God occupy and dominate the pages of the Bible in a series of stories that coalesce into ideologies and histories which implicitly and explicitly contrive to regulate women's voices and movements, remaining suspicious of women's creative power and agency as affiliated with darkness and sin.

Mary Daly argues that the myth of the Fall of Adam and Eve, although largely portrayed as unimportant by various theological strands in terms of the social relationships between 'man' and

COSMOLOGIES OF DARK FEMININE SOUNDINGS 5

'woman', is, on the contrary, responsible for a 'malignant image' of gendered relations and female identities. She argues that the dark 'nature' of women is 'deeply embedded in the modern psyche' and is a myth of femininity that 'undergirds destructive patterns in the fabric of our culture'. For Daly, 'Literature and the mass media repeat the "temptress Eve" motif in deadly earnest, as do rationalizations for social customs and civil laws, such as abortion legislation, which incorporate punitive attitudes towards women's sexual function' (Daly, 1986: 45). In these terms, women are haunted by the shadow of a mythology that essentializes their nature as already predisposed to a dark devious morality that must be both punished and controlled. The two key areas of focus for this control are fixed on her voice and her sexual reproductive system. Both of the implied 'mouths' of that body which is designated 'Woman' lead to a darkness that authorizes the regulation and stalking of her acquisition of knowledge, her voice and language, and her womb as it offers the ability to bear life. The feminization of darkness and the darkening of the feminine produces cultural and social processes whereby women are encouraged and/or forced to internalize a legacy of patriarchal judgement and an inheritance of blame, guilt and 'sin' that they inherit through 'socialization processes', so that 'she' 'is conditioned to live out the abject role assigned to the female sex' and 'actually appears to "deserve" the contempt heaped upon "the second sex"' (Daly, 1986: 49). To interpret dark feminine sound (in music and text) is thus always already hermeneutic in that one must necessarily follow a religious logic to understand how, at the core of sin and darkness, feminine mythologies are inextricably linked to the material being of 'Woman' and her (regulated) vocal body at the site of her 'mouths'. Gilles Deleuze and Félix Guattari note the *theft* of the girl's body so as to fabricate opposable organisms and impose upon her an entire prehistory – which includes of course *her* original sin:

> The question is fundamentally that of the body – the body they *steal* from us in order to fabricate opposable organisms. The body is stolen first from the girl: Stop behaving like that, you're not a little girl anymore, you're not a tomboy, etc. The girl's becoming is stolen first, in order to impose a history, or prehistory, upon her. The boy's turn comes next, but it is by using the girl as an example, by pointing to the girl as the object of his desire, that an

opposed organism, a dominate history is fabricated for him too. The girl is the first victim, but she must also serve as an example and a trap. (Deleuze and Guattari, 2003: 276)

The darkening of the feminine and the first theft of the girl's body are themes that emerge as key moments in the cosmologies and epistemologies of Western culture and music discourse, moments that nevertheless fade like phantasmal chimeras in subtle discursive processes of erasure. Part of this book is dedicated to revealing and retracing in music and music discourse the historical, cultural and ongoing darkening of the feminine that has served as the foundations upon which 'Woman' is constructed, a figure who serves as an 'example' and 'trap' for 'Man'. Imagine the ominous sound of the fall of Eve. The sound of her fall does not necessarily have an impact sound in that there is no 'big bang' body slam thud as she hits the ground. Instead, as representative of 'Woman', Eve's fall is the darkening and fall of all women in the cultural equivalent of an everlasting, descending Shepard tone, spiralling downwards forever. Whilst 'Woman' falls and falls, like Alice perpetually tumbling down the rabbit hole, 'Man' is also caught up in the implications of the fall and out of grace with his Father, the Almighty. In terms of sound and music, his concomitant post-fall suspicion of 'Woman' translates into a suspicion of women's voices and music, so that he becomes enmeshed in a cultural and historical tension between the desire to be moved by music, and the threat that music effectively effeminizes by eliciting emotional and affective responses that are contrary to legitimate rule and power, properly fathered.

Between revulsion and desire: Man's struggle

Heartbreak, shivers, tears, goose pimples, hair standing on end, these are the psychosomatic polygamous partners of loss, rage, violence, melancholy, grief, fear, lust and desire, all emotive affectations sensed as 'dark' and underpinned by the assumption that human life has a 'dark side'. Music, charged with the role of expression, in possession of physiological effects, and loaded with notions of catharsis and pathos, is accorded a dark side which parallels that of

COSMOLOGIES OF DARK FEMININE SOUNDINGS 7

human life. Tears falling and skin raising, darkness manifests itself in the erections and depressions that move within an internalized subjectivity and across the surfaces of the body, apparently finding 'expressive outlets' through making, dancing and listening to music, as well as taking advantage of the inlets of music's arresting ability to enter bodies: *moving* you. Music's power has been perceived through encounters with thresholds of possibilities, posing metaphysical and ontological questions to do with being, space and time, prompting philosophical theorization and mathematical calculation on the relationship between senses, pitch vibrations and celestial sounds as they reverberate with the harmony of the cosmos (Pythagoras's 'Music of the Spheres'). This divine cosmic power intersects with mystic speculation on the Dionysian propensity of music to channel disruption and dissonance, particularly during the Middle Ages and its belief in the *diabolus in musica*, as embodied in the so called 'devil's tritone' which negates 'a sense of modal or tonal stability' (Scott, 2003: 130). As Christopher Partridge has discussed, manifestations of this 'Dionysian excess' and 'Luciferian energy' have continued in abundance in popular music in its broadest sense, particularly since the 1960s (Partridge, 2016: 509–30).[1] That music has elicited such interests and investments is testimony to the kinds of thresholds of understanding and experience that are tussled with in the writing and voices of music lovers who attempt to talk about encountering and/or transgressing a limit, whether that be the ineffable limits of language or social taboos, having been carried by sound into heaven or hell, into the oblivion, ecstasies, bliss, *jouissance*, cosmic connections, erotic and sensual pleasures of music. The power and potential sensuality of music performance has been recognized, theorized, repressed and harnessed across centuries of Western discourse in religion, politics and philosophy where, broadly speaking, music and singing are presented as that which have an alarmingly paradoxical presence: in the same breath, music can both heal and cause pain; conform to, exercise and subvert dominant ideologies; destroy and create; torment and console; generate peace and arouse violence; provoke an epiphany and dull the critical senses into stupor. Historically, prominent philosophers such as Plato and later, Augustine, advised ideological regulation and the means of control over threats presented by music and its effect (and affects) on institutional subjects, insisting on the dangers of certain sounds, music and instruments in terms of transgression of law (music could be exploited by the Devil). Theodor Adorno of the Frankfurt School, from a notably different critical, temporal and cultural perspective, famously links the threat of fascist ideologies with cults of popular music and argued that the popular music consumer can be divided into two socio-political types of behaviour – the 'rhythmically obedient' or 'emotional' type. Of the 'rhythmically obedient' type, he writes:

> They are most susceptible to a process of masochistic adjustment to authoritarian collectivism. The type is not restricted to any one political attitude [...] repression and crowd mindedness overtake followers of both trends [...] as the standardized meter of dance music and of marching suggests the coordinated battalions of a mechanical collectivity, obedience to this rhythm by overcoming the responding individuals leads them to conceive of themselves as agglutinized with the untold millions of the meek who must be similarly overcome. Thus do the obedient inherit the earth. (Adorno, cited in Rietveld, 1998: 257)

Adorno's views on popular music (considered by Rietveld in the context of repetitive beats and the dance music of the politicized free party rave scene of the 1990s in the UK) extend and elaborate on the anxiety around the potential of music to produce obedience, to homogenize and standardize. By way of challenging Adorno's disparagement of popular music, popular music studies, in particular as a multidisciplinary field, responds to, analyses and, in varying ways, nurtures an understanding of the resistant potential of song and sound as a political and social tool that makes meaning and produces affects, creating real, positive, tangible social change that moves against oppressive power. In turn, Bruce Johnson and Martin Cloonan's *Dark Side of the Tune* (2013) is an attempt to challenge what is presented as a general positivist propensity of popular music studies, through a series of chapters that study the ways in which popular music, noise and sound elicit and arouse violence: to this extent, the dark side of the tune is characterized predominantly by violence. Pop's dark side might also be considered through the cult capital, transgression and power of 'stars' such as that of the rock god who, as cult leader, is mythologized and idolized through repeated messages and mantras adopted by fans that financially and personally invest in individual and shared rituals and fantasies.

Rupert Till's *Pop Cult: Religion and Popular Music* (2010) analyses in detail what he describes as the implicit religions and cults of popular music, noting the repetitive brainwashing activities of the music industry, the establishment of 'ritualized activities', the use of drugs, transgressional sex practices and other cultic activity: 'Pop cults have often involved specific clothing that identifies members; suicides by cult members and/or leaders; and reverences to new forms of paganism including Satanism' (Till, 2010: 8). As Till also discusses, the delineation of dark sound across America and Europe (such as rock and heavy metal) is somewhat indebted to ideas about pre-Christian pagan history, as well as the demonization of African-American music, particularly the blues, which were mythologized as the 'Devil's music'.

In general, the paradoxes and potentialities of music have prompted, across epochs, a common concord around attributions of value via qualitative evaluations, dividing music and sound into moral and ideological principles through the concept of good and evil mapped across light and dark. As anxiety around sound and its political application and moral meaning or social value seeps and weeps across centuries of Eurocentric and Western music discourse, the imagination of the philosophical writing subject appears somewhat permanently beseeched by a shared fear that Man may be overwhelmed by violent and/or manipulative seductive sounds, producing involuntary actions and manipulating the body, soul and spirit of the individual, and of society. Under such circumstances, feminine mythologies are frequently deployed in music discourse to signal the dangers of music and sound. The seminal example of this deployment can be found in Homer's poem the *Odyssey* ([675–725] 2003), which describes the great adventures of the hero Odysseus who, amongst the terrible perils he faces, must encounter and sail past the Sirens. These are monstrous bird-women creatures who possess beautiful 'honey-sweet' voices which apparently (according to Circe) lure men to their inevitable deaths. Famously driven by curiosity and the desire to hear these voices, and with pre-warning from the enchantress Circe, Odysseus's cunning allows him to listen to the voices of the Sirens and experience an ineffable and aesthetic pleasure denied to all others on the ship, without it ending in his death and failure to return home. This heroic survival, and Odysseus's successful return having navigated the threat posed by Sirenic voices is a narrative that resounds across music discourse in representations that gender the irresistible seductive voice as feminine whilst precipitating a sonic gaze that fetishizes and objectifies voices and songs perceived as feminine, beautiful and deadly.

Wherever nervousness around music and singing (and the potential dangers thereof) bubbles to the surface of the text, the ensuing moral panic reveals the core perception of a vulnerable body, open and porous, unable to prevent itself from being 'touched' by music. As the discourses on blues, jazz and rock and roll have demonstrated, this darkened 'touch' may be gendered but also racialized and sexualized through the language of contagion and contamination. Centralized images of a strong yet vulnerable body are invariably gendered as male, and that which poses a potential threat (from the margins of this centre ground) gendered female, and this dynamic is underscored by the ambiguous proclivity for being physiologically, intellectually and emotionally sensitive to sound's 'touch' as it moves through a series of fluid waves across the body and into the open ear. In movements of melodic contours, music carries a risk of effeminacy that threatens by virtue of unseen fluid waves which materially and spiritually undulate against the foundations of Man, corroding the demarcated parameters that define and distinguish the Man of Faith (religion) and the Man of Reason (enlightenment). None of this anxiety, however, diminishes the attraction to music and sound but, on the contrary, only excites desire as it seeks to encounter the risk and adventure of tabooed voices, and of the eroticized, regulated threat presented by music, frequently represented in the form of the performing singer. In part, the superimposed seduction that haunts representations of female singers has to do with a historical reaction to, not only suspicion over, the powers of the sirenic singing voice, but also women's presence on the stage and perhaps the ideological assumption of what Jean Baudrillard referred to as women's expertise in seduction through sign and artifice (Baudrillard, 1991). Permeating music discourse, the conjunction between seduction, the feminine and darkness convulses with a highly charged resonance, amplified in performative contexts and accentuated when the locus of attention explicitly focuses around what can be seen and what can't be seen, what is lit and what is darkened. On stage, Woman is held in a locked gaze that has always already anticipated the condition of womanliness to be defined by masquerade and the tools and methods of veiling and revealing, located as her expertise

(Rivière, [1929] 2015). Her essentialized being is paradoxically a condition of not being, or at least ambiguity, since she is conjured through the condition of masquerade, veiling, mystery, artifice and illusion, all belonging to the realm of shadows and dark ambiguity. I wish to pick up on what I will propose is the historical and cultural association between Woman, femininity and darkness as it weaves between historical narratives and representations embedded within culture and discourse about sound and music. Far from being a peripheral topic of discussion in music, the gendered dimension of dark sound has had huge ramifications for the perception of music's social value, cultural meaning and, specifically, the ways in which the extreme threshold experiences of music and its transgressions have been conceptualized. The association between women and the dark has evolved and endured over time (pre- and post-Enlightenment), paradoxically accruing truth through what has been framed in culture as the inverse of fact or reality: myth. Through feminine archetypes and mythological figures such as the Sirens, feminine or rather feminized soundings are continually reinvigorated by the dualism of light and dark when it is underscored by the clever Odyssey-like navigation of music's charms.

Voyages into the dark

Journeys into the dark, and from darkness to light, plot a familiar series of points in 'cosmogenetic narratives' and the development of Western civilization (Bronfen, 2013). Within these narratives, the correspondence between light and knowledge develops as distinguished from the dark (and its partnership with the unknown) via notions of movement and specifically voyages through or into the dark. Elisabeth Bronfen's *Night Passages* (2013) navigates a series of voyages that she describes as the 'cosmogonies of the night', narratives that in Western culture, connect stories from Greek mythology, Judeo-Christian religion, Enlightenment philosophies and psychoanalysis across networks of nocturnal states and night-time fantasies. Generally speaking, these discourses invariably configure 'knowledge' in relation to 'diurnal' rationality, whilst the unknown/unknowable is conjoined with the darkness of nocturnal realms. Voyages into the dark materialize in the discourse on sound and music and intertwine with the dense tangled dark cosmogonies within mythology, religion, philosophy and psychoanalysis. From this inchoate blend, I wish to weave a text that formulates an argument that perversely privileges the feminine in terms of focus and potential, whilst questioning how the cultural and historical association between women and darkness bears relevance to music practice, music discourse and the complex ways in which women are marginalized in music cultures. I'm aware that the sense of voyage in relation to the dark is suggestive of a mapping project that recovers the marginalized; I'm aware also that the argument that women have been excluded is, by now, an exhausting truism of the critique of patriarchy. Nevertheless, inspired by stories of origins and creation, this book, in part, seeks to tenaciously grip on to questions of how and why women are edged to the periphery of music canons and cultures, perhaps even more so when those cultures are considered to be 'dark'. A related area of interest is the way in which mythologies of the darkened feminine emerge in music discourse when it attempts to speak of extreme, ineffable immersive, sublime, off-the-chart experiences. That is to say, the dark feminine appears to be useful to the conceptualization of threshold experiences in music and the borderline between what can and cannot be said. Seeking to trace the dark feminine and its use value at these thresholds, my enquiry is taken to the edge of patriarchal cartographies as they map light and dark across the psyche, the body, language and music, in passages to the furthermost regions. And so, the notion of movement and journey becomes important to the cosmology of dark feminine sound.

Sigmund Freud's psychoanalysis constructs theories of the modern self and the psychic apparatus by narrativizing voyages into the 'darkness' of the unconscious. This 'nocturnal side of the psyche' emerges and develops from a dark point of origin (which remains unknown and unfathomable) and holds within it the drives, desires, affects and impulses that are repressed from entry into diurnal consciousness. The darkest of these drives is the death drive since it 'compels the subject to move beyond earthly life and return to his inorganic origins' (Bronfen, 2013: 88). Repression requires that a continuous exertion of pressure is maintained to ensure the protection of the ego, but nevertheless these drives take shapes that press forward into the consciousness and become symptoms that trace the repressed and 'unpleasant desires' in the conscious realm (Bronfen, 2013: 88). That this dynamism between light and dark, the conscious and unconscious might be considered as a 'passage', is underscored by Freud's spatial analogies whereby the unconscious is conceptualized as an entrance hall in which 'mental impulses jostle', connected with a 'narrower room, a kind of drawing room – in which consciousness too resides' (Freud, cited in Bronfen, 2013: 89). A watchman acts as a censor on the threshold between both spaces, directing permissible and impermissible admission (Freud, cited in Bronfen, 2013: 90). As Bronfen makes clear, the spatial conceptualization of the psychic apparatus and the mapping of the psyche crucially involves a sense of threshold between conscious and unconscious, light and dark, and the interactive passage between them. According to the modern cartography of the self, acquiring knowledge of oneself and the Self requires crossing a threshold into a previously unchartered 'dark continent'. But, as Freud himself revealed, the mapping of the psyche depends upon a dark unknowable origin that cannot be jettisoned and a 'dark continent' that is femininized. He writes:

> We know less about the sexual life of little girls than of boys. But we need not feel ashamed of this distinction; after all, the sexual life of adult women is a 'dark continent' for psychology. But we have learnt that girls feel deeply their lack of a sexual organ that is equal in value to the male one; they regard themselves on that account as inferior, and this 'envy for the penis' is the origin of a whole number of characteristic feminine reactions. (Freud, [1926] 1969: 38)

Freud uses the image of a 'dark continent' to illustrate the lack of knowledge about female sexuality held by an unassuming 'we', a reference and appeal to himself and other (male) scientists of the mind: this 'we' in effect designates the voyagers. The notion of a dark continent sets up a threshold between chartered and unknown territories; beyond this threshold, the analyst imagines passages to the female mind and body conflated as the off-the-chart realm of female sexuality. Insinuated in the journey, as yet neither fully explored nor properly mapped, is the dark side of the psyche and the dark interiority of her sexuality, both of which imply a dark amorphous space. Freud goes on to translate his/the lack of knowledge about the 'dark continent' into a more prominent absence that is the lack of a sexual organ *deeply felt by girls.* This feminized black hole not only excuses a lack of knowledge, but also allows the analyst to stabilize a known home territory from which he intrepidly negotiates the edge of the unknown, at the very threshold of sexual difference (and arguably, the curse to yearn for her husband bestowed unto Eve by God morphs into penis envy and a lack for which girls feel inferior, as diagnosed by the psychoanalyst). Yet, if this passage into darkness signifies a negativized dark nothing, it is also the darkness that leads to gestation and the possibility of birth, of creation. Indeed, Freud links the first sight of the Mother's genitals with darkness and the fear of castration. Drawing on Greek mythology, Freud uses the decapitated head of Medusa to illustrate the horrifying symbolism of the female genitals, suggesting that on seeing the Mother's genitals, the infant boy discovers the absence of the penis (Freud, [1922] 2003). His terror on 'discovering' the threshold to this 'dark continent' is offered consolation through the possession of the penis and a 'stiffening' that reassures him of his possession.

Many of the narratives that establish links between exploration, movement and the dark do so from a real and abstract white patriarchal occupation of light as it circumvents centralized territories of being and knowledge, whilst simultaneously demarcating the realm of that central light from the dark unknown, rendered still and waiting to be discovered/colonialized/civilized and so on. Ranjana Khanna critically reads psychoanalysis as a colonial discipline that stabilized Western European male subjectivity in relation to a 'colonized, feminine and primitive other' (Khanna, 2003: ix). Of the 'deeply felt lack', Khanna writes that 'his lack of knowledge has been displaced onto her lack of penis' for which she must bear the shame (Khanna, 2003: 49). Khanna draws attention to parallels between Freud's female 'dark continent' and the legacy of metaphoric 'dark continents' as they reference Africa. Her critique notes the importance of the notion of a journey of discovery and of the 'Odyssean spirit' of Freud as a travelling analyst who excavates the unconscious and who, as an archaeologist, 'unearths the genealogy of civilization' (Khanna, 2003: 62). In this respect, she particularly foregrounds the construction of psychoanalytical knowledge and raises the racially-marked primitive figures of psychoanalysis as connected with the castrated feminine (Medusa and her 'tribal routes' represent one such dark primitive feminine figure). Khanna argues that it is within this metaphor of the unknown (the 'dark continent') where Freud's concept of Otherness is formed:

> Although the Other is not intrinsically racialised or sexualised, it does seem that travel and exploration are the instigators of a theory of the Other, and in this case, the Other of man and of Europe are constructed as inferior versions of this 'self', becoming self in a castrated form. (2003: 49)

Hélène Cixous's essay 'The Laugh of the Medusa' (1976) picks up on darkness as something that women are encouraged to accept as their attribute whilst being 'kept in the dark' about themselves by an 'enormity of repression' that discourages self-exploration. She argues that women are 'led into self-disdain by the great arm of parental-conjugal phallocentrism', made to be ashamed and fearful of their own desires, intellect and bodies, to internalize a misogyny against themselves and other women in ways that ensure the silencing and isolation of women. Cixous also notes the racialization of the 'dark continent' of female sexuality:

> As soon as they begin to speak, at the same time as they're taught their name, they can be taught that their territory is black: because you are Africa, you are black. Your continent is dark. Dark is dangerous. You can't see anything in the dark, you're afraid. Don't move, you might fall. Most of all, don't go into the forest. And so we have internalized this horror of the dark. (1976: 877–8)

Cixous urges a release from this entrapping silence and writes of the necessity to write, to speak, to write herself and women's bodies back into history and to perform a writing that inscribes femininity: feminine writing links with female sexuality and pleasure in ways that challenge the dominance of masculine libidinal economies. Later, Cixous urges towards movement, where women have been static, a movement towards the exploration of their own bodies:

> The Dark Continent is neither dark nor unexplorable. It is still unexplored only because we've been made to believe that it was too dark to be explorable. (1976: 884–5)

As Cixous notes and Khanna discusses extensively, journeys to the dark and the idea of its exploration conjure problematic and colonialist narratives inspired by a Eurocentric mapping of habituated known lands distinct from the unknown. One of the most famous of these adventurous voyages in literature is the journey described by Joseph Conrad in his story of a journey to Africa and to the *Heart of Darkness* ([1899] 2014). Here too, the darkening of the feminine alongside the silencing of women's voices interweaves with the racist discourse of colonial imperialism and a journey from Europe to Africa (in this case the Congo) in ways that inextricably bind constructions of gender and race to the dark.

Fascinated by the 'blank spaces' on the map

From early childhood, Conrad was fascinated with maps and in particular a region on the map marked as 'blank space'. In 1868 and at nine years old, Conrad decided he would one day travel to this mysterious unnamed and uncharted place. By the time he arrived in 1890 the blank space was named 'Stanley Falls', a part of the Congo aggressively colonized by King Leopold II of Belgium. Conrad's novella *Heart of Darkness* is based on his own journey to this dark space of his childhood fantasy. In variable contexts, both the author himself and subsequent critiques of the novella have noted the silence of women in the text and their seemingly liminal place in the narrative from which they are restricted access through limited roles and lack of intelligible speech (replaced to a large degree by obscure 'non-language'). Gabrielle McIntire has argued that the relative obscurity of women and their voices in the text, together with the territories to which they are aligned, morph into a darkness upon which the boundaries of territories and the whitened, masculinized movement between them depends, making of women in the text 'ghost-like, half-presences' (McIntire, 2002: 258). Within the text, female bodies are aligned with either Europe or Africa and they ensure a distance between different modes of being that are navigated and negotiated by the white European male traveller. This anchoring to a static space means that '[...] neither women nor Africans (regardless of gender) are capable

COSMOLOGIES OF DARK FEMININE SOUNDINGS 17

of leaving the territory that defines them' (McIntire, 2002: 263). The movement and trajectory of the European male journey relies upon an understanding of the territorial alignment of women with either Europe or Africa and their stasis: their inability to leave the territory ensures and defines stasis.

In the novella, an African woman is conflated with the dark forest and inscribed as a silent 'savage' body who is seen from a boat at the edges of the river. Described as 'a wild and gorgeous apparition of a woman', heavily adorned with glittering and trembling ornamentation, her impressive presence on the shore of the river coincides with the hush of the forest:

> She was savage and superb, wild eyed and magnificent; there was something ominous and stately in her deliberate progress. And in the hush that had fallen suddenly on the whole sorrowful land, the immense wilderness, the colossal body of the fecund and mysterious life seemed to look at her, pensive, as though it has been looking at the image of its own tenebrous and passionate soul. (Conrad, [1899] 2014: 93)

Sonically speaking, the alignment between the darkness of the woman and the soul of the land she embodies is continually reiterated via an alignment between the beautiful dark savagery of her body and an ominous 'unapproachable silence', a silence used to evoke both the forest and the foggy obscurity that haunts the river upon which they travel. Out of the silence emerge murmurs of indecipherable voices and sounds, which pierce and disturb the traveller from whose perspective the reader hears the shock of monstrous cries, piercing howls, wild roars, satanic litanies and drum beats, coming either from the shorelines of the river or the depths of the forest. Strangely, the 'wild savage' acquires an essentialized slow, becoming-imperceptible movement that is made utterly mysterious and, again, aligned with the forest, which, having ejected 'savages' on to the shore, draws them back into the depths via the inhale of the forest itself: 'I noticed that the crowd of savages was vanishing without any perceptible movement of retreat, as if the forest that had ejected these beings so suddenly had drawn them in again as the breath is drawn in a long aspiration' (Conrad, [1899] 2014: 92). From the perspective of the traveller, both the movement and sound of darkened bodies are apparently perceived as uncanny, chilling, wild, unintelligible and indecipherable, as the text works to construct and conflate the movement and sound of the static hushed breathing depths of the fecund forest and the savage and beautiful woman's body. All are witnessed, navigated and avoided from the perspective of a vessel sailing a waterway that leads to the 'heart of an immense darkness' (Conrad, [1899] 2014: 120).

Both the African woman on the shoreline of the river and the European woman who is Kurtz's 'Intended' are represented through an affiliation with silence and/or incomprehensible words. The white European woman in particular is aligned with paralysing irresolvable grief and falling tears as she, the Intended, mourns for the death of Kurtz and cannot recover. Marlowe encounters the Intended in a 'lofty drawing room' in which he waits for her to enter. The room itself is clearly representative of Eurocentric bourgeois feminine domesticity, of which the piano is a sign (the piano signified the wealth of the patriarch of the house and his daughter's skill on the piano is therefore his compliment, although, as confined to the domestic sphere, hers was always an 'amateur' performer status). The scene is described as such:

> The tall marble fireplace had a cold and monumental whiteness. A grand piano stood massively in a corner; with dark gleams on the flat white surfaces like a somber and polished sarcophagus. A high door opened – closed. I rose. She came forward, all in black, with a pale head, floating towards me in the dusk. She was in mourning. It was more than a year since his death, more than a year since the news came; she seemed as though she would remember and mourn forever. (Conrad, [1899] 2014: 114)

More prominently than the death for which she mourns, lingers her own death, between the cold monumental marble as it is associated with the sarcophagus-like piano and the pale face. She is dressed in black and evoked as a spectral figure that floats towards him at the twilight temporality of dusk. As he proceeds to describe the intensity of her sorrow, Marlowe apparently breaks with the relative silence of the occluded female characters and declares her intense need to talk; 'she talked as thirsty men drink' (Conrad, [1899] 2014: 116). Assured of her interlocutor's sympathy, the Intended's words are of Kurtz and his profound brilliance, but, as she talks, it is not the words to which the narrator draws our attention, but the sound of her voice as it resonates in this somewhat gothic scene, romanticized not so much by her amorous discourse as by an association between her voice and the sounds of nature, mystery and sorrow:

> She went on, and the sound of her low voice seemed to have the accompaniment of all the other sounds, full of mystery, desolation, and sorrow, I had ever heard – the ripple of the river, the boughing of the tress swayed by the wind, the murmurs of the crowd, the faint ring of incomprehensible words cried from afar, the whisper of a voice speaking from beyond the threshold of an eternal darkness. (Conrad, [1899] 2014: 116–17)

The nature to which the Intended is compared is altogether more gentle and pastoral than that of the beautiful savage, and her cries and silences, whispers on the wind from far away. Building towards an operatic vocal climax, the narrator discloses a lie to the reader and tells the Intended that Kurtz's last word was her name. On hearing this, the Intended reacts with a vocal cry:

> I heard a light sigh and then my heart stood still, stopped dead short by an exulting and terrible cry, by the cry of inconceivable triumph and of unspeakable pain. (Conrad, [1899] 2014: 120)

Her cry is the tragic death cry of a mourning lover, but one tricked into believing that her name was Kurtz's final utterance, when in fact the knowledge of what he actually said is kept from her but disclosed to the reader ('The horror! The horror!').

Off the chart: The dark cries and black holes of the feminine

The cry of the Intended can translate in sonic terms as a cry of jouissance since it tallies with a literary device that signals the limits of language, and the combination of 'the cry of inconceivable triumph and of unspeakable pain'. In effect, it is her triumphant painful mourning cry that brings us to the brink of what can and cannot be said in the text and so it is important that the voice takes off where words fail in the non-verbal, heart-stopping cry. Both women are aligned with their environment and both acquire a sense of sorrow and hushed silences, which are broken by non-verbal cries, and in the case of the Intended expressive of 'unspeakable pain'. Following Eve Kosofsky Sedgwick, Andrew Roberts argues that the frequent reference to the unspeakable and to the rhetoric of the unknown incomprehensible dark in *Heart of Darkness*:

> produces racist effects, since Africa, African people, and women are drawn into the symbolic black hole. [However] [t]he empty signifier is empty only in terms of the story's symbolic self – understanding; ideologically, it has a history and a meaning. (2000: 126)

Drawn into a 'symbolic black hole' (which ideologically, does have meaning) neither woman travels beyond their demarcated territories: the African woman hypersexualized and rendered savage in the narrative is mapped in opposition to the European woman and her monumentalized paleness – forever in mourning, socially dead and isolated in the cold, hard domestic sphere. At the apex of the darkening of the feminine, both femininities are divided between a wild and pastoral land, both are associated with sorrow and mourning, and both are constructed at the threshold of darkness where they are drawn into the empty signifier of the black hole at key strategic points of speechlessness, sedate or floating motion and vocal cries. As the absent presence, they cannot enter the narrative and are unable to truly understand the heart of darkness since they cannot travel or move anywhere: they are denied the knowledge acquired by white male characters who venture and communicate via intelligible language. Women remain indecipherable and incommensurable with the very notion of journey, as they are that which is to be known and conquered. Whilst African people and women are caught in an orbit of racist and misogynistic effects, the black hole of the unspeakable dark feminized cry is also the site of a potential reworking of dark matter.

Theoretical and practical alternatives to phallocentric discourse, and to the patriarchal territorialization and colonization of space, have to some extent privileged the cry that holds out the possibility of an alternative feminine language, space or domain. The female

COSMOLOGIES OF DARK FEMININE SOUNDINGS 21

voice in performance has been put forward by many as that which potentially 'defies the grammar of the patriarchal symbolic' (Diamond, 1999: 376). Others have heard this defiance explicitly in the 'scream', particularly when the scream or cry is read in terms of *jouissance*:[2]

> Screams work as linguistic signs having no particular referent outside the context in which they are uttered; the scream can be read as a kind of *jouissance*, a female body language that evades the necessity to signify within male-defined conventions and meanings. (Gottlieb and Wald, 1994: 261)

Jouissance, theoretically read through the feminine following Julia Kristeva's theorization of the signifying process, is delivered via the *chora* and the semiotic (the 'underside' of symbolic language). Present in the signifying process is a 'pre-linguistic stage of connection to the Mother', a pre-linguistic stage that allows the 'maternal' to become associated with the semiotic (Kristeva, [1974] 2002). The semiotic is in constant tension with the symbolic and is for Kristeva a site of creative and destructive resistance against the paternalism of the symbolic order. Yet the connection between the maternal and semiotic has been criticized by many feminists for its associations with irrationality, biological essentialism and the privilege accorded to the maternal, which, Janelle Reinelt argues, 'romanticises the masculine notion of sanctified motherhood' (Reinelt, 1991: 51). Put simply, the scream is heard to function as an expression of extremities, of feminine anguish, terror, or bliss otherwise unheard or unexpressed in the symbolic realm that tends to privilege a pre-verbal connection with the Mother and irrationality. The criticism often levelled at the 'scream' is that it may not 'avoid the necessity to signify', but might rather merely reinstate the supremacy of the symbolic realm by reinstalling its other: 'woman' – 'silent' and still not able to *speak* in the symbolic realm from a subjective position and/or screaming in affirmation of irrational female hysteria.

In musical terms, Susan McClary's analysis conceptualizes feminine excess and crazed vocal virtuosity as it occurs off-the-scale at the extreme higher end of the vocal composition, where others cannot follow in terms of vocal performance and technique. Her notion of feminine endings in this sense paradoxically implies no end and a kind of off-the-scale excess that, having transgressed over the edge of the frame, can't return home, as it were. The 'crazed virtuosity' of the operatic madwoman and her excessive coloratura is figured as both off-the-scale, and off-the-chart, dispersed across a darkened non-place that is the ambiguous territory of feminine vocal excess. McClary tracks the symbolic journey of Western male subjectivity through narratives of tonality and in particular the musical representation of feminine excess in dominant musical progressions that migrate through feminine passivity or madness, but always return home in resolving cadences. She suggests that the very notion of male genius depends on an ability to inhabit the excesses of feminine madness and hysteria, yet return to structure and regulation, bringing it home to resolve the journey. And this understanding of the significance of the narrative of a journey and controlled navigation is not restricted to music but extends to the history of the physics of sound as Tara Rodgers's essay 'Towards a Feminist Epistemology of Sound' demonstrates in her analysis of wave metaphors and maritime themes in late nineteenth and early-twentieth-century texts on sound. She argues that audio-technical discourse is infused with a wide-scale deployment of a 'network of analogies' linking sound waves and electricity to water waves and by extension fluidity to feminine corporeality (Rodgers, 2016: 196). Through this discourse, feminized sound waves acquire a dualistic function similar to that attributed to the cultural imaging of the maternal and of the sea, in that they are 'both form giving – enabling the very possibility of sound – and perpetually in excess of formal representation' (Rodgers 2016: 202–3). Navigating these turbulent waves depends on a detached subject who is able to observe and rationalize the feminized disturbance, its formlessness, uncontrollability and so on. Rodgers places an important emphasis on the requirement to 'observe' and visualize sound, comparing this management technique with Donna Haraway's notion of the 'conquering gaze from nowhere' as it 'refers to the consolidation of knowledge and power in those "unmarked positions of Man and White" that have characterized practices of scientific objectivity' (Haraway, cited in Rodgers, 2016: 207). Dark sound suggests the subversion of this agenda to navigate, control and prohibit the feminine, especially when those control mechanisms specify techniques that both construe and seek to regulate the 'formlessness' and excesses of feminized sound.

In search of Woman, women and the feminine

On a research mission, Christopher Cox's short essay entitled 'A La Recherche d'une Musique Féminine', places an emphasis on the question of feminine sound and asks 'Is there a musique féminine, a noise that can rightly be claimed as hers?' (2005: 11). He notes a number of different rock, punk and post-punk female artists, but eventually dismisses the traditionalist masculine format of rock and its 'rock fortress' in favour of the potential feminine domain he hears in experimental and electronic music. The sonic equivalent to Cixous's *écriture féminine* is located by Cox in the field of electronic experimental music, heard to signal musique féminine precisely because the field of electronics opens up a world beyond 'ordered and stratified' music domains. Therefore, the heterogeneity of sound offered by experimental electronic music is equated with something like Kristeva's semiotic, Cixous's feminine writing and Deleuze and Guattari's Body without Organs (BwO), in opposition to the formality and structure of music (its grammar), here paralleled with Kristeva's symbolic. His search ultimately leads him to a conclusion that draws specifically on Deleuze and Guattari's BwO and the broad range of affective relationships that can be brought about by transforming the human subject and music into a BwO which, as he says, first requires a 'becoming-woman' and thus a 'dismantling of the libidinal investments that characterise Man and Music as norms' (Cox 2005: 13). This means that women, never fully integrated into the symbolic or the norms of music, are pre-disposed to a privileged relationship with electronic music because of the sonic possibilities and approaches afforded by these electronic technologies:

> From this perspective, experimental electronic music signals the becoming-woman of music; and women have a privileged relationship to musical experimentation. Here, women do not follow but lead. And this musique féminine offers a glorious world of noise that is hers and, via his becoming-woman, man's as well. (Cox, 2005: 13)

No sooner than the placeless marginalized feminine apparently acquires a privileged sonic domain, she is obliged to share it with 'man' through both of their 'becoming-woman' in a route towards the BwO, led by women.

In terms of music history, the question of the whereabouts of women has been asked of various canons as they pertain to a broad range of classical, folk, popular, electronic and avant-garde music categories. For instance, and following the critical logic of Linda Nochlin's essay 'Why Have There Been No Great Female Artists?' ([1971] 2003), Marcia J. Citron's *Gender and the Musical Canon* ([1993] 2000) critically analyses the received canon of classical music and the ways in which canon formation and music discourse are ideologically constructed and strategically exclude women. Other key texts in this regard include Christine Battersby's *Gender and Genius* (1989) and Susan McClary's *Feminine Endings* (1991), both of which deconstruct the conceits of music discourse and representation to demonstrate how the notion of musical genius is the preserve of male ability and subjectivity. There is a growing body of research and critical commentary by writers and activists in sound and music, often musicians and sound artists themselves, broadly dedicated to a feminist critique of representation and issues of exclusion and which seek to redress a 'knowledge gap' concerning the work and impact of women in music and sound across genres (amongst them for example, Bayton, 1998; Davis, 1999; Downes, 2012; O'Brien, 2012; Reddington, 2007; Rodgers, 2010; Whiteley, 2000). Issues around gender identification, the label 'Woman' or 'female' are issues that permeate this discourse and elicit various strategies, particularly when considering a woman's 'voice'. Vocalizing and speaking 'as a woman' is bound up in a legacy of feminist theory that, in particular, foregrounds the significance of performance and voice. For instance, Joan Rivière's psychoanalytical study, published in 1929, suggested that 'womanliness' is worn as a mask, in reaction to the castration complex (Rivière, [1929] 2015). Womanliness as a masquerade is extended and adapted in the work of Luce Irigaray, who proposed that the excessive mimesis of the feminine might be adopted as a playful strategy in order to undermine the assumed neutrality of *Truth* and gender (Irigaray, [1974] 1985). Judith Butler's work on 'gender as a performative act' is less inclined towards the idea of volitional play and critiques the 'regulatory norms' of gender identity, insisting that gender is real only to the extent that it is performed. By foregrounding the 'performativity' of gender over its 'expression', Butler unravels the 'measures' of 'true gender identity' so that any notion of 'true or false, real or distorted acts of gender' may be 'revealed as a regulatory fiction' (Butler, [1988] 2003: 399). Importantly however, Butler is at pains to point out that there are repercussions and strict punishments for those who deviate from or contest the 'script' (2003: 401) and that, in fact, the performativity of gender should not suggest voluntary choice, but rather, repetition of 'oppressive and painful gender norms to force them to resignify. This is not freedom, but a question of how to work the trap that one is inevitably in' (Butler, cited in Kotz, 1992: 83–4).

Bearing in mind these differences in approach to what it means to speak, play and perform 'as a woman', Kimberlé W. Crenshaw's development of 'intersectional feminism' (1989) draws attention to the need to consider social stratification, discrimination and differences along the lines of race, gender, class, sexuality, disability, age and so on, complicating further the notion of speaking 'as a woman' and critically revealing the assumptions of various (white) feminist theories as reiterating the marginalization of black women, women of colour, disabled women, trans women and working-class women. Alongside important publications, writers and scholarly attention, dedicated networks and blog entries have emerged and evolved in ways that create network communities that share information and opportunities related to an inclusivity agenda and women in music, giving rise to (impermanent) groups which host and organize live and virtual events broadly categorized across performance, discussion, release and publication, music and sound technology workshops, with an emphasis on direct/indirect critiques of sexism in the music industry, and the promotion of intersectionality, diversity and inclusivity (OMNII, Her Noise, Ekho: Women in Sonic Art, Loud Women, Goldsnap, Women in Sound/ Women on Sound, Feminatronic, Loud Women, Women's Audio Mission, The F-Word, WITCiH, MusicTheoryExamplesbyWomen. com, The World is Listening, MzTek, Girls Like Us, The Girls Are, She Shreds, etc.). A common thread between these critical discourses ties together various critiques on the processes of 'gendering', such as the labelling of 'female' singer-songwriter, drummer, bass player, DJ and so on alongside a weighing up of the advantages and disadvantages of women-only festivals and/or the idea of compulsory quotas. In many ways, this growing body of work and the mass amplification of critical feminist voices on these issues, facilitated by social media, is energized by a crossover of interests (not unproblematic) in theory and practice, in academia, sound art, music, composition, performance, journalism and activism. To that extent, this work can be thought of as a diverse, matrixal movement with no central organizing point, connected through differing approaches to historiography and the 'mapping' of marginalized voices from differing perspectives, critically contextualized through intersectionality and social, geographical and economic privilege.

Direct challenges to male-dominated music canons reflect the importance of dismantling hierarchical structures and a reorganization of cultural and aesthetic value. Anne Hilde Neset's paper 'Tangled Cartography' ([2007] 2011), featured on the 'Her Noise' website, specifically critiques the dominant mapping of music and sound histories that have been presented in Western music canons, such as rock, classical and experimental music, in cartographies that pay allegiance to key male musicians within each field, ('Beethoven/Elvis/Beatles'). Noting the status of Pauline Oliveros, for example, Neset writes: 'Female composers are not so much written out of history as squeezed out of sight, in the hazy peripheries of continents yet to be conquered' ([2007] 2011). In her essay, Neset talks about how the Her Noise Map developed through a list of initial names and gradually grew into an uncentred rhizomatic mapping of female artists. She writes:

> It [the Her Noise Map] is incomplete, sprawling, non-hierarchical and with a spread energy. It doesn't have a centre, there is no nucleus. The map is in no way an attempt to define history or make a definitive statement. Omissions are admitted. The map gives, at a glance, an inroad into the hazy continent that is female experimental composition, punk, electronics, sound art, performance, and is there to remind how densely populated it is with female artists. We took perverse delight in making the links and groupings mysterious and opaque, but at the same time tried to use some sense in the construction. [...] the crux of the Her Noise Map is that it has no Jerusalem, no Beatles and no beginning or end. It doesn't have a story, it has a myriad of interlinking and contradicting narratives. It is a momentary snapshot of a pulsating labyrinth of women in sonic experimentation. (Neset, [2007] 2011)

This notion of being squeezed into the hazy peripheries by a dominant force and of mapping, exploring and colonial conquering is important to the conceptualization of dark sound and the ways in which, as I shall argue, female bodies and soundings are construed to signify both the shadowy edge of darkness, and the darkness of the unknown: the black hole. Important, because it underscores not only the ideological forces that err towards the erasure of female bodies from (music) histories or the higher echelons of musical value in hierarchal terms, but also how it anticipates the desire to territorialize the darkness that is the non-place nothing of the marginalized. That is to say, darkness in music discourse and aesthetics particularly, although by no means exclusively, has value in terms of the cultural capital accrued through 'outsider' narratives and 'cult' status. And this value of dark sound affixes itself so assuredly to maleness and masculinity as to suggest darkness is actually the domain of 'Man' as opposed to 'Woman'. Far from marginal in any simple sense, music's 'dark side' has developed a strong semiotic and affective cultural presence and the developments of these expressions (rage, violence, melancholy, alienation, addiction, eroticism) acquire a cultural capital and credibility that, despite the dark's historical and cultural associations with women, tends to accrue around a kind of dark sound canon that privileges masculinity. At times, darkness emerges explicitly like a word broken out of repressive bondage, as in Nick Kent's *The Dark Stuff: Selected Writings on Rock Music* (2013), George Lipsitz's *Footsteps in the Dark: The Hidden Histories of Popular Music* (2007) and Dave Haslam's *Life after Dark: A History of British Nightclubs & Music Venues* (2015), all of which are texts that appear to find in the word 'dark' (as noun and/or adjective) a useful connective tissue between language, music, outsider narratives, marginalized identities and subcultural scenes. I want to argue that the very notion of a 'mainstream' and an 'underground' with an attendant dark underbelly of subgenres, is experienced differently by female artists, fans and the feminized who operate in the shadows of 'mainstream' music cultures as well as 'underground' subcultures, who are in effect marginalized across the board in terms of (sub)cultural hierarchies bound to an ideological logic of what is valuable and authentic. Arguably, certain kinds of nods to 'inclusivity' agendas do not so much unseat the structures of power, but colonize and capitalize from a darkness that designates identities always already less than – in the shadows.

Herein lies the notion of the territorialization of the dark, as it instills a dark canon that perceives itself differently to the centre/mainstream and yet which is structured by the same occupation and rearticulation of hierarchal values and gendered principles that cannot but privilege masculinity, even if this privilege sneaks beneath the surface of a curated work made by women and/or 'marginalized' groups.

A rhizomatic non-hierarchal matrix of musicians who make dark sound forms and grows across the following pages. Amongst the artists whose work connects through these soundings are voices that seem to particularly imprint sonic impressions of dark themes onto the fleshy palimpsests of listening subjects, artists whose recordings and performances rise and drop to create the dynamic range of dark sound, among them: Nina Simone, Edith Piaf, Eartha Kitt, Diamanda Galás, Nico, Patti Smith, Grace Jones, Siouxsie Sioux, Kim Gordon, Cosey Fanni Tutti, Björk, PJ Harvey, Anna Calvi, FKA Twigs, Nadine Shah, Lingua Ignota, Fever Ray, Junko, Anna Von Hausswolff, Moor Mother, Savages, Pharmakon, Paula Temple, Bridget Hayden, Sharron Kraus and Mary Hampton. These artists offer a plethora of ways to conceptualize dark sound through music practice that embodies dark themes and aesthetics across a diversity of genre-hybrids and approaches. Far from considering this conjunction of the feminine and the dark as a pathology, these artists and musicians have deliberately situated their practice at this very juncture in a positively valorized aesthetic move that articulates and challenges how the dark is construed. Dark sound initiates enabling movements in a dark 'ex-centric' space between and outside mainstream and underground territories. Implicit within the critique of the mapping, journeys and canons of music discourse, these artists introduce an ambiguity of location – where does one 'place' artists who move in the shadows? This rhizomatic intersectionality moves away from the notion of centre/margins and towards a different comprehension of the potential of 'dark sound' to change what 'we know' about gender, music and the world. The case studies featured in this book position and direct the conceptualization of the potential of dark soundings as well as draw attention to the significance of raising darkness in an era increasingly referred to as 'dark times'; environmentally, politically, culturally, nationally and globally. 'Dark' and its synonyms have a seemingly endless currency as climate emergency is declared across the world and the flames rise, life burns and the land dries and dies. In these times, the 'dark' seems to proliferate across literature, film, media, politics, culture, as well as music, growing in frequency and duration as if, in an Attali-like economy of 'noise' (1985), the word 'dark' was a cry not only of the past and present, but a prophecy of the future. James Bridle in his *New Dark Age: Technology and the End of the Future* (2018), argues that the word 'dark' alludes to the hidden operations of power and the nature of a crisis focused on technology alongside our inability to think the network: 'that which was intended to enlighten the world in practice darkens it' (2018: 10). More than indicative of a troubling ignorance, a 'chasm' of knowledge caused by oversaturation of information and the degradation of critical thought, Bridle finds hope in the connections between the dark and its possibilities, its freedoms and equality. Nevertheless, the meaningful agency that comes from 'acknowledging this darkness', is orientated towards 'new ways of seeing by another light' (Bridle, 2018: 11). This 'new light' is appealing, but more problematic than it appears given its correspondence with both theological and enlightenment conceits. On the other hand, are there not forces that are indisputably dark, and isn't the distinction of 'light' as indicative of hope, thought and knowledge vital to challenging dark forces? Whilst this may be the case, the light is also embraced, relished even by the rhetoricians of dark forces.

In many media reports across the world, the evolving sense that 'dark forces' are on the rise corresponds with the movements of a reinvigorated right-wing and the notion of 'dark' relished by its academic, corporate, governmental and social media branches which gravitate towards a 'new light' – a dark light. It is undoubtedly risky to relish the dark from this perspective given its use-value for and association with fascistic ideology. In his essay, 'Ur-Fascism' (1995), Umberto Eco discusses his childhood memories of Italian fascism, the first right-wing dictatorship to take over Europe and the 'first to establish a military liturgy, a folklore, even a way of dressing – far more influential, with its black shirts, than Armani, Benetton, or Versace would ever be' (Eco, 1995: 3). Eco lists fourteen features of Ur-Fascism (or Eternal Fascism), including the syncretism between cults of tradition, traditionalist mystique, spiritualist and occult writings that, whilst different in practice and belief, lead back to the same overriding primeval truth.

Alongside anti-intellectualism (action over thinking: 'Thinking is a form of emasculation' (Eco, 1995: 6), the rejection of modernism, enlightenment, age of reason, Eco lists the 'cult of heroism' linked to the 'cult of death (heroic death)': 'The Ur-Fascist hero is impatient to die. In his impatience, he more frequently sends other people to death' (1995: 7). The hero's power translates through warfare and given warfare is not permanent, the will to power transfers to sex and 'sexual matters': 'This is the origin of *machismo* (which implies both disdain for women and intolerance and condemnation of non-standard sexual habits, from chastity to homosexuality). The Ur-Fascist hero tends to play with weapons – doing so becomes an ersatz phallic exercise' (Eco, 1995: 7–8). Notwithstanding this necessary note of caution, I write this book in a time when the darkness is utterly vital to the fight against the hidden operations of power and at a time when the darkness and dark sound is under threat. The artists featured here say something about the dark that is cherished, that is vital to life, love, thought, compassion, freedom, music and the imagination and that reconfigures notions of space, time and knowledge: something of this force of energy is cultivated and harnessed in dark sound. This being said, I present dark sound as a movement in the shadows.

1

Rewiring love-sick text and listening for the presence of the dark lady

Leonard Cohen's album *Old Ideas* (2012) features a track entitled 'Darkness' in which the lyrics establish the dark as a contagion caught by the body and mind: 'I caught the darkness, it was drinking from your cup / I caught the darkness drinking from your cup / I said is this contagious? / You said just drink it up' (Cohen 2012). Post-transmission of the disease (darkness), the song reflects on the cause and effects of a body driven by a compulsion to drink the darkness from 'your' cup. The addressee denoted by 'your' can be interpreted as a deadly lover who transmogrifies into both the cup or vessel that carries the darkness, as well as the darkness itself, the fluid that is drunk. The lyrics conjure an image of an unnamed dark lady who Cohen addresses as 'baby' and 'you' (Cohen's heterosexuality and relationships are frequently commented on in stories and commentary about him). She shifts like poison across the song, stealing time (the future, the present and the past) and depriving the poet of hope. Drinking, drugs, and sex, conflated into one fluid, toxic darkness, signifies the internal corruption of the amorous poet as his open mouth 'drinks it up'. 'It', the darkness, generates enough ambiguity within the song as to resonate with the historical notion of music itself as contagion, a 'catchy' tune, a seductive song, liable to breach the guard of the subject by entering the vulnerable open (male) ear (when it is without wax, rope, a mast and an obliging crew). Stuck in the head and caught by the body, attention is also drawn to the song itself as a carrier comparable to the dark lady: both are carriers and mediums of the darkness. Having acquired incredible fluidity, the darkness spreads uncontrollably backwards and forwards along a linear timeline, infecting not only the present and the future, but even the past, a time typically understood as a poet's reliable source of romantic undisturbed nostalgia, which can inspire and reinvigorate a sense of identity and selfhood. Even this well of memory is contaminated; the poet succumbs to a sickness that infects all sense of time, health and hope at the moment that he relents to the vocal bidding of the dark lady, who says 'just drink it up'. Of course, this isn't exactly the voice of the dark lady as such, but that of Cohen's ventriloquism, thrown through his close microphonic vocal intimacy with characteristic deep resonant timbres in poetic speech-song. Later in the song, during the blues-spiritual organ solo, in the background of Cohen's close vocal foreground, a set of female vocals join with harmonious, ethereal 'oohing' and proceed to both precipitate and echo the lines of his vocal verses. These grouped female vocals, of course, inhabit space in the stereo-image, but they do not take up the primary space of the song and remain distant in relation to the close proximity and domain of the lead Cohen vocal. Given their sonic, timbral and melodic character, their arrangement in the song and in the mix, these female vocals are not so much representative of the central dark feminine presence, but rather a ghost track of the poet's consciousness made from a series of alluring sonic shadows rather than the dark lady herself. During the final line of the penultimate verse, Cohen initiates a lyrical manoeuvre that redistributes the perverse sick power of the darkness by attributing the severity of the contagion to himself, 'I caught the darkness, and I caught it worse than you.' At this point, the trajectory of the song is explicitly revealed: he now carries and bears the darkness, whether that be love, addiction or pain; in any case, Cohen caught it worse than the 'you' addressed. This textual shift importantly masculinizes the melancholy of his love-obsession-addiction sickness and raises the extra significance of his suffering whilst, all the while, the dark lady remains silent and/or foiled by the poet's strategy to contain and territorialize the darkness, a darkness she had previously possessed via the logic of her textual construction. Cohen's song is effective in establishing a darker, more meaningful melancholy beyond that of the general platitudes of hopeless love-sickness. The subject of the song both ascribes darkness to a feminized other, thus becoming her victim, yet the subject is also able to seize the force and implied extreme states of the darkness as his own, claiming it as a territory by which he moves beyond her and any sense of impotency: he suffers and bears a heavier darkness, more than her, *worse* than her.

This strategy (which is not to say that the author is necessarily fully conscious of it as devised intention) is comparable to what is uncovered in Juliana Schiesari's *The Gendering of Melancholia: Feminism, Psychoanalysis, and the Symbolics of Loss in Renaissance Literature* (1992), in which she painstakingly discusses the historical privileging of male melancholia in artistic and literary canons that construe a more valuable and elite male-authored melancholic genius. Her argument suggests that in opposition to the greater significance and cultural value ascribed to male melancholics and their creative expressions of grievance, sorrow and loss, for women, far from the kudos of articulate alienation and outsider narratives, the melancholic position is deemed 'normative, thus reducing women to an essentialized and therefore inconsequential lack' (Schiesari, 1992: 75). Schiesari traces a history and discourse wherein male melancholia is linked to a privileged male narcissism that has acquired a sense of moral superiority, hyperconsciousness and sensitivity; the potential genius being that male artists are able to represent and express grievous loss, translate it and produce it as culturally valuable and credible art and aesthetics. Such a male subject is able to aggregate a loss from the lack attributed to femininity so that he perceives himself as the body that truly feels the 'open wound' and bears the 'stigmata of melancholy', a wound therefore gendered male and expressible in 'great' sorrowful literature, art and music that reflects the loved and valued image (Schiesari, 1992: 41; 166). For women and feminized queer bodies, the problem is not only that their melancholia, suffering, sorrow and tears do not acquire the same cultural value, but that they are consigned to inarticulate, devalued forms of expression. Schiesari writes of the differences between 'empowered' expressions of loss and those devalued within the signifying economy:

This implicitly empowered display of loss and disempowerment converts the personal sorrow of some men into the cultural prestige of inspired artistry and genius. At the same time, such an impressive translation of lack seems persistently denied to women, whose association with loss or grief is expressed by less flattering allusions to widows' weeds, inarticulate weeping, or other signs of ritualistic (but intellectually and artistically unaccredited) mourning. (Schiesari, 1992: 12)

When it comes to heteronormative love-sick melancholy, the canon of dark sound and poetry is replete with dark ladies, demonized women and femme fatales, who make frustrated and miserable victims of their lovers and admirers. However, despite the familiarity of the image, this chapter focuses on how the dark lady is conjured in 'love-sick' poetic text and questions to what extent she has been captured and muted by the kinds of textual bondage that weaves through the secret life of the love song discussed by Nick Cave: 'I have taken possession of you the love song whispers' (2000). In his lecture, Cave recognizes within the love song (and the love letter) the power of words to bind and contain the object of desire. Given this power and the gendered dimension of devalued expressions of sorrow, loss, melancholy and addiction within the signifying economy, the key question moves to voice and sound: what, if anything, can be heard of the dark lady, does her silence in the text specify feminine dark sound as a kind of hushed sonic shadow, or is there something else to be heard that might constitute dark feminine sound? With this in mind, it is noteworthy that the dark lady occurs within the love-sick text as that which evokes the limits of language and tests the poet's ability to really 'capture' her being in words. Therefore, the struggle to discern the dark lady occurs at the breaking point of what can and cannot be held by the text in a signifying economy that arguably privileges the melancholic words and expressions of heteronormative masculinity. So, I begin by returning to the text of a grand master of literature, William Shakespeare and to his love-sick sonnets about a 'dark lady' who he wishes to 'have' and over whom he wishes to exert power – with words, effectively entrapping her within a web of darkening love-sick text. Encouraged by Cohen's 'Darkness', I approach both text and song as potential carriers of the presence of the dark lady, a presence listened for.

The darkening power of Will's wilful words

Love-sick poetry bursts with vivid evocations of dark ladies. From William Shakespeare's dark lady of the 'Sonnets' ([1609] 2009) to the 'Darkness' caught by Cohen after 'drinking from the cup' (2012), fragmented and multiple configurations of the dark lady rise and fall in sonnet and song, like malevolent apparitions torturing the feverish desire of the man-made-mad. She materializes in song through seductive and mysterious sirenic feminine archetypes, stirring desire and threatening the stable subjectivity of those she seduces. Being driven mad with desire, the lover's loving dreams of total union morph into night sweats, irrational compulsions and a violent will to power over the other ('*libido dominandi*') who is difficult if not impossible to contain (Barthes, [1977] 1990: 121). Characterized by ambiguity and allusiveness, the dark lady is assigned the temporality of night-time and consigned to marginal places, just out of reach. Her mysteriousness causes an awkward shadow to dominate over the image of her corporeal form, suggesting that sexual 'union' does nothing to ease the fatal malady of desire, but rather takes the subject further into the black hell of a deathly unrest that, at best, results in an amorphous immersion in repulsive shared lies, flattery and shame. Flitting between fragments of adoration, paranoia and curses, befitting of the fragments Roland Barthes referred to as a 'lover's discourse' ([1977] 1990), the dark lady sonnets appear to bequeath the confused passions of an amorous subject who claims to love the object of his 'affections'. Shakespeare is sick of it and in sonnet 147 of the dark lady sonnets (127–54), he writes of his fever and illness:

> My love is as a fever, longing still,
> For that which longer nurseth the disease,
> Feeding on that which doth preserve the ill,
> The uncertain sickly appetite to please.
> My reason, the physician to my love,
> Angry that his prescriptions are not kept,
> Hath left me, and I desperate now approve
> Desire is death, which physic did except.

Past cure I am, now Reason is past care,
And frantic-mad with evermore unrest;
My thoughts and my discourse as madmen's are,
At random from the truth vainly expressed:
For I have sworn thee fair, and thought thee bright,
Who art as black as hell, as dark as night.

(147.1–14)

The dark lady is a figure that shifts between the sequence of Shakespeare's dark lady sonnets (127–54) and forms one part of a love triangle that also includes a young man and the speaker, a triangle also elaborated on in the preceding young man sonnets (1–126). Although the connection between the speaker of the sonnet and writer is debated, we can assume the speaker-subject is Shakespeare himself, writing in a cultural context wherein love poems form part of a 'private dialogue' intended to court and seduce (and in this case perhaps provoke) the addressees as 'performative utterance' (Bell, 2010: 294–5). Written to be read out loud, the sonnets anticipate vocal delivery, gesture and audience (albeit a dubiously 'private friends' audience) and, in so doing, draw further attention to the musicality and aurality of poetry as it speaks of both the writer's craft, his vocal performance and the performative context. Heterosexual and homosexual desire weaves through the young man and dark lady sonnets, prompting uncertainty as to the addressee of each particular sentiment, so that the reader is at times uncertain whether it is the dark lady or young man that is referenced, spoken to and of: the desire in this sense is not easily tracked. Picking up on this ambiguity of desire and address, Ilona Bell's 'Rethinking Shakespeare's Dark Lady' questions moments in the sonnets which are assumed to be directed to and reflective of the dark lady and she formulates an argument that raises the possibility that such lines may in fact be reflective of the duplicity of the alluring young man as well as Shakespeare's disappointment and anger at his own complicity in sordid, scandalous events (Bell, 2010: 308). Nevertheless, there are unambiguous moments of resentment directed at the dark lady and Bell's critique highlights the violence simmering within the text and the poet's apparent threat to misrepresent her.

A master of the craft, deeply aware of the potential mechanisms offered by the technologies of language and its controlling/seductive

LISTENING FOR THE DARK LADY IN LOVE-SICK TEXT   37

devices and also of the privileges of a patriarchal cultural context, Shakespeare intermittently threatens the dark lady with exercising his technological and contextual power in response to his sexual frustration, here forewarned as 'madness'. As Bell argues, he seems to threaten to misrepresent her should she continue to reject him, and his threats also suggest that society would believe the bitter and mad slandering that would inevitably follow his rejection:

> Be wise as thou art cruel; do not press
> My tounge-tide patience with too much disdain,
> Lest sorrow lend me words, and words express
> The manner of my pity-wanting pain.

(140.1–4)

> For if I should despair, I should grow mad,
> And in my madness might speak ill of thee.
> Now this ill-wresting world is grown so bad
> Mad sland'rers by mad ears believed be.

(140.9–12)

Bell makes the point that in fact the mad slander and rumours have been believed, over centuries, in that 'editors and critics continue to assume that the lady was a sexually voracious married woman, perhaps even a whore' (Bell, 2010: 301). In effect, the writer threatens to use not only the power of words, but the power of *his* words as indicative of a special alliance between his unique craft, performative poetry (the musicality and affection of words) and the patriarchal context of his performative utterance, i.e., a context that is always already waiting to confirm *who* the dark lady (and ladies) really are beneath the mystery of darkened female sexuality. To this end, the sonnets guide a focus on the dark lady's deviant sexuality (for she is the 'bay where all men ride', 137.6), and her darkness is articulated with frequent reference to 'blackness' made all the 'blacker' in significant contrast with the 'fairness' of the young man on whom Shakespeare lavishes compliments of beauty in preceding sonnets. As Bell suggests, links can be drawn between this violence of representation, its 'mad' believers at the time of performance and publication and the assumptions of scholars since then who believe that the dark lady is/was indeed, 'reprehensible', 'unforgivable', 'cruel', promiscuous, seductive: 'The widespread "revulsion" for the dark lady (Greenblatt, 2004: 255) has prevented scholars from seeing crucial, clarifying links among the dark lady sonnets themselves' (Bell, 2010: 311). In this sense, the poet's words entrap the dark lady in an enduring characterization, muting her 'voice'. It is in the lover's discourse of these sonnets, a language that apparently communicates and expresses love for a unique being, where a textual alchemy occurs that drowns out *her being* and (con)figures this dark lady within a vast textual weave of feminine darkness. Between the unique and the general, the actual dark lady and the cultural configuration of the dark feminine, the bondage of this discourse binds and looks to monumentalize its object whilst articulating the complex melancholy-desiring subject, who professes love and moreover the torture of his love-sickness. Under such circumstances, the 'voice' and audibility of the dark lady is drowned out by his articulate and performed text. This being said, the 'madness' of the text (more accurately expressed as manipulative technical precision) and the writer's threats acknowledge the social vulnerability of the dark lady and also hint at a conflation between patriarchy, *logos* and his poetic mastery, as they enable an alignment between his sonnets as performative utterance and the effects of imposing (W)ill, also here implying the power of a love-spell, or rather a curse, that lasts for centuries. And, indeed, earlier sonnets have placed an excessive emphasis on *will* as it cascades between the writer's name, her will, his will and possibly that of the young man (and perhaps also the young man's name), culminating in the final lines of sonnet 136:

> Make but my name thy love, and love that still,
> And then thou lov'st me for my name is Will.

> (136.13–14)

What's in a name? Woven within this name is the power of performative utterance as active agency with effect. The (W)ill of a grand literary master moves under the guise of love with an intention to express the ability to harm the loved other if her will will not give up and relent to sleeping with him. The performative utterance of Will also, however, speaks of a tension that belies a repressed aurality, in that Shakespeare's sonnets and the discourse about them, opens up the shadowy dimension of the dark feminine in which the dark lady, and the theories about her identity, resonate as part of a spun, (un)sounding sexualized darkness.

The black and white of love's sight

Perhaps agitated by the mysteriousness of the feminized darkness, much has been made of distinguishing the true identity of the dark lady, with researchers making historical claims based on relationships in Shakespeare's personal life, noting implications from these sonnets that she is skilled at playing the virginals and has a dark skin complexion, all of which, according to some historians, mean that the lady is well-educated and likely to be Italian or of Mediterranean origin. Whatever the truth of her identity, the dark lady as a figure of cultural imagination and intrigue appears to run the gamut between misogynistic fantasies of purity and corruption (the virgin/whore dichotomy), historical excavations of 'real' people, and the cultural resonance of racialized and sexualized feminine darkness that precedes and follows her, so that she is drawn between multiple identities: married (corrupted) young woman, deceitful and promiscuous temptress, courtesan and brothel owner. Whoever the dark lady *really* was, she has become and perhaps always was after being subjected to such textual 'flattery', less 'real' and more wraith-like, shifting between temporal and textual dimensions, appearing and disappearing amongst the vast blur of literature's multiplicity of virtual dark feminine figures cast out to a shadow realm on the edges of the master's romantic limelight. With this in mind, in addition to the issues with historical accuracy, given her historical and contextual relationship to patriarchal power and bearing in mind social scripts and issues of agency and representation, the notion of uncovering the dark lady's *real* identity is questionable, if not impossible. Quite aside from uncovering the dark lady's true identity, I am interested in the relationship between the darkening of a lady (singular) and ladies (plural) as an image and identity constructed by the poet through the gaze of his text and the recurring deployment of 'blackness':

> For I have sworn thee fair, and thought thee bright,
> Who art as black as hell, as dark as night.

> (147.13–14)

When the dark lady is at her darkest (and when the poet is at his most acerbic), the word 'blackness' consistently recurs as a word that embodies her darkness. She is a mistress with wire-black hair and a 'dun' complexion, with 'raven black' eyes, compared with mourner's eyes. Aligned with (his) love-sickness and with death, as opposed to the invigorative jargon of a loving dedication, the dark lady is situated in opposition to others fair in complexion, without enlivening rosy lips and cheeks (130. 1–6). And yet, despite the contrast with atypical beauty, and the fact that the writer himself has noted 'with mine eyes' a 'thousand errors' (141. 1–2), along with the fact that he does not love with his eyes, the poet insists on his absolute obsession with the dark lady as a hopeless and tormented man in love. In contrast with unproblematically beautiful female muses of romantic poetic ardour, much in these sonnets is dedicated to ensuring the woman of his desire is explicitly denied the attributes of 'objective' beauty. In being able to love the lady, despite her being 'black as hell, dark as night', the poet has complemented himself with the ability to see something others do not, as well as the integrity of heart to love this blackest, darkest of women, essentially surreptitiously highlighting his own brightness. And if the poet's language is a clever critique of the platitudes and clichés of other love poetry dedicated to women, the dark lady is a figure conjured in order to economize on the culturally understood marginality of blackness, darkness and the historical suspicion of female sexuality, accruing a cultural capital of sorts by which the poet distinguishes critical as well as loving integrity: he doubles up on the capital of conjoining 'blackness' and 'dark lady'.

Kim Hall's essay 'These Bastard Signs of Fair: Literary Whiteness in Shakespeare's Sonnets' (2010) makes a series of important points about the relationship between the poet's language and the praise of 'fairness' and beauty lavished on the young man in the sonnets that precede the dark lady sonnets, where Shakespeare sets up his love triangle. Hall interprets in Shakespeare's writing an anxiety over legitimacy, bloodlines and inheritance coupled with a highly significant fear of a 'deadening, over-used language of praise' (2010: 77). Shakespeare's anxiety and critique reveals itself particularly in sonnet 68 when he decries 'the bastard signs of fair' as language which is elicited by the false 'cosmetic' beauty of women. Or in other words, an illegitimate 'fairness' haunts women and the banalities of the language used to praise their beauty. 'Fair' women are after all *painted* lily white and rosy red. In response, the gendered and racialized opposition between white and black, true and false, natural and cosmetic becomes crucial to establishing the genuine beauty of the young man in sonnets 'haunted by the spectre of a possible Africanist presence (the dark lady)' (Hall, 2010: 66). Hall reveals the usually hidden processes by which an aesthetic and ideology of whiteness is produced and naturalized within both the sonnets and a wider context of poetry and art which promote white, winter, snow, blond, lily-like purity as 'fair beauty'. She notes that the naturalized processes of constructing whiteness and its beauty has an especial relevance to the colonial ambitions and economy of England. As portraits of Queen Elizabeth demonstrate, whiteness and transcendent metaphors of light establish Christian superiority and a privileged class and so the young man's fair beauty must prevail: 'His beauty is described in terms of Christian transcendence: it has no "holy bower". It can be "profaned". He is a "better angel" and "a saint"' (Hall, 2010: 79). Whereas the dark lady returns us back to the material body, devalued as 'black' and therefore racialized, gendered and lower class, bearing in mind, 'In early modern England, blackness becomes the mark of bodies – be they female, African, Welsh, Jewish, Irish or lower class' (Hall, 2010: 80). In this context, 'black' and the designation of 'dark' might apply to social categories and qualities other than, and as well as, skin colour. The poet resorts to fairness and pure whiteness to develop a particular kind of superior English male identity; both spiritually transcendent and naturally beautiful. The young man's truly ineffable beauty is set in opposition to the debased dark lady and in the process of constructing this opposition in writing, the poet distinguishes himself as possessing the insights and legitimate literary skill that enables him to notice and articulate the depth of character and difference between these beauties, the young man and the dark lady. In effect, the oppositional value he creates raises the value of his own beautiful language, turmoil and insights as the preserve of a great male author.

On the precipice of a risk he has manufactured, the suffering lover, past all cure and rendered blind in one respect, nevertheless implicitly claims to see and desire something that eludes others via the ineradicable dominance of his heart, whilst he apparently compulsively agitates the painful bondage that draws him ever closer to his inevitable demise at the mercy of her blackened cruelty and seduction. His suffering and self-pity orchestrate the beating love-sick heart of these dark lady sonnets and it is the erratic pumping of his heart, one moment adrenaline pumped and the next depressed, that orchestrates the rhythm of male desire in relation to a dark, black, cold, cruel and indifferent figure that moves slowly or remains static like a statue around which his fatigued passion dizzily orbits. His heart's drumming meter intends to dominate the temporality of the sonnets, whilst the subject's desire is built around the edges of a black hole that the dark lady, through surreptitious ideological processes of representation, has become and through which the subject is apparently threatened with total annihilation. Considering the apparent dominance of the poet's voice and the regulating meter of his heartache, it is difficult to imagine the sound or 'voice' of the dark lady. Nevertheless, the cultural ambisonics of the dark feminine and the repressed uniqueness of the dark lady herself resonate within the blank spaces/black space of the text.

The dark lady's black sound

The will(s) of Will(s) does not constitute an all-out silencing of the dark lady, more a muffling of her soundings that every now and then find a connection to the 'speakers' of the sonnets, creating signals that redirect the elicited curiosity about the dark lady to focus on the gaps between her representation and beyond the intentions of the speaker (author). Tuning in, as it were, to the aurality of the dark lady sonnets, is to begin to listen to elements of the dark lady that might elude the powers of the poet; moments when dark(ened) feminine sound comes through in the word 'blackness', in the consistent reference to his blindness, in the intentionally mysterious conjunction, 'dark lady', and particularly in references to music and voice and the discovery that the dark lady is a musician:

How oft, when thou, my music, music play'st
Upon that blessèd wood whose motion sounds
With thy sweet fingers when thou gently sway'st
The wiry concord that mine ear confounds,
Do I envy those jacks that nimble leap
To kiss the tender inward of thy hand,

LISTENING FOR THE DARK LADY IN LOVE-SICK TEXT   43

Whilst my poor lips which should that harvest reap,
At the wood's boldness by thee blushing stand.
To be so tickled, they would change their state
And situation with those dancing chips
O'er whom thy fingers walk with gentle gait,
Making dead wood more blest than living lips.
Since saucy jacks so happy are in this,
Give them thy fingers, me thy lips to kiss.

(128.1–14)

Within the sonnets, references to sound build in a derogatory
nature. Although it is implied that she is a musician, the dark lady
is not credited with any particular sublime musical talents which
might rationalize and elicit poetic dedications to the familiar figure
of the female muse, nor does she possess a delightful 'tongue's tune'
(141.5). Her supposed lack of audiovisual beauty, a lack that does
not nourish the senses, somewhat heightens a vivid sense of the
sickness of a heart that cannot be regulated by reason, endorsing
the amorous subject's claims to a kind of 'blindness' innate to the
suffering of his love sickness. Following Fred Moten's approach to
the photograph, the question becomes how is it possible to listen
to this sonnet's sound, the dark lady's soundings and the darkened
feminine voices that extend beyond it; how might we 'attune
oneself to a moan or shout that animates the photograph with an
intentionality of the outside' (Moten, 2003: 208)? In this case, how
can we listen and sense the 'silenced difference' (Moten, 2003: 205)
of the dark lady, the outsiders and the repressed cultural ambisonics
of the dark feminine? Consequently, questions migrate away from
who she is, what she looks like, or the nature of her relationship to
Shakespeare and towards what and how she sounds as a meaningful
affective vibration within a muted cacophony of darkened feminine
sounding suppressed within the text as unsounding sound. Difficult
to hear anything at all, considering that even the sonnet based on
her musicianship seems doomed to muteness.

Despite making explicit references to her music and voice,
Shakespeare arguably navigates subtle distraction away from her
sound whilst appearing to refer to it, appealing to the reader to
identify with his gaze. Sonnet 128 reveals that the dark lady is a
musician, skilled at the virginals we assume, an instrument gendered
and sexualized to the extent that its name may be etymologically

related to 'virgin' and often played by young women. Even here, however, despite the inference of sexual innocence, she is already circumvented as promiscuous with a sensuality conjured and spent between her body and the instrument, specifically via hands that touch the instrument. Attention is drawn to loving intimate gestures of 'sweet fingers' and the 'tender inward of thy hand' as they gently move across jacks and wood and strings; except the poet's jealousy is agitated by her motion and he expresses this by animating the materials and surfaces of the instrument as blessed in relation to her motion and then admonishing the 'dead wood', 'more bless'd than living lips' (128.12). Jealousy then moves to sardonic resentment, suggesting her bodily movements are wasted on the wood in a false gesture of sensuality where there can be no desire of any value, not between the dark lady and her instrument: the lady's musical desire, a desire that doesn't enlist the poet is unthinkable! Strangely perhaps, he has no desire for those hands and fingers to touch him, rather, he is happy to dismiss the hands in favour of the lips he demands to kiss: 'Since saucy jacks so happy are in this, / Give them thy fingers, me thy lips to kiss' (128.13–14). One might suppose the last reference to 'jacks' plays on the connotation of a plurality of men in conjunction with devious promiscuity, represented by her hands. In contrast, the poet's integrity is measured by his understanding of the value of her body, fragmented into an economy of debased physical erotic sensuality in contrast to the much more valuable lips, which are of love and higher spiritual principles hinted at by the virtues of her mouth from which issues her soul/voice. At the very moment her mouth is conjured and a voice inferred, she is muted by his romantic kiss. However, the attention drawn to the relationship between the hands of the dark lady as she plays the instrument, underscores the very desire and problematics the lover would seek to absent by raising the form of both her desiring sensual body (despite/in spite of his gaze) and the threat to his listening subjectivity.

What the poet references and cannot suppress is the 'grain' of the body in the 'performing' limb, her unique materiality and erotic sensuality as it beats against the surfaces of the instrument. This bypasses the rules and constraints of his ocular-centric and poetic textual interpretation with a performance, neither ugly nor beautiful, that will not 'reinforce him' or express his erotic desire, but 'destroy him': he dissolves (Barthes, [1972] 1977: 276). Post-performance reflection, the text only partially relents to his attempts to reinstall the bulwark that protects the subject's imaginary from total annihilation; blown up by the performance, the text cannot help but partially reveal that the writing engaged with darkening the unique dark lady (text wired into the general dark feminine) has driven the writer's desire into a black hole of his own creation: a limit that is the limit of his power and agency, and a space beyond his intention. Driven by a sense that there is something that exceeds his words, a 'beyond words' indicative of the frustrations of the lover's discourse (how to speak about what one loves?), the writer subject's egocentric desire seeks to triumphantly frame and objectify the lady through darkness and blackness whilst exceeding the limits of other writers and poets who are condemned to clichés of beauty. He does this successfully, up to a point. His writing presents a complex melancholy craft that criticizes the rhetoric of a lover-poet's praise (written by those other lesser writers), injecting a sense of masterly agency dominated by his libido disguised as a love-sick subject, who is particularly at risk of harm and endless sorrow since he 'loves' a dark lady rather than an easy-to-love fair beauty. In other words, he needs the black hole of the dark feminine to specify both the limits of the lover's discourse, his greatness, his illuminated melancholic integrity and the risk posed to his being. Although the risk is manufactured, the dark lady threatens to topple the poet's dominance through a darkness that eludes him and an alliance with her sound. With an ear bent towards the aurality of the sonnet, it is possible to perceive how the hierarchy, agency and economy of his desire is contingent upon the blackness and darkness of the lady who should remain image-object. However, what explodes through the suppressed aurality of the dark lady is a blackness, or a dark sound that cannot be said, and that must not be uttered because it is the othered absent sound on which the supremacy of his subjectivity depends. Dark sound in this respect makes audible the gap that his writing both desires and resents. The only thing that might rescue his agency is light, comprehensible in religious, gendered and racialized terms, deployed to re-establish the dominance of a beautiful white (melancholic) male. But the dark feminine sound that is blackened produces not blankness/nothing, but polyphony that seeps through the colour black in ways that confound the binary hierarchal logic of light and dark. When he speaks about her sound, he is forced to admit the limits of his understanding, that being 'The wiry concord that mine ear confounds' (128. 4). As Moten has written about Billie Holiday's 'Don't Explain', the dark lady is on 'another register of desire':

> He [Forrest] imagines her reading what he already knows, but her wisdom, as he knows and would actively repress, cuts that wisdom. She's on another thing, another register of desire. And that grained voice elsewhere resists the interpretation of the audience when the analytic positions are exchanged. (Moten, 2003: 104)

The darkness confounds and cuts the lightness upon which both his transcendence and the transcendence of the white fair young man implicitly and complicity depend. If it were not for the aurality of that 'darkness' which cannot be expressed, the white light of the sonnet would be blinding, allowing for a reassuring sense of the ineffable migration of dominant, beautiful white light. However, the 'unfair' beauty has not remained mute and confounds the writer's eyes and ears in music and sound not reducible to his lover's discourse. His regular reference to obscured sight and blindness, disguised as a virtue of his genuine loving heart, hints at the anticipation of his own death, that is to say the death of the author's predominant intentions over the meaning of the text (Barthes, [1967] 1977), especially as brought about by its soundings as opposed to the visual means by which he primarily bases his judgements of beauty. Moreover, in the very fact that this is a lover's discourse dedicated to a so-called unnamed 'dark lady', there is an underlying acknowledgement beset by the notion of romantic ineffability, that the writing, in seeking to express love, approaches a difficulty that borders the limits of language as well as the general clichés of love that threaten to diminish the poet's technical prowess and power.

Through the blackness, darkness and sound of the sonnet, the melancholy and darkness that the lover's discourse had sought to territorialize returns to the lady, with value. This sonic desire and melancholy has seeped through the interstitial semiotic blend of an audiovisual dark feminine, eliciting not only image, but timbre, body and tone through the rich significance of colour. Elizabeth Harvey discusses the chromatic in early modern culture onto which 'discourses of race would graft themselves' and writes that, in early modern culture, 'Colour was more than the shade of skin visible to the eye; it was the expression of an entire bodily composition that included a relatively opaque interior' (Harvey, 2010: 315). In contrast with the interpretation of blackness and darkness as nothingness or silence, blackness here connotes the secret interior of the female body and the colourful chromaticism of the dark lady of the sonnets. Harvey foregrounds Kristeva's association between the 'chromatic apparatus' and rhythm in language: 'each functions outside of the symbolic dimensions of language, as an excess or a residue of meaning that cannot be processed within the existing linguistic or representational systems' (2010: 323). In effect, the 'colours' and chromatics of the dark lady's sound, meant to be suppressed, can be conceived of as 'a language of the passions, sexuality and the unconscious, a world that subtends, participates in and also continually escapes the regulations of symbolic language' (Harvey 2010: 326). As audible and affective excess beyond the holding conventions of language, the aural imaginary is encouraged to encounter the sexualized and racialized figure of the dark lady. Her blues, her unique grain and desire is, as Moten writes of Billie Holiday, 'on another register' (2003: 104). Here, in the gaps of the poet's language, its white space and black holes, the 'dark lady' musician introduces not only darkness and blackness, but dark sound and, in so doing, she infects the logic of her making and containment and, in defiance of his power, raises the body and grain of the female femme musician. It is noteworthy therefore, that when Federico García Lorca conceptualizes the integrity and affect of 'dark sound', he does so by reintroducing the body of the voice as it sings and importantly, the figure that exemplifies this dark sound is a female singer, La Niña de Los Peines.

Dark sound and the singer's body

Inspired by singer Manuel Torre who claimed: 'All that has black sounds has duende', Federico García Lorca's essay 'Play and Theory of the Duende', ([1933] 2010: 56–72) proposes that 'dark sound' materializes in and through '*duende*', a Spanish word that Lorca develops in relation to art, particularly music and singing, as a way of evaluating the spirit, emotion, expression and movement of an artwork or performance that either does or doesn't have '*duende*'. Lorca makes a direct attempt to articulate some of what produces and connects *duende* in art, without subjecting the mysterious energy of all that has dark sound to the conceits of intellectualism. To do this, he foregrounds the opposition between mind and body, raising the significance and quality of the body (and its spirit) over the ruling principles of the intellect. In the essay, intellectual production is represented by the Muse situated in opposition to *duende*, so that the figure of the Muse appeals to intellect and form, whilst *duende*, on the other hand, moves through the visceral struggles of body and spirit. Although Lorca perceives the possibility of *duende* in all art, his writing especially privileges dancing, music, singing and spoken word poetry and, in this respect, he specifically connects *duende* with Andalusian folk music and the expressive *cante jondo* vocal style of flamenco music. According to Lorca, Andalusian culture is made up of a people who recognize the presence or absence of *duende* to the extent, they will say of a piece 'This has much *duende*', and in southern Spain, when *duende* arrives through the voice and body of a dancer, is 'greeted with sincere cries of *Viva Dios!* – deep and tender cry of communication with God by means of the five senses' (Lorca, [1933] 2010: 62). In this context, Lorca considers the relationship between the national and ethnic identity of Andalusian people and a cultural history of torment and struggle, including the suffering during and after the Spanish Civil War. He writes:

> Spain is, at all times, stirred by the duende, country of ancient music and dance, where the duende squeezes out those lemons of dawn, a country of death, a country open to death. (Lorca, [1933] 2010: 64)

Duende is repeatedly associated with death and the pain of an individual and collective wound, the physical assertion of the self and a people against political oppression and religious dramas of sacrifice and worship. In this, there is something that is significantly connective about dark sound, created and caught between the generation of 'an almost religious enthusiasm' brought about by the communication of a feeling, wired through the mysteries of dark sounds: 'Those dark sounds are the mystery, the roots that cling to the mire that we all know, that we all ignore, but from which comes the very substance of art' (Lorca, [1933] 2010: 57). If music has *duende*, it will be heard and felt by an audience and if it doesn't, its lack may be felt as indifference or the 'discovery of a fraud' and consequently dark sound is perceived as the embodiment of sincerity in music and movement. Lorca chooses a specific performance to illustrate a voice that induces dark sound and this voice belongs to a female singer who manages to 'banish her Muse' and transgress the paralysing effects of the judgemental gaze of 'experts', thereby traversing into the sincerity of *duende* and dark sound:

> La Niña de Los Peines had to tear apart her voice, because she knew experts were listening, who demanded not form but the marrow of form, pure music with a body lean enough to float on air. She had to rob herself of skill and safety: that is to say, banish her Muse, and be helpless, so her duende might come, and deign to struggle with her at close quarters. And how she sang! Her voice no longer at play, her voice a jet of blood, worthy of her pain and her sincerity, opened like a ten-fingered hand as in the feet, nailed there but storm-filled, of a Christ by Juan de Juni. (Lorca, [1933] 2010: 62)

When singer La Niña de Los Peines 'banish[es] her Muse', she displaces the dominance of intellectual learning and instruction and instead opens up a space inside her vocalizing body that requires and inhabits the process of struggle, making body, sound and performance vulnerable, particularly to pain. According to Lorca, she gets up to perform 'like a madwoman, trembling like a medieval mourner' and beings to sing 'with a scorched throat, without voice, breath, colour, but…with duende' (Lorca, [1933] 2010: 61). Here the safety of a well-rehearsed, well-known vocal rendition is sacrificed in order to bring about a physical, embodied emotional darkness, imagined by Lorca as a vocal 'jet of blood'. Her openness, characterized in the excessive figure of the possessed 'madwoman' and lamenting, dirge-singing medieval mourner, is what allows for the unrepeatable and inventive quality of *duende*, a quality that will only appear if the possibility of death is conjured somehow in practice, on the performative precipice of madness, mourning and a hot 'scorched' throat. A performer's proximity to death, pain and struggle provides the vitality and blood-letting of the vocal sound as if 'anger, bile and tears' ultimately connected wounded bodies to something beyond mortality and to the ultimate link that will bring bodies closer to God (*Viva Dios!*). Dark sound singing also acquires a kind of exquisite tenderness through its apparent ability to navigate an escape from this world and towards an intimacy with nature, night-time, the sublime and the cosmological: 'Behind those black sounds, tenderly and intimately, live zephyrs, ants, volcanoes, and the huge night, straining its waist against the Milky Way' (Lorca, [1933] 2010: 71). However, it is not so much an ultimate blissful transgression from earth to cosmos that is on offer, but more of an evocation of precipices that present both the threat of an edge and the 'delights' of a subject caught up in duende, 'fighting the creator on the very rim of the well' (Lorca, [1933] 2010: 67); neither transgressed or resolved, this verge threatens the subject with a deep fall into the pit, such are the terrible delight and throes of dark sound. Consequently, dark sound draws the sincerity out of the subject by leading them to this 'edge' in that the song itself opens up to mortality and to the terrible verge of death. La Niña de Los Peines is the figure that Lorca uses to exemplify this song. On the precipice of life and death, a figure of a singing woman, banishing intellect and physically open to bloody painful streams of vocalizations, sounds the manifestation of the *duende* of southern Spain; linking female singer, death, pain and national identity within the dark vocal soundings of her performing body. Although Lorca provides other examples and analogies for *duende*, the singer stands out as a body on the edge of death, deeply immersed in *duende*. As such, the soundings of the 'dark lady' are not suppressed in this text, as much as used to exemplify the genuine performative embodiment of dark sound and the mysteries of *duende* at the edge of the sayable. This fringe of contact with darkness, so frequently evoked to express the quality or indescribable qualities of affective art and heightened emotion, appears in many ways to be bound to a female figure, a singer, musician. Having witnessed La Niña de Los Peines's vocal performance, Lorca privileges her voice as a way of describing the indescribable in an essay that seeks to point beyond its own intellectual, communicative, textual limitations and towards the feeling of *duende* in dark sound.

Dark singing presence

Each of the cases discussed here – Cohen, Shakespeare and Lorca – all in some way situate dark feminine soundings at the edge of a text which seeks to ruminate on the power and limits of text itself. But

LISTENING FOR THE DARK LADY IN LOVE-SICK TEXT 51

what is it about this limit as it corresponds with a sense of 'darkness' that particularly evokes female voices, singers and musicians? In a final turn towards the voice of a female singer aligned with dark sound, Edith Piaf and her words about her relationship with songs and practice become relevant, since she appears to point to an important threshold in singing practice that is both a vocal openness to death (a darkness of being) and exceeding the limits of language. She writes:

> My songs! How can I talk about my songs? Men, however much I've loved them…they were still 'the others'. My songs are myself, my flesh, my blood, my head, my heart, my soul. Yes, how can I talk about them? (Piaf and Noli, 1990: 88)

In a 'ghosted autobiography' collated as dictated memoirs by journalist Jean Noli during the last year of her life, Piaf alludes to the difficulty of talking about music and insists on the inextricable relationship between her songs and every physical, emotional, spiritual and mental aspect of herself, thereby establishing an indissociably visceral body of songs connected through heart, blood, soul, singing and performance. The romantic ardour of Piaf's exclamation is compelling. On one level, her coherent body of flesh and song may be perceived as the absolute truth of a successful artist and singer, whose performative presence cannot be replaced and whose powerful affect on the audience is caught up in the idea of a unique, individual soul, romantically expressed in the embodied voice, performed live. Nevertheless, as has been raised by many who discuss the uncanny necromedia that disassociates voice from body and allows voices of the dead 'to speak', something inevitably does threaten to dissociate the flesh and blood of the singing songful body: that something being in this context both recording technology and, of course, death itself (see Young, 2015). And yet, even via a recorded medium and following the death of this singer, the '*duende*', or dark sound, of her songs, thought to be vitally attached to vocal embodiment, manages to transmit beyond the life of her body and via the song and recording medium itself. Recall the infamous media audiovisual memory that resurrects her standard signature performance black dress, the gestures of her hands and face and her voice itself, these all contribute to an intensification of hearing the body in the voice as it sings, of hearing 'dark sound'. Despite the death of the singer and therefore the ineradicable knowledge that this body is dead and gone, Piaf's dark sound persists via the recorded inscription of her body and voice, not just 'open to death' as Lorca has said of *duende*, but opening a channel between life and death. Despite the inevitability and knowledge of Piaf's death, the vocal affects of *duende*, dark sound, the grain, all of which refer to the body, survive within the medium as the vocal corporeality of a dead body that one could regard as a dark feminine presence.

Singers in particular work at the threshold of being and non-being, aware of the recurrence of death in the stories they tell as much as the 'bringing to life', as Walter Benjamin has written of the storyteller.[1] Piaf herself expands on the notion of the 'storyteller' by touching on the resuscitating powers of song and by drawing attention to the words of the song as they breathe life into *les gens* – the folk. Piaf says: 'It's the words that interest me first of all [...] for in each song I try to make the people live' (Piaf and Noli, 1990: 8). In Piaf's speech-song style that tells the story of *les gens*, there is the echo of a recognition of an 'aesthetic of meaning' that Barthes recognized and so loved in Panzéra's '*naked voice, à voix nue*' and the tradition of the folk song. Panzéra's singing, for Barthes, cultivates the folk song (in secret): 'For if the folk song was traditionally sung, *à voix nue*, that is because it was important to understand the story: something is being told, which I must receive without disguise: nothing but the voice and the telling: that is what the folk song wants' (Barthes, [1977] 1991: 284). As Benjamin writes of storytelling and as in Piaf's sense of the importance of telling the story, incarnations of people and their lives are not just about 'bringing to life', but also, if not more so, about the appearance of *death* in the story and the faith that the storyteller has in its regularity (Benjamin, 1969). Performing songs for Piaf is about both the defiance of death and the immersion of self and others in the full acknowledgement of the grievous conditions of mortality: '*Non, je ne regrette rien!*' At the same time as Piaf admits the difficulty in talking about her songs (and perhaps a feigned unwillingness), she also seizes the absolute vitality of language and summons the fringe of contact between language, bodies and music, in songs that tell stories about people, that breathe life into death and usher death into life. Piaf's voice raises the body (and bodies) in song, resurrects herself and others time and again, via a grain of the voice inscribed in sound and text, invoking the troubling shadow of dark feminine presence and desire that is both of the body and exceeds it.

2

At the frozen borderline of a music lover's discourse

The dark white voice

Since, when words are no longer worth saying,
what can one do, except sing?

(Vladimir Jankélévitch [1961] 2003: 117)

Music, like signifying, derives from no metalanguage but
only from a discourse of value, of praise: from a lover's
discourse [...].

(Roland Barthes [1977] 1991: 284)

Hanging out at the edges of what can be said, the discourse that attempts to talk about music is frequently preoccupied with the limitations of language. Like any lover struggles to talk about their love, like any lover tussles to do justice to the unique singularity of love, a music lover's discourse stretches to overcome generalizations and to articulate experiences of bliss, intimacy, affect, immersion, elicitations of tears and shudders, without stifling or betraying the beating heart, goose pimples and blood rushes of music's touch. Ultimately, a music lover might give up on the struggle and be forced to admit music's ineffability, compelled to acknowledge that music is in fact too great to be uttered. Under these circumstances, discourse is forced into silence, stunned at its own insubstantial meaninglessness. Indeed, as Paul Hegarty suggests, this admission is arguably part of an inevitable trajectory in a discourse that wishes its object to exceed the powers of language: 'All music, and a considerable amount of music criticism, wishes music (or noise) to possess a certain ineffability, wishes it to be beyond the powers of language' (Hegarty, 2007: 162). Such wishing hints at an implicit critique of music discourse when it inhibits and locks down meaning rather than honours what music lovers sense, which is that music has the potential to exceed and transform that which is known and can be discussed. In this respect, what can be learnt, experienced and derived from music is positioned as vulnerable to the 'powers of language' when they are perceived to be deadening. And yet, at the same time as this threat is acknowledged, a music lover has faith in music's ability to exceed attempts to grasp it as an object of study, to pin it down to description or analysis. Amplifying the wishes and desires inferred by Hegarty, it is possible to detect within music discourse the charged faiths and guarded commitments that music is in fact ultimately ineffable and, consequently, too great to be spoken about. Haunted by these clandestine undercurrents, it is as though music discourse, possessed by tricky occulted characters that relish its secrets, works to undermine the work of speaking, ultimately driving towards its own muteness, the end of speaking about music. The question then is of the relationship between the powers of language and ineffability, or rather of meaning that can live or die, as language might live or die, as language might breathe life into a subject or suffocate it. For many writers, concerned as they are with the powers of language, ineffability is vital to the production of meaning. Judith Butler, for example, considers these powers in terms of violence, suggesting that 'the violence of language consists in its effort to capture the ineffable and, hence, to destroy it, to seize hold of that which must remain elusive for language to function as a living thing' (Butler, 1997: 9). This implies that the violence of language, when it attempts to capture the ineffable, is a violence directed not just towards the ineffable, but inwardly towards itself in destructive death drives compelled towards a nihilistic void. Toni Morrison elaborates on the necessity of the ineffable with respect to language that bears a political responsibility to what can never be said. She writes: 'Language can never "pin down" slavery, genocide, war. Nor should it yearn for the arrogance to be able to do so. Its force, its felicity is in its reach toward the ineffable' (Morrison, 1993). Considered thusly, the ineffable is not only vital to the life force, effectivity and momentum of language and its meaning, but also integral to a political commitment to the unspeakable. Seeking to find ways of articulating the complexities of what is at stake when music is (or isn't) spoken about, two music lovers, Vladimir Jankélévitch and Roland Barthes, produced writing particularly attuned to the tensions between music, language and the ineffable and into this tension both philosophers introduce the body … and love.

A music lover's discourse

Music, writes Barthes, derives from a lover's discourse, a discourse of value and praise, or in other words, a discourse that allows itself to be changed and effected by that which is loved and, with this in mind, Barthes's essays are not so much 'on music', but, importantly, titled 'Music's Body': this body remains crucial to all Barthes's music-loving essays. Reflecting on listening to 'the andante of Schubert's first trio' one evening (Barthes sets the nocturnal scene of the amorous encounter), he implies the impoverishment of language and music's ineffability by proposing: 'What else is there to say about what one loves except: *I love it*, and to keep on saying it' (Barthes, [1976] 1991: 286)? However for Barthes, importantly, loving music engenders a discourse of evaluation as opposed to compelling one to admit the generalization that all music is ineffable, or that we should love all music. Indeed, rather than wholeheartedly committing to either music's ineffability or the conceits of a music discourse, Barthes appears to set up a critical liminal position with a question that characterizes the concern of all his essays, but which emerges explicitly in 'The Grain of the Voice', where he asks, 'Are we doomed to the adjective? Are we faced with this dilemma: the predicable or the ineffable' ([1972] 1977: 180)? For him, the ineffable is one side of a dualistic predicament that writing about music encounters: the predicable or the ineffable? To tackle this dilemma, one of the most striking strategies of Barthes's evaluations is the necessity of opposition. This is particularly prominent in 'The Grain of the Voice' where he discerns between two types of singing voice. On the one side of his evaluation is the deadening culturally-coded vocal emotion that is the phenosong, the example of which Barthes finds in Dietrich Fischer-Dieskau. On the other side, Barthes positions the singer Charles Panzera, whose singing Barthes loves and values through the 'genosong' and the concept of a voice that has 'grain'.[1] A voice with 'grain' works dynamically at the fringes of voice/body/language to produce ongoing, vitally alive, radiant meaning that is *signifiance* as opposed to closed signification. In the 'grain', one hears the body of the voice as it sings and is immersed in a generative process of meaning-making that takes the listener to a threshold, beyond the bulwark that protects the subject and into states of jouissance, wherein the subject is lost in untranslatable ecstasy. With the 'grain', Barthes attempts to engage the 'impossible account of an individual thrill' ([1972] 1977: 181), not to express or represent feelings, but to focus on the materiality of language as it encounters voice in the genosong, 'where melody actually *works on* language – not what it says, but the voluptuous pleasure of its signifier-sounds, of its letters' (Barthes, 1977: 182). In effect, his writing explores how language identifies itself with the sensual labour of the corporeal grain in a signifying process he calls the 'second semiology'. For Barthes, the first semiology is interested in 'the system of notes, scales, tones, chords and rhythms' and is organized through the principles of traditional modes of music interpretation. The second semiology is interested in tracing the body that beats within the materiality of sound and text and this requires the listener/writer to follow the 'effervescence of beats' (Barthes, [1975] 1991: 312). On one level, Barthes's proposition is maddeningly inaccessible in that there are no explicit instructions, certainties or formulas of analysis to follow. However, his writing is determined to challenge the annulment of the body in music criticism and, for him, it is the erotic relationship between music's bodies, between the body in the voice as it sings, the body in the hand as it writes and the pads of the fingers as they beat the piano keys, that changes the discourse itself and destabilizes the speaking subject in moments of musical jouissance.

Following the body in Barthes's writing, one begins to discern the influence of Jankélévitch's *Music and the Ineffable* ([1961] 2003), where romanticism (and Romantic composers) poignantly linger in a text that also advocates for the importance of love and the body in writing about music. Jankélévitch proposes a scenario in which a

AT THE FROZEN BORDERLINE OF MUSIC DISCOURSE 57

pianist is asked a question and proceeds to respond to the question by playing the piano; the pianist has not verbally said anything and yet says something, without 'saying'. This is what he highlights as the 'manual response' of the pianist and it insinuates an underlying argument that the meaning and mysteries of music exceed the discourse *on* music and it also, crucially, insists on the importance of the body as part of the production of music's enlivening meaning. The central argument or manoeuvre of Jankélévitch's text is to base an understanding of music on what he refers to as music's 'ineffable Charm', which directs the listener away from the 'the intolerable chatter about music' and wrests music away from the conceits of '*logos*', thereby releasing music from its dimming authority (Jankélévitch, [1961] 2003: 142). According to Jankélévitch, the violence of *logos* attempts to seize and know what, for him, remains the unknowable mystery of music: the 'ineffable Charm'. An ineffable silence is for Jankélévitch the absolute silence of *logos* – but not of music. Ineffable silence is rather the enabling context in which the many different languages and voices of music may emerge. Whereas Barthes explicitly challenges the ineffable, Jankélévitch embraces ineffability as essential to the conceptualization of music's potential in relation to both the body and language and to its ability to unfurl the conceits of *logos*. Despite the appeal of the idea of the 'ineffable Charm' of music and the foregrounding of a physical manual response in the form of music practice and performance, the key strategy of this chapter is to repeatedly question whether the 'ineffable' does actually unfurl those conceits or whether it harbours some of the violent powers that it is apparently distinguished from. Whilst the ineffable might maintain unsayable and elusive meaning (of music in this case), its deployment may also harbour potential violence in terms of what the ineffable attempts to hush, seize, know, silence, hide, monumentalize or destroy: to kill as a living thing might be killed. In other words, the violence of *logos* and the powers of language are not necessarily challenged by ineffability if one considers, for example, the theological understanding of *logos* that refers to the Word of God, in relation to ineffability as etymologically tied to God, His unspeakable name and religious prohibition (*what must not be uttered*). In this respect, far from challenging *logos*, ineffability encourages and compliments the reverence and authority granted to grand Christian patriarchs and the word of the Father.

Similarly problematized here, is the music lover's discourse, with its inextricable connections to ineffability alongside its deeply gendered and sexualized romantic rhetoric and aesthetics. Although the romantic heart of a lover's discourse might wish to deny it, power is at play in the lover's discourse in terms of how it distributes praise, attributes value and implies what is deemed ineffable in a relationship between the speaking amorous subject and an apparently foregrounded adored (silent) loved other. All lovers wish for the violence of their discourse to be disguised as an integrity of the heart, wish that the loved object reflect a flattering image of ineffability. And yet, despite the appeal of both Jankélévitch's and Barthes's loving writing about music, this chapter suggests that when music is praised and valued, when it apparently transitions from words to blissful beyond words, or to the ecstatic liminal fringes of contact between bodies, gender matters a great deal. In fact, both writers, in order to create qualitative distinctions and generate valuable meaning in their writing about music, depend on feminine figures and mythologies. Moreover, these feminine mythologies converge with the occurrence and deployment of light and dark to insinuate value that has an ideological basis in the construction of a light/radiant feminine in opposition to a dark feminine. I am interested therefore in the borderline between what can be said about the music one loves and what lies beyond the limitations of language. However, this chapter is particularly orientated towards questioning and revealing the dark side of ineffability and the music lover's discourse arguing that both depend upon a dark feminine that appears to function within a dynamic between language and music as a sign of death, or as a gap in meaning that confounds the writers.

Although engaging with loved text and music, this writing takes a darker turn in offering a bleaker critical perspective on the music lover's discourse and the kinds of value that accrues at the threshold of supposedly transformative potential, when music is apparently released from the will to hold and contain its meaning. To this extent, I want to question not only the processes by which the light and dark feminine are constructed, but also the value of the dark(ened) feminine to an audiovisual music discourse as it bespeaks the desire for music to be ineffable, meaning too great to be uttered (its godly aspect) as well as the lesser recognized implied taboo (not to be uttered/forbidden/risk). My focus in this respect is on the configuration of a mysterious and dark feminine voice, frozen at the borderline between language and the ineffable rather than released from it and therefore contra to the production of meaning positively appraised by Jankélévitch in the form of 'ineffable Charm' and Barthes with his concept of 'signifiance' (the ongoing plurality of meaning). This focus leads to a voice and an album I love, Nico's *The Marble Index* (1968). In the form of reviews and commentary, the lover's discourse that builds and accumulates around Nico's mythology (the vast majority of which is written by men) and specifically this album, offers ways of reading the occulted principles of a music lover's discourse as well as what Barthes in his discussion about the romantic song would briefly refer to as the 'dark voice'. Ultimately, the recalibration of the music lover's discourse reveals a hidden dark side and forms of desire that are usually disguised by a complex identification with light, truth and moral integrity. Under the cover of transparency and light, the processes that gender, sexualize and racialize within the music lover's discourse and the language of ineffability appear neutral, not ideologically informed. Eventually, however, following the traces of dark feminine mythologies, the music lover's discourse reveals a tapestry of Christian theology, philosophy and music epistemology that has spun a feminized voice of evil and/or death at the brink of what can be characterized as the dark oblivion of music at the edge of and beyond language: this is not the ineffable beyond, but a chasm which is configured as music's cold dark void. Intriguingly, the void is testified to in the lover's discourse about Nico's *The Marble Index* as a deathly hole that a listener falls into, as a depressive stasis which is the antithesis of the transformative potential implied by Jankélévitch's ineffability and Barthes's second semiology.

Sonic epiphanies and the light and dark of a music lover's discourse

Based on a monthly column in *The Wire* magazine, *Epiphanies: Life Changing Encounters with Music* (2015) is an anthology of short essays that presents individual accounts of specific moments of 'music's transformative power'. The collection features writing about subjective encounters with music that have changed the life of the writer, altering their reality and perception. Transformations such as these, apparently subjective, but also curiously often shared with others, are therein accorded the term 'epiphany' to suggest the magnitude of each specific experience and its effect on the listener. The word 'epiphany' acquires its cultural gravitas through the implicit undertones of a religious and/or spiritual connection, foregrounding both vision and light in that, etymologically, epiphany is linked to ideas of being able to see the 'manifestation of Christ', of 'something coming into a view', an appearance of a deity, a sudden perception or insight; 'to show' and 'to shine'. The mysterious radiance of sensual and supersensual sonorous epiphany is underscored in the editor's introductory notes in which he writes:

> Epiphanies, sonorous or otherwise, come in many forms. They can be instant or elliptical, numinous or traumatic, sensual or philosophical, or all these things and more. They recalibrate the world and illuminate routes to other ways of being. (Herrington, 2015: 13)

A sonorous epiphany *illuminates* routes to other ways of being and the insight on offer bequeaths an intoxicating contradictory blend of sudden realization and intense mystery, leading to the potential for something else, previously unseen. The radiance of this sonorous epiphany resonates with the radiance, jouissance, eroticism and effervescence of Barthes's second semiology and, moreover, with the transformative effulgent melodies and tones of Jankélévitch's ineffable Charm.

Light is important to Jankélévitch's conceptualization of music's ineffable Charm, and the sonorous epiphanies thereof and in many ways Jankélévitch seeks to challenge a legacy of discourse that has imagined music as essentially nocturnal, bound to femininity and female sexuality and thus regarded as 'mysterious' from the perspective of a male subjectivity aligned with the unconcealed light of reason. Of this legacy, he summarizes the perspective of masculine rationality:

> A man who has sobered up, a demystified man, does not forgive himself for having once been the dupe of misleading powers; a man who is abstaining, having awakened from his nocturnal exhilaration, blushes for having given in to dark causality. Once

AT THE FROZEN BORDERLINE OF MUSIC DISCOURSE   61

morning has returned, he disowns the pleasurable arts themselves, along with his own skills of pleasing. Strong and serious minds, prosaic and positive minds: maybe their prejudice with regard to music comes from sobering up. (Jankélévitch, [1961] 2003: 3)

To venture into the night of music is to risk the shame of becoming intoxicated, to be moved beyond one's control emotively towards the maelstrom of the feminine irrational (hysteria, sexuality, tears). Dark bewitching music belonging to time, spaces and mythologies of night, offers tempting nocturnal aesthetic pleasures of which one (Man) must remain cautious and enjoy with appropriate precautions in place (being strapped to a mast being one such clever precaution). Boldly, Jankélévitch attempts a rescue mission and decisively wrests music from its solely dark feminine figuration so as to provide the hope that mythical feminine figurations of 'light' can bring. His reading splits music between two feminized potentialities embodied in the divide between the mythical Muses, who are representative of the path towards Truth and the ineffable mystery of music (light); and the Sirens, who bewitch, flatter and, in essence, derail the dialectic (dark). Jankélévitch's move is apparently motivated by a critique of those who would moralize against the perceived musically induced corruption of masculine will and reason, and who would further advocate holding out for the protection of science against the 'intoxications of the night and the temptations exercised by the enchantress appearance' ([1961] 2003: 2). As part of his critique, Jankélévitch makes explicit reference to the relationship between misogyny and the grudge against music as it demonstrates suspicions of (feminized) pathos and music's propensity to derationalize and to drive even the wisest and serenest of men mad. In the opening pages of *Music and the Ineffable*, Jankélévitch presents a hung-over Enlightened Man as he shamefully remembers, once morning returns, the night before when he lost control and gave himself over to 'dark causality'. For his part, writing in the 1960s, Jankélévitch treats the eagerness to resist the dark temptations of music and night with suspicion and writes:

The Puritan grudge against music, the persecution of pleasure, hatred of seduction and spells, the antihedonist obsession: in the end, all these are pathologies, just as misogyny is pathological. ([1961] 2003: 10)

Puritan grudges aside, despite his explicit recognition of misogyny and his willingness to rescue music from *logos*, Jankélévitch, out of an apparent necessity, deploys the Muses and the Sirens as representative of a divide between enlivening virtues and deadening enchantments. In contrast to the creative, inspiring virtues of the Muses, it is the Sirens, those half-bird, half-women expert singers, who are, typically, lumbered with the responsibility of causing the fear and shame of both pilgrim and Enlightened Man whenever he is seduced by the dark 'influence' of song, moved beyond his self-control and therefore effeminized. In this case, the Sirens 'reroute, mislead' and ultimately 'they derail the dialectic, the law of itinerary that leads our mind towards duty and truth' (Jankélévitch, [1961] 2003: 10). In other words, the Sirens become the necessary fall bird-girls for the misogynistic baggage of music discourse as Jankélévitch, in approaching the ineffability of music, is forced to deal with a legacy of suspicion around music's ability to transgress and bring about liminal experiences that are associated with dark feminine voices and (feminizing) intoxicating musical oblivions. This is, of course, not the first time that the Sirens are constructed as a useful Other to Man's enlightened subjectivity, nor the first time that they are made to embody the dangers of the seductive pleasures and indulgent oblivions that music can bring.

In his effort to make a qualitative opposition that distinguishes the ineffable movements of music from static darkness, Jankélévitch's dependence on the feminine as that which usefully encapsulates inspiration or destruction is relayed in two mythopoetic feminine figurations: the Muses and the Sirens. In the processing of this coded dualism, Jankélévitch attempts to rescue music's mystery from being swallowed up entirely by 'death's sterilizing inexplicability', whereby music descends into a black hole after which nothing can be said and meaning is evacuated. He introduces a third mythological feminine creature in the form of Medusa so as to contrast the 'untellable' as opposed to the 'ineffable'. The ineffable opens up the cosmos to the infinite and inexhaustible multiplicity of meaning that can rightly be called 'musical', whilst the untellable is the condition of a blackened despairing non-being/death:

> Death, the black night, is untellable because it is impenetrable shadow and despairing non-being, and because a wall that

AT THE FROZEN BORDERLINE OF MUSIC DISCOURSE 63

cannot be breached bars us from its mystery: unable to be spoken of, then, because there is absolutely nothing to say, rendering us mute, overwhelming reason, transfixing human discourse on the point of its Medusa stare. And the ineffable, in complete contrast, cannot be explained because there are infinite and indeterminable things to be said of it: such is the mystery of God, whose depths cannot be sounded, the inexhaustible mystery of love, both Eros and Caritas, the poetic mystery par excellence. (Jankélévitch, [1961] 2003: 72)

Here, the difference between stasis and movement is applied directly to an opposition between the black night of music as it overwhelms discourse and meaning (a transfixed static state and despairing non-being), and ineffable music as it produces inexhaustible mysteries of love, God and, in effect, the ongoing movement of meaning. The switch here from the use value of the Sirens, a three-part bewitching vocal troop with dark deathly voices, to Medusa, whose stare transfixes the viewer and turns them into stone, further underscores a deathly mute stillness and presents an interesting transferral of focus and power from audio to sight. Both the Sirens and Medusa are loaded with deathly effects and their voices and eyes symbolize cutting repercussions for the vitality and mystery of music and music discourse. Whether by voice or eyes, singing or staring, the mysteries of love are thwarted by the Sirens and Medusa. Nevertheless, however terrifying and transfixing in their deployment, these dark feminine figures bear the traces of a troubled heteronormative male desire that wishes to penetrate the mystery of the dark feminine. Nestled underneath the implicitness of that desire is an ever more subtle fear of both 'impenetrable shadow' and of being penetrated by sound, rendered mute, as in, without words, without 'knowledge' and silent. Although Barthes's figures of light and dark differ and are perhaps more difficult to trace, a comparable dark muteness that is the arrest of meaning haunts his lover's discourse. In Barthes's music lover's discourse, connections between bodies are key to the enlivening and production of meaning. This is nowhere more vital than when 'the Mother' occurs in connection with the listening body, a connection that can be considered via a radiant intimacy in a text that lovingly reaches between bodies, between life and death.

The luminous shadow of the Mother

Barthes's evaluations of music are based on listening to the *body* in music, or rather the encounter between body, text, and music. Music's body, as it emerges in Barthes's text, has an umbilical cord that can be traced back to the maternal through Julia Kristeva's writings on the pheno/geno text, jouissance and the semiotic chora (Barthes credits the work of Kristeva). At times the mother explicitly appears in his texts in a series of references scattered across the body of his music essays. Of the most intense of these references is the moment where the 'Mother tongue' explodes in an essay about Schumann, a composer whose music Barthes loved:

> To remain with Schumann [...], the explosion of the *Muttersprache* in musical writing is really the declared restoration of the body – as if, on the threshold of melody, the body discovered itself, assumed itself in the double depth of the beat and of language; as if, with regard to music, the mother tongue occupied the place of the *chora* (a notion adapted from Plato by Julia Kristeva): the indicating word is the receptacle of *signifying*. (Barthes, [1975] 1991: 310)

It is the ongoing process and plurality of meaning that Barthes hopes to relieve from the tyranny of the signified by following the 'body in a state of music' ([1975] 1991: 312). And, as Barthes turns to the specificity of his unique relationship with Schumann in the essay 'Loving Schumann', the umbilical relationship to the maternal is made explicit as the epitome of solitary intimacy, in which there is a musical refuge that expresses pre-Oedipal and choric space:

> This is a music at once dispersed and unary, continually taking refuge in the luminous shadow of the Mother (the lied, copious in Schumann's work, is, I believe, the expression of this maternal unity). (Barthes, [1979] 1991: 298)

There is comfort in the lied, the comfort of refuge in the luminous shadow of the Mother and the dream of pre-separation unity and wholeness. In conceptualizing Barthes's 'maternal methodology', Barbara Engh draws comparisons between this umbilical relation and the 'umbilical cord' that Barthes refers to in his *Camera Lucida*

AT THE FROZEN BORDERLINE OF MUSIC DISCOURSE 65

where he conceives of the affect of the photograph as though being 'touched' by the radiations of a body as they occur between his own and that of the body that 'was there' (Engh, 1993). Barthes discusses the feeling of such connection with his own mother as he reflects on a picture of her in a winter garden photograph as likened to the 'last music Schumann wrote before collapsing', according to both 'my mother's being and my grief at her death' ([1980] 2000: 70). The maternal connection continues when he writes: 'A sort of umbilical cord links the body of the photographed thing to my gaze: light though impalpable, is here a carnal medium, a skin I share with anyone who has been photographed' (Barthes, [1980] 2000: 81). With both kinds of musical and photographic 'touch', Barthes refers to the radiance of light as it establishes and expresses the connective tissue between bodies, across time and space and between the past and the present.

Schumann's music takes refuge in what Barthes calls 'the luminous shadow of the Mother' and the emitted light of the maternal, though impalpable, establishes intimate contact – he is 'touched' and able to dream a dream of maternal reunification. The radiance of the maternal continues in his essay 'The Romantic Song', where Barthes begins by setting the night-time scene of listening to Schubert. During this encounter, Barthes draws the reader close by revealing his internal dialogue and allows us to hear his ruminations on the limits of language: 'What is there to say about what one loves except I *love it*, and to keep on saying it' (Barthes, [1976] 1991: 286). Barthes, listening to the unassuming romantic song, once again, returns to the maternal and to a special kind of radiance, one that is emergent in the lieder of Schumann and Schubert, both of which embody, for Barthes, 'the incandescent core of the romantic song' ([1976] 1991: 289). Immersed in this radiance, Barthes begins to question the 'feeling' of the romantic song, and his writing shifts the mode of questioning from the 'music itself' to bodies in a state of music, so that his questions migrate towards affect and address and he asks of himself:

'What is it that, in my body, sings the lied to me listening?' It is everything that resounds in me, frightens me, or makes me desire. [...] for the lover as for the child, it is always the affect of the abandoned subject that the romantic song sings. Schubert loses his mother at fifteen; two years later his first great song,

Gretchen at the Spinning Wheel, utters the tumult of absence, the hallucination of the return. (Barthes, [1976] 1991: 288–9)

The lied's space is one of solitary intimacy that ultimately comes back to subjectivity and the imaginary image of oneself who loves, desires and loses something, someone. One sings the lied to oneself, to the wound of loss or nostalgia opened by the lied, as a separated child or lover; 'the lied's space is affective [...] its true listening space is, so to speak, the interior of the head, of *my head*: listening to it I sing the lied with myself, for myself' (Barthes, [1976] 1991: 290). In this respect, the romantic song draws the listener to an imaginary space that is exquisitely painful and, as Barthes recognizes, has an 'imprisoning' effect to the extent that one is trapped in a deep intimacy with the image of both oneself and the desired lost other. Hallucinating and fantasizing in this space means being subject to the memories, landscapes and moods that acknowledge one's abandonment and the 'irremediable absence of the beloved' at the same time as being 'touched' by them, bathing in the luminous shadow of the lost other. Inevitably in this respect perhaps, given his closeness to love and loss in the lied, Barthes's ruminations on the romantic song are tinged with the threat of a darker turn toward disconnection and death. If Barthes's maternal luminous shadows are difficult to trace, his 'dark voice' is barely perceptible and yet it emerges as part of the vicissitudes of the evaluation as the anti-human, anti-body, anti-desire ominous undercurrent of the romantic song, which engenders not love or connection or comfort, but utter disconnection from bodies ever more distant: the end of desire.

The disconnected, end of desire dark white voice

The 'heart' of the romantic song, or indeed its 'incandescent core', offers a comfort or a refuge in the sense that one may be brought closer to one's self and the lost other, bringing about some kind of 'contact'. However, the lied has a dark side which Barthes expresses and admits in the idea of the lied's interlocutor as the self's double, a reflection which is the cut-off and fragmented self, corrupted and overwhelmed by an ugly narcissism:

AT THE FROZEN BORDERLINE OF MUSIC DISCOURSE   67

In short, the lied's interlocutor is the Double – my Double, which is Narcissus: a corrupt double, caught in the dreadful sense of the cracked mirror, as Schubert's unforgettable *Döppelgänger* puts it. (Barthes, [1976] 1991: 290)

Barthes's cracked mirror fragments the 'hallucination of the return' of the lost other and opens up several ways of reading the romantic song as 'dark'. There are echoes here of many separating moments: of birth itself, as the infant is pushed from the dark sound world of the mother; of Lacan's mirror phase and the moment in which the infant realizes it is separate from its mother and (mis) recognizes itself; of Freud's uncanny as embodied by the 'double' or *döppelgänger*; of the pain felt by Narcissus who falls in love with his own reflection and despairs upon realizing he cannot have what he desires – himself. And yet, when Barthes explicitly talks about a division that haunts the romantic song, it comes as a 'dark voice', one that he is adamant does not refer to the division of the sexes but, rather, divides between the 'dark voice of super-nature, or of demonic nature' and 'the pure voice of the soul, not insofar as it is religious but simply human, all too human' ([1976] 1991: 288). Referring to Schubert's song 'Death and the Maiden' ('Der Tod und das Mädchen'), Barthes writes:

The diabolic evocation and the maiden's prayer here belong to the order of the sacred, not of the religious: what is suggested, what is here vocally put before us, is the anguish of something that threatens to divide, to separate, to dissociate, to dismember the body. The dark voice, voice of Evil or of Death, is a voice without site, a voice without origin: it resonates everywhere [...]: in every case, it no longer refers to the body, which is distanced in a kind of non-site. ([1976] 1991: 288)

The song 'Death and the Maiden' (1817), composed by Schubert (before his quartet of the same name) and based on a poem written by Matthias Claudius, is written in the key of D Minor and features two vocal parts: the maiden (Das Mädchen) and death (Der Tod.). It begins with a dark melancholic theme that proceeds slowly through a repeated rhythm, creating an impression of a funeral procession up until the moment that the maiden begins to sing. The maiden intervenes with phrases sung significantly quicker (*etwas geschwinder*) and in a higher vocal register, providing a feeling of urgency and youth in resistance to the inevitability of the funeral motif. She pleads with death to leave her alone: 'Oh! Leave me! Prithee, leave me! Thou grisly man of bone! For life is sweet, is pleasant.' After a significant and ominous pause, the dark theme returns, and with it the voice of death whose vocal part is delivered significantly slower, according to the tempo of the previous funeral march, and with a prolonged focus on a low D. *He,* Death, reassures her to take his hand and as a friend he encourages her to rest: 'Within my arms shalt softly rest thee'. Death's offer to the maiden perversely echoes the refuge offered by the lied's connection with the maternal. Moreover, in this song occurs a double of sorts that echoes Barthes's fragmented cracked mirror image: the vocalist sings *both* the part of the maiden and of Death, a voice with two acoustic images, a voice that expresses both the plea for Death to leave and Death's offer of comfort. Consequently, the voice is required to inhabit two roles: one of life and youth and the other of death in a series of uncanny reflections.

Although the text of the song prescribes explicitly gendered roles, Barthes contends that the romantic song in general forgets the Oedipal dramas of Western operatic vocal roles where father, mother, son and daughter are 'symbolically projected' on to bass, mezzo, tenor and soprano and further that the lied emerges instead from the 'unisexual', from the human body as it appeals to the 'any body' that sings, promoting in effect humanity and the human body as the familiar site of the romantic song. Instead of being haunted by sexual division, gender roles and Oedipal triumphs as in opera, Barthes claims that a different division haunts the romantic song: that of the 'dark voice' as it emerges from an unfamiliar non-site without origin and threatens to divide and dismember the human body. The dark voice may 'resonate everywhere' as in Wolf's 'Glen of *Freischütz*' or become 'motionless, suspended' as in 'Death and the Maiden', but in each case 'it no longer refers to the body, which is distanced in a kind of non-site' (Barthes, [1976] 1991: 288). Bearing in mind Barthes's distinction between the phenosong and the genosong, between the over-coded expressive sung vocal and the voice which has 'grain' (the body of the singing voice), the dark death voice of 'Death and the Maiden', emerging from a non-site, seems to propose something that exceeds Barthes's reading (his evaluation) of voices and therefore reaches the limit

AT THE FROZEN BORDERLINE OF MUSIC DISCOURSE   69

of his opposition, arguably because the dark voice without origin and desire exceeds the gendered and sensual body that Barthes so depends on for the 'erotic' relationship between his listening body and that of the singer/musician; without that, there can be no desire or jouissance. The dark voice is neither ideologically expressive, nor is it *signifying* at the level of the grain as it rubs between music, voice, language and body(bodies).

The dark voice of death in this respect seems to mean the end of meaning, even for Barthes's second semiology. It also appears to suggest an 'unsexed' voice, genderless, bodiless and desireless. Barthes's emphasis on the singing voice of the lied is explicitly 'unisexual' and 'human', but there are a few discreet references in his music essays which imply that this loved up human body is haunted by a disembodied dark voice without a familiar site that is the voice of evil or death. The threat posed by the dark voice seems to pose the fear of underlying *disconnections*. In his essay 'The Romantic Song', Barthes talks about the 'anguish of something that threatens to divide' and, after reassuring himself that the dark voice is the exception, he returns to the comforting originating heart of the romantic lied which comes from the familiar site of 'the singer's – and hence the listener's – body', because the lied makes meaning 'only if I can always sing it, in myself, with my body' ([1976] 1991: 288). In other words, the dark voice holds out no image of oneself and one's body and it lacks the narcissistic function and any comforting umbilical cord leading back to the lost Mother. Another poignant threat of disconnection between the singer, the listener and language occurs in the essay 'Music, Voice, Language' and is related in a passage that precedes another loving dedication to Panzera's voice and the old French language. Barthes writes:

> there is no human voice which is not an object of desire – or of repulsion: there is no neutral voice – and if sometimes that neutrality, that whiteness of the voice occurs, it terrifies us, as if we were to discover a frozen world, one in which desire was dead. ([1977] 1991: 280)

The dark voice therefore may be interpreted as something that has exceeded the codes of 'humanity' as they refer to love, erotic relationships, national identity and objects of desire and reached the limits of a lover's discourse, finding a parallel with Jankélévitch's bewitched, transfixed, blackened untellable end of meaning.

When desire is dead, something is disconnected from the luminous shadow of the Mother and from the enabling inspiration of the Muse. All loving intimacy severed, in place of the human voice is what Barthes describes as a 'terrifying neutral whiteness of voice', a voice cut off from the luminous maternal and the umbilical cord to choric meaning and therefore all potential jouissance. For a brief moment in his writing on music's body, Barthes opens up the possibility of the occurrence of a terrifying neutral whiteness of voice, 'as if we were to discover a frozen world, one in which desire was dead'. Freezing in this regard recalls the Medusa-like stare warned against by Jankélévitch and aligned with the black night, untellable arrests of meaning. However, something in Barthes's description pushes this further and bequeaths a void which freezes the world, being and desire. Alongside the icy imagery, this whitened neutral version of a disconnected 'dark voice' can be discerned in the lover's discourse about Nico, where the writing about her and *The Marble Index* gathers at the 'cloudy borderline' of the album, at the limits of what can be said. Drawing parallels between Jankélévitch's blackened feminized untellable (cultivated through the mythology of the Sirens's voices and Medusa stare) and Barthes's supernatural non-site dark voice of death coupled with the neutral white voice cut off from maternal radiance and desire, the music lover's discourse about Nico amalgamates and reveals the dark feminine mythologies upon which these voices and looks depend. As the writing about Nico and her album stretches to articulate this amalgamation, it exposes the dark side of itself, not only the violence of heteronormative and gendered aesthetic sensibilities, but also the racialized aesthetics of the lover's discourse which here bespeaks a whitened beauty. Nico's music reflects these sensibilities back on to the discourse itself, revealing for a moment the terrible neutral whiteness that attempts to freeze the apparent object of its love. In this respect, the album exceeds that which would enshrine and incarcerate it; in a Medusa-like manoeuvre, *The Marble Index* reflects the power of the gaze back on to the gazer, the power of the discourse back to the speaker and acts as an audiovisual mirror that casts a disturbing reflection on to the music lover's discourse, threatening to transfix its techniques and arrest its ideologically-laden desires.

Nico's cryogenic beauty

In the track 'Frozen Warnings', singer-songwriter Nico heeds proximity to a cloudy, frozen borderline: 'Frozen warnings close to mine / Close to the frozen borderline'. The spectre of a mirror follows in the lyrics, 'Into numberless reflections / Rises a smile from your eyes into mine', drawing the listener to the threshold and reflection of a wintry phantasmagoria. Music journalism and commentary has clustered over the years at the brink of what can be said about the album, culminating in swathes of articles about Nico, but all of which can be interpreted as a series of attempts to deal with a fascinating audiovisual reflection of a music lover's own (heteronormative) desire, a desire that wishes to speak itself. There is perhaps nothing exceptional in this given that such encounters are so often the impetus for saying or writing anything about music. However, tuning into the listener's desire, Theodor Adorno, in less than generous terms and characteristic of his strident critique of popular music and the culture industry, suggests that gramophone listeners are orientated around providing themselves with a flattering reflection of their own image:

> What the gramophone listener actually wants to hear is himself, and the artist merely offers him a substitute for the sounding image of his own person, which he would like to safeguard as a possession. The only reason that he accords the record such value is because he himself could also be just as well preserved. Most of the time records are virtual photographs of their owners, flattering photographs. (Adorno, 1990: 54)

To this degree, writing about the record might be interpreted as the clarification of that image. Nevertheless, something about Nico and her sound in *The Marble Index* disturbs the 'virtual photograph' of the listener and appears to agitate the lover's discourse into an unusual overdrive. This is partly because the album forces the evaluation of Nico to transition from the visual, where she, an ex-model, is highly valued in terms of hyperbolic expressions of beauty, to the audio, where the signifiers of her beauty are much more ambiguous as the ear interprets a low contralto drone-like voice that is prone to aesthetic interpretations of ugliness, slurring disconnection from standard channels of communication and darkened with the potential affect of fear. As well as the unnerving shifts between an unambiguous beautiful image and ambiguous unlovely vocals, some kind of response is also elicited in Nico's transformation from model icon, infamous muse/object of the male gaze, to singer-songwriter and musician, with agency. Set to oscillate between the sound of Nico and her visual image, writing about her has had to find a way of negotiating the all-out marbleized stasis of 'ice queen' and her more aesthetically troubling unnerving soundings where voice and song is heard to 'drone'.

A 'drone' refers to a long, sustained low sound, a single tone or sustained group of pitches and is a term that recalls monotony, humming, buzzing, vibrations and, in a sense, a sort of desireless sound that 'drones' on, sometimes lagging, without an easily locatable momentum driven by desire. It is a sound that lends itself to the notion of non-meaning or nonsense in that it lacks an active agency and the necessary organization of spaces in-between sounds, which provide language with meaning. A drone is thus generally perceived as a dull ongoing sound or noise. Etymologically, drone acquired its sonic meaning in the early sixteenth century, meaning 'deep, continuous humming sound' and is related to threnody, from the 'Greek *threnodia* "lamentation", from *threnos* "dirge, lament"' (Etymonline). Feeling drone in the body, physiologically, can therefore produce an uncanny affect as it lacks subjecthood and has no meaningful intention of verbal meaning, but nevertheless vibrates the body in a way that resonates with drudging 'low' tones and closeness to death. John Cale is largely credited for developing the drone sound of the Velvet Underground which featured Nico, whilst the other founding member Lou Reed, 'brought rock and roll sensibility' (Demers, 2010: 107). From the perspective of this dual combination, Joanna Demers suggests that Nico complemented the band because her voice was an amalgamation of two tendencies: 'a soft contralto that could be soothing or strident dependent on how much Nico pushed it' (2010: 107). In classical terms, the contralto is the lowest register of the female voice, which Demers draws on to describe Nico's vocal range, amended by a sense of contextually characteristic timbre, varying from smooth to strident. Understandings of Nico's voice, imagined as a variable intensity between drone and rock 'n' roll, have employed terms such as 'deep', 'monotone', 'cool', 'glacial', 'dissonant', 'cold' and 'melancholic'. These understandings have, over time, constructed a dark feminine mythology that has attached itself to timbre and pitch, to focus on the cold drone contralto of Nico's voice as it meets the much foregrounded beauty of her looks. In *The Marble Index*, voice and harmonium move slowly through drones and low contralto pitches, towards the cold of the track 'Frozen Warnings' and the pounding 'doombells' and 'midnight winds landing at the end of time' in the track 'Evening of Light', creating the generally accepted deathly dark and fearful beauty of the album. During the making of *The Marble Index*, both voice and harmonium were apparently a source of musical antagonism from the perspective of tuning, owing perhaps to Nico's hearing issues (it has been suggested she was deaf in one ear) and heroin addiction. Cale, in his capacity as song arranger, was reported in one interview to have said that Nico insisted on playing whilst singing despite it being out of tune and that this resulted in the requirement to find compatible instrumental voices and a lot of overdubbing (Cale, cited in Pinnock 2015). And yet, the hypnotic droning voice and harmonium persist, insist, in fact, on a psychic landscape of melancholy at the brink of an album that has been interpreted as the sonic realization of a 'death wish'.

The strategies for transitioning between gaze/beauty and ear/unlovely effectively involve the translation of Nico's image into her sound where the death wish can be surreptitiously romanticized. Language about Nico's looks habitually monumentalize her figure by evoking untouchable iconic beauty from which a pale white light radiates and by promoting nicknames such as 'moon goddess' in a series of monikers that mysteriously glow and foreground her Germanic nationality, blond hair, blue eyes, chiselled features and pale skin. Commenting on *The Marble Index*, one article posits a mysterious winter twilight and ethereal radiance that encompasses both the sound and image of the album. In 'Nico: A Conversation with Danny Fields', David Dalton remarks:

> Nico was astonishingly beautiful, radiating an ethereal, icy image that made her seem like some kind of exquisite replica created by the doyennes of high fashion, a quality her unearthly voice seemed to underline. All this seemed astonishing enough, if a bit ephemeral. Then came *The Marble Index*. At that point we

realized, not only did we not know Nico, this was someone quite other, someone whom we would never know. (2002)

The 'we' that is appealed to here assumes a collective of unknowing lovers, invested in the mystery of never knowing Nico, the exquisite replica, the unknowable other. Decades earlier however, after the release of *The Marble Index*, one of the most famous writers of the music journalism canon, Lester Bangs, had already established the problem that 'we would never know' and worked on it in an article entitled 'Nico: A Kind of Frozen Purity' (1971). Bangs conjures an aural winter landscape in his review of Nico's work, which 'continuously sharpens a lens focused on her dark separation until it all but glows in its very impermeability, with a kind of frozen purity' (Bangs 1971). Glowing with a frozen purity, Bangs's use of audiovisual imagery conflates Nico and her sound into a series of glaciers, distinguishing remoteness by engendering a composite blend of winter light and darkness, season and temperature and drawing on cultural mythology to situate Nico at the mystical edges of an image of remote snowy landscapes haunted by the light and darkness of the north. This is in order to say something about Nico's sound and the artist herself, as well as his listening relationship to it. Following the explicit temperature gauge of the lyrics in 'Frozen Warnings', a combination of chilling timbres and tones and arrangements without a clear tonal centre, materialize in his writing about her and are filtered through notions of emotive indifference, painlessness and a sound without desire. He thereby draws on a mythology that pushes Nico further and further into an igloo album of physical, temporal and spatial estrangement. Indeed, what Bangs hears in 'Frozen Warnings' is 'a very specific song about human estrangement'. He further notes, 'The irony of it is that the glittering beauty of the music makes alienation seem like Shangri-La, an arctic clime of perfect insulation. Nico intones the words like a benediction, safe in the bosom of her gleaming steppes snow-leagues distant from the pain of contact' (Bangs, 1971). Another review by Bangs entitled 'Your Shadow Is Scared of You: An Attempt Not to Be Frightened by Nico' ([1983] 2003) features extracts from a conversation with his girlfriend about the album, as both attempt to wrestle with loving the deathly acts of negation heard in *The Marble Index*, where you 'might begin to wonder if you are not the junkie, a junkie for a glimpse of the pit' (Bangs: 206). The woman

AT THE FROZEN BORDERLINE OF MUSIC DISCOURSE 75

to whom Bangs refers (his girlfriend at the time) hears Nico 'lost in her own blackness' and between them both they hear acts of '*de-creation*' and negation:

> She is a black point hole in space with one point left. [...] 'It's empty, it's black, it's alone, it's a whirlpool, an eddy, it's nothing,' but it's not nothing, it's her that's nothing. [...] She wants to mutilate it [an insect] too because it's another act of negation, because it snuffs more light out of her star. (Bangs, [1983] 2003: 209)

Black and white, dark and light: this is the stark audiovisual imagery of the album's negation that the lovers struggle with at the edge of a fascinating black hole. Decades on, the glistening snow of winter and its parallels with wilful isolated psychology and avant-garde outsider innovation continues; Tom Pinnock writes: '*The Marble Index* gives voice to a psychic landscape of immense loneliness, a wintry place, lit occasionally by a haunting Alpen glow, but otherwise darker than anywhere rock music had ever been or in future would much care to venture' (2015). Reviews of Nico consistently evoke a cold and dark audiovisual imagery, from mystical priestess litanies and austere prayer funeral-like melancholy that characterize her voice, to a cold indifference that draws connections between Nico's body and a bleak, desolate aural landscape of snow and ice. Across the landscape of *The Marble Index*, the sonic shadow of Nico resounds amongst other elemental forces: John Cale's orchestration, affective electric shiver production, Cale's arrangements organized from overdubs of improvised recordings, Nico's harmonium drones; all swirl around steadfast timeless vocal melodies in a storm that eventually crystallizes notes at various points in the vast space of a wild extensive winter plain and on the edge of a 'black hole', reaching an uncannily calm deathliness that elicits shudders: her 'de-creation'. Within a track such as 'Frozen Warnings', the egocentric desire of the performing and listening subject is decentralized and the rhythmic beat killed, buried or lost. Heart turned to ice, a series of pulsed tones that have no audible attack blend as oscillating notes rising and falling, going nowhere, droning on in oceanic swells and whirlwind gusts that swirl across the aural/aurora scene of the album's imaginary (Nico compared the sound of the harmonium with the sound of wind).

Out of time: The hyper-white voice and its dark other

Temporality is a primary area of focus in a discourse about an album that makes assertions such as 'Nico is an anachronism in the modern age – a projection of not just one but countless eras past' (Watson, 1985). Julian Cope's reflection on the album notes the correspondence between the out-of-time temporality of the album verging on what Nico would present in the final track 'Evening Light' as the 'end of time' and Nico's 'lack of respect for musical rhythm' and time-keeping (turning up days late), as a lesson to be cherished in an age obsessed with scheduling: 'throw away your time-pieces and embrace *The Marble Index*' (2007). The Velvets complained about Nico's timing issues with, for example, her tambourine playing, so even earlier in her singing career there is a sense of her timing being an issue. Discourse on *The Marble Index* processes and amplifies a focus on time, correlating the album's temporality with the 'timelessness' of romantic lieder and folk, as well as its apparent movements against the light of the future, drawing back to the 'dark ages' and to an imagined time before the Enlightenment. Pushing backwards on a linear timeline, her sound and vocal intonation are affiliated with Gregorian chant and pre-Christian mythology in an album compared with the spatial-temporal dark ambience of the Middle Ages. Bangs writes that Nico's 'aura' of loneliness is 'so distant' as to be 'positively medieval', whilst Dalton makes direct comparisons with the sanctity of mystic composition and liturgical singing: 'And then came *The Marble Index* where you have what sounds like Hildegard of Bingen singing mystic hymns from an interior Middle Ages in the middle of the 20th century' (Dalton, 2002). Vivid sonic imagery draws from a spatio-temporality that migrates from vast arctic plains to architectural gothic vacuity, through German '*volk*' and idealized accounts of a 'pre-Christian' past, ushering in pagan mysticism woven from Germany's dark past. Simon Reynolds describes the 'sonic *mise-en-scène* of the album as conjuring 'dark draughty castles of Bavaria or Bohemia, with shadows, cast from guttering candles, flickering against the walls' (Reynolds, 2007).

Alongside the ambience of German Gothic cultural history, Reynolds makes specific reference to Nazi ideology, to Nico's reported racism and to an incident where Nico violently attacked a black woman. In doing so, he makes explicit what others have inferred or dreamt, in that he draws attention to the ties between the mythological darkness of Nico, Nazi ideology and the narratives of Nico's racism, which bind together to produce the perception of the dark sonic spaces of the album and its 'Aryan aura' (Tweddell, 2011). Whitened dark emptiness, edges, holes and voids within the album correspond with observations of Nico's personal 'inner void' and, in turn, the horrific cultural history that recalls her early childhood experiences and traumas in Germany as a child sheltering from and escaping the bombings of the Second World War, a war which apparently led to the death of her father from shell shock (Reynolds, 2007). Nazis haunt Nico's biography and early life and phantoms of Nazi ideology are also controversially invited by Nico herself, particularly, for example, when she caused an audience riot in Berlin by singing the 'Das Lied der Deutschen' ('The Song of the Germans'), which prompted shouts of 'Nazi' from the crowd who hurled bottles until she left the stage (Young, 1999: 90–2). In terms of the discourse about Nico, the undercurrents of connections with Nazi ideology and racism do nothing to exhaust the fantasy of her but, on the contrary, exacerbates Aryan fantasies in a way that, following Susan Sontag, might be described as the spectre of 'fascinating fascism' (Sontag, [1975] 2013). Writers, assuming a variable distance, make regular inferences of Nazi ideology, with some bolder than others: 'her blonde Aryan aura offsetting the dark, junkie image of the band', which is put together with the supposed possession of a cold and 'difficult' temperament (Tweddell 2011). Through a combination of cultural mythology, history, bio-mythology and sonic affects, Nico magnetizes descriptions of northern wintery whiteness as if her voice, construed to monumentalize 'the cold white feminine', offered the avant-garde a fascinating frozen borderline, beyond which lies the unmapped dream of the Hyperborean. The audiovisual imagery in the discourse about Nico uses a combination of dark and light metaphors and continuously reiterates the cryogenic freezing of the album, this having ramifications for how one might listen for the construction of gender, race and sexuality in a wider context of a sexualized and racialized aloof dark feminine sounding.

Her 'iciness' corresponds with an unsexing that translates as impenetrability and frozen bodily fluids and this is perfectly exemplified in Simon Reynolds and Joy Press's figuration of rock's ice queens. Press and Reynolds describe *The Marble Index* as 'one of the most harrowing and death-fixated albums in rock history' (1996: 301). Chilling ice queens are isolated, cut-off beings compared with Lady Macbeth who, in William Shakespeare's play *Macbeth*, appealed to 'the spirits that tend on mortal thoughts' to 'unsex her' – 'relieve her of gentle femininity':

> Ice is the opposite of all that women are supposed to be: warm, flowing, giving, receptive. Like Lady Macbeth the Ice Queen has unsexed herself, dammed up her lachrymal and lactation ducts. She offers cold, not comfort. Her hard surfaces can't be penetrated. She is an island, an iceberg. (Reynolds and Press, 1996: 300)

This corresponds with an unsexing that repeatedly infers an 'unsexing' of atypical femininity measured by nurturing maternalism. 'Unsexing' as a cutting off from the maternal body and feminine sexuality is pushed further in relation to her drug-taking. The appeal of the fantasy of Nico's impermeable iciness is offset by the frequent reference to her heroin addiction, where one is invited to imagine the impenetrable queen regularly penetrated by a self-destructive needle loaded with an opiate injected into the veins, further underscoring images of a cold desire-less body, droning in desire-less space, hungry only for more cold oblivion. All this is brought together in a quote from Reynolds and Press, who make a series of oppositions and analogies that bring together a bleached, white Aryan sound underscored by a frigid expanse with a drive towards the living death of 'Absolute Zero'.

> The Velvets went straight from folk-rock to whiter-than-white noise, bypassing R&B's body-heat. On solo albums, Nico goes even deeper into a wasteland of arid, ascetic, Aryan sound [...] 'Nibelungen' describes a world drained of affect, bleached of colour; again, she longs to be 'asleep'. [...] its hunger for narcosis, its frigid expanses, recalls William Burroughs's description of the junkie's quest for a metabolic 'Absolute Zero'. The only way to erase doubt and kill pain completely is to enter a *living death*. (1996: 300–1)

Nico's vocal body is ardently mythologized through the gloaming of winter and the frigid impenetrability of a white cold nothing that is the absolute negative of life and desire. Driving towards death, her voice opens up to a vivid image of a stark winter landscape where nothing survives and which opens up both a 'terrible inner void' and a 'hole you fall into' (Mohawk, cited in Gill 2007): an absolute zero that is the black hole of a dark sounding that can be considered through the drone and Nico's low pitch vocal soundings.

Sonic whiteness of voice

Antagonized by Nico's musical innovation and dark 'beauty', hidden ideologies usually suppressed beneath the music lover's discourse surface to reveal the ordinarily invisible 'white sonic identity' and usually inaudible sonic markers of whiteness, so that what is intermittently revealed by Nico's sound and, moreover, the discourse about it, is the socially-constructed ideological system of what Jennifer Lynn Stoever has called the 'listening ear', which 'normalizes the aural tastes and standards of white elite masculinity as the singular way to interpret sonic information' (Stoever, 2016: 13). In Stoever's comparative critical analysis of the epistemological language developed to record and evaluate the white opera singer Jenny Lind ('The Swedish Nightingale') and the black opera singer Elizabeth Taylor Greenfield ('The Black Swan'), Stoever notes the 'qualities' bestowed on Lind's vocal-body as a 'vessel for whiteness', produced in language that orchestrates correspondences between Lind's performance and 'Nordic whiteness [...] at the apex of the American racial spectrum' (2016: 98). A proliferation of adjectives focused on vocal timbre and performative gesture work are used to establish Lind's performing body/voice as 'carnally desirous' yet 'corporeally transcendent' in terms of white supremacy. As a result, Lind is perceived as a disciplined vocal performer, in control of a 'clear', 'pure' voice with an 'intellectual understanding of lyrics', with 'crisp intonation' and accurate timing (Stoever, 2016: 98). Greenfield, in stark contrast, is hypersexualized as 'thrilling and abject' and scrutiny is focused on her contralto and low vocal pitches, sounds interpreted and directed to confirm both her blackness and masculinity. Although much of the Nico mythology finds parallels with the Hyperborean fantasies of the north and the white feminine body as a vessel for a 'purity' of race, her low voice, as it blends with harmonium drones, resonates with some of the racial and gender anxieties that drive the timbral adjectives used to classify Greenfield's voice as black, hypersexualized and masculine. To handle the incommensurability of looks (unambiguously beautiful, light) and voice (potentially ugly/not pretty, dark) and to set conceptual parameters for a voice/album in possession of soundings that potentially threaten to feminize masculinity as well as to masculinize and/or transsexualize the beautiful white female body as an object of desire, Nico's voice-body is sent to the farthermost regions of the north, to be unsexed as a frozen void of nothing, pure and indifferent. It is distinguished from the gender clichés of connected loving Motherhood (her 'de-creation') and idolized as a mysterious priestess at the frozen borderline of what cannot be said: a 'suicidal' void on an edge where masculinity senses a threat:

> It was a short album, mainly because [producers] Mohawk and Haeny couldn't listen to much more than half an hour of it. 'It kind of made us want to slit our wrists', Mohawk recalled. '*The Marble Index* isn't a record you listen to. It's a hole you fall into.' (Gill, 2007)

This album as a 'hole you fall into' once again returns to the void and to the dark voice of death, white/neutral and non-human. The question of what makes this album terrifying for commentators and producers can be brought together in the conceptualization of an audiovisual mirror, not exactly the flattering mirror of the Velvet Underground's 'I'll Be Your Mirror' ('reflect what you are'), but a different kind of mirror reflecting disturbing fragments of images. Buried beneath the construction of Nico's white beauty is a notion of pure origins that leads to a fantasy of the Mother tongue and the Mother country as it gives birth to pure white beings, at the beginning of time, before the corruption of Christianity or foreign bodies. However, the Mother at the frozen borderline is not radiant, full of the plenitude of compassion and reassuringly maternal, but disconnects, does not bear fruit, doesn't invite you into her arms, doesn't want you (interpreted as 'desire-lessness'). A frenzy of beautiful, dark, cold metaphors and adjectives proliferate across the articles about Nico and *The Marble Index*, as the lover's discourse senses, in the dying gothic ardour and winter light of its own imagery, an end without jouissance and without the choric radiance of the Mother and the refuge offered by her luminous shadow. Constitutive then of a disconnection with the Mother's lost body and Mother country, this whitened voice cuts the desire for connection, depresses that desire. Discourse here can no longer gravitate towards the transcendent ineffable light of the beautiful white male or the Father-son dyad, because Nico's album is an end without light, a dark, white feminine with an inner void. The shudders and shivers within the text as it approaches Nico's frozen borderline belie connections between darkness and a white, low, droning female voice which is the absolute zero of the dark feminine, absolute cold, impenetrable, impermeable abyss. In a Medusa-like return of the gaze, Nico's acoustic mirror, if looked at and listened to directly, threatens to reveal the gendered and racialized void that has been created by the hideous violence of a white supremacist Hyperborean fantasy nestled within the discourse about her, reflecting a voice within the discourse itself that can neither love or be loved, a hidden voice of hatred that attempts to turn the object of appraisal to stone, to adored monument. This is the dark white voice Barthes referred to, but one that *is* all too human, a voice racialized and gendered at the limits of what can be said, a voice that reflects the hideous ugly neutrality of white supremacy disconnected from feeling for the other. Unloving, unlovable, unspeakable, not ineffable … and the narcissistic body, teeth chattering and shivering, recoils from its cold stare and compassionless reflection.

3

Open to the demonic

A sonic articulation of desire

Holes are not absences where there should be something else.

(SADIE PLANT 1998: 57)

*Too little, too much, too empty, too full:
The suppression of female sexuality has always
been a matter of regulation and control.*

(SADIE PLANT 1998: 202)

As a matter of the regulation and control of female sexuality and desire, Western religious, philosophical and scientific discourses have constructed Woman as both lack (a hole 'where there should be something else') and as vessel (carrier). An open empty body, Woman is both carrier of and subject to a whirl of forces, the nature of which have changed and developed within the dominant beliefs and epistemologies of each given epoch, yet remain consistently focused on what has been construed as the open mouths of her body, meaning that the womb, female genitalia and the voice are all subject to scrutiny. Gathered around the openness of the female body, these discourses fantasize about the sexual pliancy and penetrative availability of women, the contradiction being that although apparently 'open', the female body and sexuality also produces anxiety in so far as it is regarded as an 'unknown', which, in Sigmund Freud's terms, is conceptualized as the 'dark continent' of female sexuality (Freud [1926] 1969: 38). Studies that seek to penetrate and explore this dark unknown have created a female body that, as object of investigation, drifts across centuries of time, swept up in discourses on demonic possession, melancholia, madness and irrationality, hysteria and wandering wombs; all such ailments and conditions converge on the mouths and spaces of the open female body, essentialized in a paradox of being, 'too empty, too full' (Plant, 1998: 202). 'Hysteria' itself is, of course, derived from the Greek word for uterus, *hysterikos* and considered to be a nervous disease/neurotic condition peculiar to women. Beset with paradoxes, these discourses can be characterized as the struggle to produce authoritative knowledge on an object that is simultaneously sexually titillating and revolting, desired and feared. Such combinations of feelings are particularly pronounced in the comparisons drawn, via images of 'open' mouths, between the female body and the female voice. In her essay 'Gender of Sound', Anne Carson argues that writings from as far back as Antiquity elucidate ways in which the upper and lower 'mouths' of women's bodies are conflated and contrived as disorderly and in need of regulation. Carson locates this relationship in Ancient Greek and Roman medical theory, noting that a sexualized conflation between female vocal mouths and genitalia from this early moment in the history of human anatomy theory, was explicitly perceived via a perception of the sonic quality of female voices, more specifically in pitch (and inferred timbre): 'defloration causes a woman's neck to enlarge and her voice to deepen', whilst a virgin is in possession of a pure higher voice (Carson, 1995: 131). Voice in this respect is heard as sonically embodying a very direct material connection with female sexuality; timbre and pitch in this respect informs how the listener hears the *type* of openness available to them (naive youthfulness or sexual knowingness), alongside the aesthetic terms of how the vocalist looks (and might feel). Consequently, female voices are heard and perceived according to fantasies that fetishize the link between female voice, open mouths, throat and body, revealing in acoustic code the terms of her sexuality and appeal. These terms might therefore be considered a sonic equivalent of the gaze, one that objectifies the female voice in anticipation of the image and feel of a body. Alternatively, and in accordance with the conflict between desiring and despising, the female voice elicits revulsion, fear and abjection by rendering disorientating spirals of chaos from a grotesque gaping mouth.

Edgar Allan Poe's short story 'A Descent into the Maelström', published in 1841, illustrates a relationship between male travellers sailing on turbulent seas and a terrifying feminized whirlpool hole exuding hideous noise. Textually, sound features are vital to conjuring the sublime magnitude of this oceanic spiralling maelstrom and the threat it poses to the male protagonists who, trapped, spiral in its orbit. From the whirlpool emerges a 'loud and gradually increasing sound, like the moaning of a vast herd of buffaloes upon an American prairie'; the waters rage and 'hiss' in broad heaving convulsions until there comes an encounter with a 'mouth' and an 'appalling voice':

> The edge of the whirl was represented by a broad belt of gleaming spray; but no particle of this slipped into the mouth of the terrific funnel, whose interior, as far as the eye could fathom it, was a smooth, shining, and jet black wall of water, inclined to the horizon at an angle of some forty-five degrees, speeding dizzily round and round with a swaying and sweltering motion, and sending forth to the winds an appalling voice, half shriek, half roar. (Poe, [1841] 2016: 10)

As the reader spirals downwards, in terrifying proximity to the mouth of this gleaming jet-black wall of water, described as the 'terrific funnel', what is heard in the dizzying chaos of the dark waters are the kinds of voices that connote and associate animality, wild nature and disorderly feminine sexuality through moaning, hissing, shrieking and roaring, brought to bear through the historical evolution of the demonic possession of 'witches' and gendered 'hysteria'. Feminist music and sound theorists such as Susan McClary ([1991] 2002), Barbara Engh (1996) and Marie Thompson (2013) have discussed the relationship between hysteria, madness, the 'wandering womb' and the sound of disorderly female voices, attempting to recall the construction of hysterical vocal soundings as signifiers within wider cultural and historical narratives on feminine 'noise', threatening to both seduce (Sirens) and agitate the male ear (Harpies), with voices devoid of semantic content and which issue from a misogynistically imagined wet, feminine 'mouth' and lashing tongue. The threat of descending uncontrollably into this noise is to fall, irremovably (unless you are lucky and clever enough to strap yourself to a barrel) into the disorder, unreason and non-meaning of feminine din: idle chatter, scolding tongues, hysterical screams, shrill shrieks, and so on. An open hole, the female voice-body is 'too little, too much, too empty, too full' (Plant, 1998: 202), the carrier of nothing and brewer of erratic potential, which, left uncontrolled, threatens the Father's phallic logic with the hysteria of a 'wandering womb' and the soundings of disorderly feminine excess. Accordingly, her open body is deemed prone to leakages of excessive over-emotional expression with a tendency to chatter and generally produce a disorderly shrill din, painful to the male ear. To that extent, her holes and open mouth(s) have been historically conceived as problematic and requiring the kinds of policing that has always sought to control, domesticate and silence the voices of women. This has led to a sadistic array of severe and ideological 'treatments', such as the painful 'scold's bridle' fitted on to the heads of 'nagging' wives as punishment for the terrible 'tongue lashing' of their suffering husbands, preventing them from bothering them any further with their vocalizations. 'Gossipers', scolds and women with 'riotous' voices could all be fitted with a scold's bridle (sixteenth and seventeenth centuries), which was an iron frame that enclosed the head and contained a gag that pressed on the tongue and prevented the wearer from speech or eating – such that if the tongue moved it could be cut or lacerated by the device. The tortured wearer of this device was led and paraded through town as a form of public humiliation and to serve as a warning to all (lower-class) women and those who might 'speak out'. It was also still used in the so called 'Age of Reason' in Europe and particularly by European slave-traders on African captives (Federici, 2014: 101).

Of the discourses and histories that have opened up women's bodies as vessels via conflated upper and lower mouths, psychoanalysis is particularly implicated. Here, in the development of the study of the unconscious/conscious mind, Woman has been theorized as the keeper of castration and made to bear the ultimate lack that is the abjected void of humanity's incompleteness. Her sexuality therefore, as Luce Irigaray argues in 'This Sex Which Is Not One' ([1981] 2000), is construed through a 'hole-envelope' that specifies 'vaginal passivity', alienating woman from her desire as she is rendered both 'beautiful object of contemplation' and the body with a sexual organ that 'represents *the horror of nothing to see*. A defect in this systematics of representation and desire. A "hole" in its scoptophilic lens' (Irigaray, [1981] 2000: 263). The primacy of the phallus is reiterated through the unconscious and conscious exclusion of female sexuality and desire via processes that articulate woman as the signifier of lack, the gap and this has repercussions particularly for the female body and voice: woman's speech, desire and agency is null and void in relation to a phallic language that privileges masculinity and male speakers within a logic of phallogocentrism. In such circumstances, as Hélène Cixous has discussed extensively and particularly in her 'Laugh of the Medusa' (1976), the problem for women has to do with expression and with how to relinquish female sexuality and desire from its repression as lack, as nothing, within the terms of the symbolic order. For the purposes of this chapter, I am interested in the strategies that both contain Woman, women and the feminine within the 'logic of lacking and passive "hole"' (Irigaray, [1981] 2000), as well as the strategies of female musicians who articulate desire. In both respects, I propose that the demonic and the Devil is a technology that can be used to reiterate woman as an open vessel that is predisposed to darkness, or as part of a strategic appropriation of those terms where sound and voice is fundamental to articulating otherwise suppressed desire. Here, singer-songwriter and guitarist Anna Calvi becomes a focus, particularly her track 'The Devil' (*Anna Calvi*, 2011). Calvi creates alternative blues-rock music that recalls the semiotics and affects of the association between Woman, female sexuality and the Devil in performance, sound and image, raising in particular the notion of desire as it pertains to darkened demonized sexuality.

The Devil as regulating technology

The Devil is part of an evolving series of technologies of control that have contributed to the social degradation, torture and deaths of women whilst legitimizing the regulation and punishment of women and feminized, demonized bodies. The Devil and ascriptions of the demonic have been deployed amongst an arsenal of ideologies to rationalize attacks on women, whilst the discourse of demonization also in many ways served to legitimize the slave trade and the colonialization of the 'New World', demeaning and oversexualizing women and people of colour to effectively ensure their exclusion from the social contracts of freedom and paid labour: in short, demonization works to authorize the denial of selfhood. In the sixteenth and seventeenth centuries, hundreds of thousands of women across Europe, usually peasant women, were accused of witchcraft and 80 per cent of recorded cases of deaths via execution for witchcraft were women (Federici, 2014: 179). These women were believed to carry within their bodies either an insatiable lust that led to pacts with the Devil and/or moral/mental weakness that allowed the Devil sexual access to them. Either way, demonologists and witch-hunters persecuted the female body through a demonic spatialization that made of her a penetrable open body, specifically orientated around her vagina, cervix and uterus:

> The accused were stripped naked and completely shaved (it was argued that the devil hid among their hair); then they were pricked with long needles all over their bodies, including their vaginas, in search for the mark with which the devil presumably branded his creatures (just as the masters in England did with runaway slaves). Often they were raped; it was investigated whether or not they were virgins – a sign of innocence; and if they did not confess, they were submitted to even more atrocious ordeals; their limbs were torn, they were seated on iron chairs under which fires were lit; their bones were crushed. (Federici, 2014: 185)

Women were subjected to torture, drowned, hung or burnt at the stake on the basis of accounts that insisted upon their biological disposition to evil and marks of the Devil. As Silvia Federici convincingly argues, the history of the persecution of women as witches should be read as part of wider European state and ruling-class agendas evolving through feudalism and the beginnings of capitalism, colonialism and imperialism, as well as part of a quelling of (women's) peasant resistance: a significant threat in order to effectively keep rebellious women quiet. Federici draws correspondences between land privatization, labour quests and anxiety over population declines, with the strategic demonization of birth control practices, of female midwifes (who would be replaced by 'trained' males), of 'deviant' sexual practices outside of procreation and the domestication of the female body that ensured both their economic and social dependence on men and the continuation of their unpaid labour of procreation, women thus being, in effect, enforced to bear the labour force required for European capitalism. Historically, wombs and vulvas have been the ultimate site of investigation and suspicion since they signify a woman's proclivity for seduction, her ability to host unseen life and her general weakness in relation to evil. In the fifteenth century, the *Malleus Maleficarum* (*The Hammer of Witches*) ([1487] 2011), written by Jacob Sprenger and Henrich Kramer and published in Germany, was a treatise that endeavoured to establish a fundamental belief in the existence of witches. This is a demonology text that defines the practice of witchcraft and stipulates 'remedies' for the victims of witchcraft whilst guiding the processes of prosecution and accusation by outlining methods of confession extraction, torture and death to be used in the persecution of women and men in Europe across the sixteenth and seventeenth centuries. In this, the text traces the pain and anguish of those accused of witchcraft and who underwent appalling torture and deaths. The disposition of women to witchcraft is articulated in this misogynistic diatribe in its contention that women become agents of Satan due to their innate uncontrollable carnal desire, weakness of spirit and 'openness'. Indeed, throughout the extensive literature written by 'intellectual' men on the study of witches, a key concern was whether the witch could become impregnated by the Devil during her sexual relations with him. As Federici highlights in her extensive study, the discourse of the witch-hunt linked witches with prostitution primarily through the premise that both sold themselves (one to the Devil, the other to men), and both symbolized abject, non-procreative sexuality (the attack on such sexuality also included homosexuality). That music, sounds and dancing were implicated in the discourse of demonization is illustrated particularly by representations of the Sabbath, which included dancing, feasting, orgies and also, specifically, by the demonization of native Americans and Africans. From the fifteenth to nineteenth centuries, the conquest of the 'New World' and creation of the Atlantic slave trade saw those whom European colonialists and slave-traders sought to colonize and enslave invariably being charged with 'devil-worship' and demonized through missionaries', slave-traders' and other European travellers' reports of savage sexuality, 'barbaric' languages and an 'inordinate fondness for music and dancing' (Federici, 2014: 200). The sexualized and demonized body thus inherits a relationship with sound and music that is based on the hyper-sexualization of a (non-procreative) body deemed primitively promiscuous and disorderly and the host of chaotic, barbaric, diabolical, sexualized, sinful dark sound. Such dark soundings are part of the essentialization of demonized bodies and relate directly to sexuality.

The sounds of possession

When the soundings of demonic possession and female hysteria are conjured, they are superimposed over female sexuality, body and voice, making the inferences of demonic possessed women rich in sonic and vocal excess such as incoherent repetitiveness, improvised chaos, noise, static, feedback, fevered breathing, abrasive croaks and the glossolalia of a body possessed by spirits. The nature of the spirits or supernatural beings that possess the body fluctuate ambiguously between the divine and the diabolical, in that, since from at least the Middle Ages, women were regarded as potential vessels for the supernatural, be that the Devil or God. Under such a principle, unification with the divine Father could be attained by women through singing: the 'woman as vessel, wherein the divine intones its harmonies' (Muessig, 1998: 152–3).[1] The body is important in this case because to unify with God in such a way, to become His sonorous vessel, the woman is sexually 'pure', a virgin. Ruth Evans's analysis of the virgin martyr narratives contends that the chaste virgin body embodies the puritanical values of Christian ideology and represents 'the wholeness and unchangingness of the body of the church, the *corpus verum* (true body)' (2003: 174). She goes on to argue that the pure white female virgin body functions in the twelfth and thirteenth centuries in relation to the xenophobic construction of purity's 'other', so that 'the virginity texts themselves are sites where the chaste female Christian is constructed through her opposition to the Jew' and this anti-semitism continues through into texts of the fifteenth century:

The early fifteenth-century *Middle English Life of Edith of Wilton*, an exemplary virgin, is a 'vengeance miracle' that explicitly deploys the opposition between the classical, intact virginal body and the grotesque, gaping body of the Jew to construct a fantasy of English Christian purity. (Evans, 2003: 172)

Hagiographies of virgin martyrs are full of tales of divinely infused knowledge in necessarily chaste 'pure' (white) bodies, as opposed to any notion that women were actually educated or able to learn as their scholarly male counterparts learnt.[2] This is an ideology of denial that stretches into the twentieth century, where the mythology/popular narrative of Robert Johnson's blues guitar virtuosity replaces legitimate study and education with the idea of Johnson's skill having derived from selling his soul to the Devil. The gendered and racialized dimensions of the body as vessel seek in this way to deny intellectual capacity and stabilize the gendered, sexual and racial terms of what constitutes a pure and impure vessel.

This opposition between a pure and impure body is significant to the blues and its controversial adoption of church music, spirituals and the glossolalia of Evangelicalism, Holiness and Pentecostalism. Teresa Reed argues that the blues style of addressing God and the Devil developed during the early twentieth century (up until the 1950s), at which time oppositions emerged in African-American religious culture between the sacred and the secular, good and evil, sanctity and sin: 'From this perspective, music was either God's or the Devil's, with little to no grey area in between' (Reed 2003: 90). Artists such as Mississippi John Hurt, Memphis Minnie and Blind Lemon Jefferson were blues singers who crossed the divide between sacred and secular by writing, performing and recording for *both* the gospel and blues market (although the litigations and cultural prohibitions of this divide meant that these artists were forced to perform under pseudonyms) (Reed, 2003: 159). Angela Davis makes the point that although black women's blues draws on the spirituals of church music, it refuses to mimic the church's ideological marginalization of women's lives and condemnation of taboo subjects such as female homosexuality. Instead, through a fearless and fierce discourse, artists such as Gertrude "Ma" Rainey and Bessie Smith insist on female sexual agency, valorizing as opposed to condemning a connection between spiritual and sexual joy denounced by the church that, as Davis discusses, had taken on the Christian dualism of 'spirit "good" and body "evil"' and which 'played a pivotal role in valorizing that aspect of racist ideology that sexualized the ascription of intellectual and spiritual inferiority to black people' (Davis, 1999: 131). The result of this is that the battles within women's blues require from the artist and their music an ability to not only inhabit contradiction, but to challenge the very dualistic thinking on which it is based through intellect, irony, humour and a highly developed consciousness of gender, race, class and sexuality. In other words, female blues artists had to negotiate issues of identity as they emerge in the aesthetics and effects of music and the social realities of a complex series of lived experiences of violence and oppression within heteronormative white patriarchy, as well as navigate the context of male dominance within the church and the violence against women within socially and economically oppressed black communities. Davis argues that blues women resisted and challenged the binary logic of good and evil onto which gender, race and sexuality are grafted, asserting a sexuality and articulating a desire through the blues in ways not necessarily clear to the hegemonic frameworks which sought to contain these singers. Davis writes:

> The blues were a part of a cultural continuum that disputed the binary constructions associated with Christianity. In this sense, they blatantly defied the Christian imperative to relegate sexual conduct to the realm of sin. Many blues singers therefore were assumed to have made a pact with the Devil. [...] Blues singers were (and to a certain extent still are) associated with the Devil because they celebrated those dimensions of human existence considered evil and immoral according to the tenets of Christianity. (Davis, 1999: 123–4)

And further,

> In the context of black Christianity's disdain for the blues, [Ma] Rainey's work can be viewed as a female subversion of the male Christian ministry that equated blues and sexuality with the Devil and sin. (Davis, 1999: 125)

Davis recalls the Christian dualism of 'spirit "good" and body "evil"' as a distinction that reads sexuality and, specifically, female, black and non-heteronormative sexuality through the problematic body of the singer and her vocal soundings as evil, whilst her connection with the Devil solidifies through the physical matter to which she has been associated in opposition to the higher function of the mind and intellect (masculine territories). Evil is transmitted via the secular, embodied, female, black, blues-singing voice, a blues body admonished as the connective vessel and passage by which sin and the Devil can manifest.

The strategies of the blues women identified by Davies infer the rupture of hegemonic frameworks. The blues itself, particularly 1960s white blues-rock, might be regarded as a hegemonic framework in which 'Male blues generally equate woman trouble with "devil woman"' (Whiteley, 2000: 57). In particular, white male blues-rock of the 1960s arguably offered far less potential for the articulation of transgressive female desire. This genre developed via the by now clichés of guitar rock, raising grandiose unambiguously masculine power in collective sound led by the electric guitar, heavily amplified, distorted and processed through technical prowess and performative phallic thrusts in solos that situate a hero. Whilst the singer (also a contender for lead phallic power) delivers the clichés of the blues-rock script which relies heavily on figurations of the 'devil woman' and 'black magic woman' to ensure the terms of heteronormative desire. Devil women seduce, lie and hurt and black magic women threaten to make a devil out of the male subject should he be 'blinded' by her 'spell'. The implication of occult powers held within her mysterious being is excited by 'black magic' and 'spells', as though to verify a conflation between darkness, female sexuality and to install implicit undertones of a racialized 'dark' woman, the ultimate unknown from the established dominant perspective of a naturalized, white(ned) male heteronormative fantasy. Such deployment works to essentialize, whilst at the same time trivialize the conjunction between the Devil and Woman. The devilish body onto which fantasies of control, mastery and virtuosity are projected is also an excavation site for male rock mythology since what can be retrieved and appropriated from the black magic woman are the occulted dark sonic powers and devilish feminine excess she holds within her, a power she herself cannot articulate or refine, linguistically, technically and/or musically speaking. Via his terms of engagement, the demonized burden of darkness that femininity has borne for centuries is delivered via the (guitar) craft of his maieutic approach to her devil woman sound. This installs a logic where he delivers her devil plus woman occult powers (itself the impregnation of patriarchy) appropriating and converting those powers into cultural capital, thereby acquiring devilish kudos. Following his midwifery of her dark sound, she is little more than a spent sexualized object in a broader occult fantasy of accompanying sex witches that are subservient to men with (guitar) craft who lead ritual practice and who repeat strokes that continually rearticulate androcentric devilish mastery and privileged occult knowledge. Under these terms, the Devil is a technology applied and assumed by the male subject.

Mothers and the demonic

Given the focus on wombs and women as vessel in the discourses that demonize women, the Mother is a particular site of fascination, evoking both fear and desire, shame and loss. The Mother becomes for Freud a central example of what raises strange and disturbing 'uncanny' feelings, if not the epitome of the uncanny. Having linked the uncanny with evil intent (the 'evil' eye) and the repression of fears revived by ghosts, shadows, spirits and dead bodies, Freud contends that the most 'pleasing confirmation' of the uncanny is reserved for the female genitals, which, according to his analysis, 'neurotic men' confess they find 'uncanny'. He writes:

> But what they find uncanny ['unhomely'] is actually the entrance to man's old 'home', the place where everyone once lived. A jocular saying has it that 'love is a longing for home', and if someone dreams of a certain place or a certain landscape and, while dreaming, thinks to himself, 'I know this place, I've been here before', this place can be representing his mother's genitals or her womb. Here too, then, the uncanny ['the unhomely'] is what was once familiar ['homely', 'homey']. The negative prefix *un-* is the indicator of repression. (Freud, [1919] 2003: 151)

The two unequivocal types of the uncanny derive firstly from repressed childhood complexes 'where the question of material reality does not arise' – the maternal body – and secondly from 'primitive beliefs', long thought to have been surmounted by modern enlightened man, that return to cast doubt on material reality – and in particular those beliefs related to the supernatural in the forms of ghosts and other creatures of the 'dark'. These two types of the uncanny are intimately related to the potential of the female body to host supernatural dark demonic entities as well as the 'primal' past; the Mother therefore epitomizes an ability to defer progress in that she becomes the place that *was* home, an uncanny place one must leave in order to become an independent adult. And this is what perhaps most prominently, links psychoanalysis with the witch-hunting discourses and theology developed from the Middle Ages through to the early modern period, in that female bodies are in particular posited as vessels for demonic supernatural beings as well as primal and uncanny conflicts, where a subject feels caught between the familiar and desperately unfamiliar, a longing and a revulsion for a birth and death-bearing female body. The Mother therefore is a feminine figure under extreme pressure of scrutiny based on the conflicts of male subjectivity and within the terms of a violent logic. Musically, this logic is rendered audible in 'The End' written and performed by The Doors (*The Doors*, 1967), which is a song that moves in on the lacking, desired and uncanny Mother's body. What the song finds within that holding space of the Mother made audible is demonic dark sound.

'The End' begins with the resounding vibrations of metal ringing across lightly brushed cymbals and sustained electric guitar tones. Drums and guitar develop and establish a slow meandering tempo with riffs that rotate around and return to the droning of upper and lower E dropped down to D. The continuation of the drone and the dominance of the two notes D and A (in the D5 chord) provide an openness that allows for improvisation between major and minor riffs, creating, to Westernized ears, a wandering 'exotic' ambivalence drawn further by the feel of a continual drone, the rhythmic jingles of a tambourine and the supernatural sustained-breath timbres of organ chords that follow. Hypnotic trippy effects are intensified by Morrison's LSD-stoked vocal delivery in an eleven-minute plus long song combining spoken-sung lyrics and non-verbal sounds that affectively writhe in existential wonder, murderous lust, sexual desire and death drives, evocative of what would become the primal rock mantra of Morrison's phallic ritualistic power and his eroticization of death: 'apocalyptic sex – love is sex and sex is death' (Whiteley, 2003: 134). To get to the end – the climax of 'The

End' and, arguably, to Morrison's transition from son to 'Lizard King' – an Oedipal drama is self-consciously staged in which the vocalist and band play with a steady increase in energy so that, almost clandestine, snake-like, the ego-libido of sound awakens and emerges from its trance like musical conjunction between a funeral-style march and a psychedelic sojourn without destination. Suddenly, apparently aimless individual elements wandering across the desert of the imagination come together by virtue of the narrative, focused by the walk down the hallway, coming to a door (of perception) and proceeding to take a look inside, at which point we hear a son address his parents: 'Father ... Yes, son? I want to kill you! Mother ... I want to ... FUUCCCKKK YOUUU!' Following the lead of a becoming-Dionysus rock-god and his 'scream', a collective musical ejaculation, triggered by the lyrical confession, engenders a brotherhood of followers performing a collective orgasmic release of an apparent break with the past and the social constraints of law and family to elicit the ultimate patricidal and incestual taboo. These instruments coalesce around an affective collective identity of wild masculinity and the ego to id of rebel sons released on the 'fuck, fuck, fuck me baby, fuck, fuck, kill, kill':

> Robbie (Krieger, guitar) and I were racing to keep up with John, driving and pushing each other faster and faster until we had no place left to go and exploded in an ejaculatory climax! An aural orgasm. We shot our sonic wad out onto the heads of the collective and anointed the faithful with holy chrism. (Ray Manzarek, cited in Whiteley, 2003: 131)

In accordance with the clichés of the rock-rebel, the phallic metaphor is adopted with snarling, grinning, provocative relish, endowed with a special ability to weave the deadly serious with self-congratulatory self-aware humour under the guise of performative theatre. What is interesting here, however, is the theatrical presentation of the necessity of the killing of the Father and the fucking of the Mother, metaphorically suggestive of psychologically, spiritually and physically cutting ties with both parents so as to journey into a liberated future (appealing of course to teenagers who wish to 'cut the apron strings'). In one way, this is a staged, knowingly ludicrous and sardonic take on the Oedipus myth and yet it draws from the performance a rebellious integrity that utterly conforms to the logic of the myth, in that the place of the Father is taken by the son who releases in ecstasy his unrepressed desire for the Mother, thereby replacing his Father as per the fantasy. So, despite the in-built spoof, the song cannot fully rebel against the logic of the myth since the rebellion itself is set within the terms of the overall structure of patriarchal power and heteronormative masculinity which remains intact or, rather, is intensified by the creation of a greater virile brotherhood that coalesces around the dead corpse of the old Father and the open Mother's body, encouraged by a violent logic that assumes the ultimate passivity of the female body as hole.

In terms of the temporal flow of Morrison's journey, Sheila Whiteley discerns a continuum of thought in his poetry: 'Forget your past, create your future, travel to the "end of the night" and "break on through to the other side"' (Whiteley, 2003: 133). The Mother's body in this respect is the vessel through which the past is apparently forgotten and the future created on the basis of its transgression. Her body, as well as the lesser female sexual conquests that come to stand in for the Mother, are now the hole(s) that are penetrated, the 'end of the night' that must be reached for in the darkness of her body before breaking beyond it and breaking with the desire for that body, transgressing to the greater messianic states of the phallic subject liberated from femininity. Thus, her 'hole' is the portal to other worlds, to the/His (phallic male subjectivity) future and the rite of passage through which a brotherhood of sound collectively comes together on the basis of a musical entry into chaotic ejaculatory improvisation, only to emerge in the calm outro of 'The End' which returns to the vocal chorus of the beginning: 'It hurts to set you free / But you'll never follow me / the end of laughter and soft lies / The end of nights we tried to die / This is the end.' Musically and lyrically, although devices suggest the song begins at an apocalyptic, spatial end and proceeds to explore sojourning, improvisatory possibilities heading into new unchartered futures in a sort of post-apocalyptic scenario, it actually appears to project a fairly familiar song structure, indicative of the kinds of trajectories that Susan McClary has discussed in relation to tonality and the masculine cadence. Analysing the score in opera and European classical music, McClary deconstructs the 'narrative impulses of underlying sonata-allegro form' and the semiotics of tonality as powerful hegemonic frames deeply imbricated in relationships of patriarchal power and constitutive of the strategic containment of whatever is marked as 'feminine' (McClary, [1991] 2002: 15). In opposition to any essentialist claims, McClary's understanding of the semiotic markings of feminine soundings are considered through the evolution of sounds marked as potentially taboo, deviant, ornamental, decorative, irrational, exotic and excessive in relation to the structure, strategies and narratives of musical 'journeys' with 'homing' impulses that ensure the resolution of the original tonic key and thus the dominance of the masculine protagonist strapped to the musical resolve of his strong homing impulse. Without such a chartered homing impulse guided by hegemonic musical framing and/or linguistic structure, the excessive female vocal is posited as beyond the borders of order and marginalized in the chaotic maelstrom of the irrational. Once the mouth of the Mother's body in 'The End' is discovered, the musical ejaculation occurs within that ultimate taboo dark body and we hear the (demonic) chaos of her body and the (demonic) violence of desire before the subject returns to the chorus that is heard at the very beginning, the one that now signals the past of the song, something that, considering this movement through bodies, one would expect to have transgressed beyond, to something new. But, in effect, the past returns as an apparent transgressive future, and so what is really heard is a retrograde movement with a homing impulse towards an imagined liberation from the desire for the Mother chartered by a nostalgia for an imagined past in which presides a vitally alive, potent, beautiful, mythical masculinity engaged in ritual worship as a connected brotherhood, now travelling away from the Mother and her spent body, hitting a wall at the end that enables him to continue movement into an unknown future as an adored solitary hero (he leaves us in the end at the end of 'The End'). The becoming Lizard King/rock-god of Morrison requires other men to facilitate his movement, to worship him as the embodiment of ideal manhood, whilst female bodies are the dark portals to other worlds and unknowns that they themselves can never travel to since they are, precisely, nights, portals, or islands to move through, conquer and to leave. Sexual liberation in this context involves not only absenting female desire and embodiment, but also selling the idea of freedom (including, but not exclusively sexual freedom) based on the naturalized dominance of male agency that colonizes and territorializes female sexuality with the

OPEN TO THE DEMONIC 99

notion of a lacking hole, so as to plant within her body a violent logic that legitimizes her conquest and colonizes her desire with the parallel necessity to cut with the Mother in order to move into a transgressive rebellious future. Morrison himself provides a warning sign at the end of 'The End', intoning, 'But you'll never follow me', (you'll not move with me or befriend and beat death like me). Made to internalize a misogynistic absence within herself, which is the dark end of the night, her end is the end of movement, beautiful perhaps, but nonetheless stranded in timelessness, a hole that cannot move beyond its own vacuity and a creative potential mined and expropriated.

There is a deeply entrenched colonial psychology in this understanding of the female body, darkened and dehumanized. This psychology reveals not only the racialized, gendered and sexualized dimensions of zero (0), but is also representative of the social processes that construct this hole in relation to the naturalized dominant humanness of white Man, who is free to the extent that he is able to move with desire through a predetermined space-time under the auspices of a threat he navigates, overwhelms and transgresses.[3] Threat here speaks to an obsession apparently with death, but a death projected onto the sexualized, conquered body, whilst the killer Mother-fucker appropriates mythological powers he has imagined within this host of night by becoming her death, effectively beating death by eroticizing and nullifying her body as the site of his antagonism with her power of creation; he is like a murderer claiming fatal risk by being close to a death he himself brings by moving in on the body of the Mother. This movement is encapsulated by Luce Irigaray who writes:

> Thus, unaware of the bedrock of hysteria or of his reliance upon it, he goes on in(de)finitely moving in/on the body, of his mother. She is merely a receptacle whose dimensions must be determined in case they prove threatening or in case she can no longer be overcome by the father's logic and assertion of precedence and prior existence. But he continues to feed on her undefinable potency of which *place* would be, some say, the most extraordinary store. Even intelligible matter would have some of this potency, no doubt, when it is predicated as having spatial *extension*. Furthermore, mother matter affords man the means to realize his form. (Irigaray, [1974] 1985: 166)

Whilst 'The End' can be interpreted as a metaphoric 'penetration' of the unknown, this unknown can be taken as a kind of unspecific penetration of any lacking female body leading backwards in time through the individual unconscious and the Son's relationship with the Mother from which all ties are apparently cut in 'The End'. However, despite the journey through her body, the end of the night and into an apparently unknown future, the subject in fact returns to the beginning, caught in a loop upon which his subjectivity relies and following an endless reiteration of journeys through sound, since the transgression depends upon her demonized body and its conquering. The struggle then is caught between the desire for the Mother and her abjection, i.e., the cutting off point that Julia Kristeva argues is important for the subject to distinguish itself as subject. However, the self-aware Oedipal male musician is here caught in an uncanny relationship with sound, since if, as Kristeva suggests, the realm of the semiotic chaotic affective potential of sound exists in relation to the maternal and the chora, then rebellion against the Father (symbolic/*logos*) necessarily involves engagement with the feminine, not only the externalized maternal Other, but also the repulsive, feminized unconscious, the darkness within that has been demonized over centuries.

Anna Calvi and the becoming vulva of the electric guitar

Musician Anna Calvi draws from blues-rock mythology and stylization to mix with elements of contemporary gothic and operatic drama. Calvi adopts an approach to music making that she describes as 'sound-painting' in, for instance, 'Love Won't Be Leaving' (*Anna Calvi*, 2011) and discusses 'seeing music very visually'. In an interview about *Hunter* (2018), Calvi resists boundary-drawing and any alignment with specific genres and instead reiterates thinking of song cinematically: 'I don't think about genres. I actually imagine the songs as mini films. I know that a song is worth pursuing when I can see it as a film in my head' (*Diva* magazine, 2018). Seeing music visually as an image or moving image, one can trace a relationship between the rich, dark, sonic textures of Calvi's albums (*Anna Calvi*, 2011; *One Breath*, 2013; *Hunter*, 2018), the iconography of her album artwork and the cinematography of a neo-noir dark fantasy drama or gothic western. Her performance persona in video and live performance evokes sensuality through, for example, slick tied-back hair, deep red lips and heavy black-lined eyes, with masculine red flamenco shirt and trousers, heels, matador capes, garb that corresponds with deeply affective aesthetics that draw from a gothic fantasy film-like cultural imagination. This spaghetti western, neo-noir opera gothicism seeps through the screen in music videos such as 'Blackout', 'Desire', 'Eliza', all of which educe motion in shots that pass through desert landscapes, train tracks at night and dimly-lit woods that are intermittently intercut with candlelit spaces saturated in signs of elicit diabolical passion in strong orange and yellow filters, in red velvets, chessboard floors, satins, crucifixes and skulls. All these 'mini-films' offer portals into the kinds of engulfing audiovisual darkness and surreal space-time that demonstrate parallels with her cinematic influences and the enigmatic dreamlike work of directors such as David Lynch, Gus Van Sant and Wong Kar-wai, as well as that of soundtracks for films composed by Ennio Morricone (composer for Sergio Leone's spaghetti western *Once upon a Time in the West*, 1968) and Bernard Herrmann (composer for Martin Scorsese's neo-noir psychological thriller *Taxi Driver*, 1976). The explicit dominance of red and black seeps through the affects of Calvi's music videos, album iconography and performances, dazzled with frequent splashes of gold opulence that offer decadent theatrical drama which sparkles across the vampiric and demonic dark audiovisual consciousness of her work.

Her powerful, controlled vocal delivery, sensual performativity and virtuosic guitar technique profoundly antagonize the phallic technical guitar potency inhabited by the becoming-Devil of rock's rebellious fathers and sons. It is not just that Calvi appropriates and occupies a position typically reserved for male musicians, i.e., the guitar virtuoso (the electric guitar is a primary voice in her albums, a favourite being a Fender telecaster she has owned since her teenage years, consistently tuned down a tone or semi-tone), but also that she subverts the mythology of blues-rock which constructs its 'Devil women' as object through a type of sonic gaze, to be penetrated and transgressed, a body open to heteronormative fantasies of penetration. She refutes this kind of phallus (active) hole (passive) equation. Her technical ability on the guitar allows her to bypass and retune the dimensions of the guitar body and its relationship with the body of the performer, recoding the connection between bodies to articulate queered desire that, in performance, is combined with a strong, low-register voice and a vampiric persona that come together to produce ambiguous, non-conformist gender identities and sexualities. In her album artwork and promotional material, visual attention is repeatedly drawn towards a heightened focus on her mouth, recalling the enduring chain of associations between sexuality, femininity and painted red lips, attributed in rock fantasies to the penetration and ultimate transgression of the Devil woman. Notably, however, despite the focus on the mouth, Calvi's iconography also pointedly features flashes of teeth, awakening images of vampiric hunger and desire. From her mouth issue deep vocal tones and timbres, not the cold of the undead, but demonic heat, caressing the vocal folds in warm, long breaths that invite the reorientation of desire and its movement across the senses, sound, taste, smell, touch, without the primacy of the phallus and His (acoustic) image of the object Other. Desire disperses across Calvi's performance, in the multiple fringes of contact between voice, words, strings, bodies, hands, mouth, language, creating an erotic tension in spaces arranged by sensational reverb, orchestrating an intensity of encounters that feel supernaturally dark, such as the eroticism in the track 'The Devil' wherein she intones the words: 'Wait for God / Fall for me [repeat] / And lay me down / The Devil will come'.

Between elicit orgasm and the threat of impending evil, the lyrics create trajectories of sexual, theological and metaphysical ascension and descension drawn by gestures of melodic vocal waves that invoke God and the Devil, although it is the Devil that will inexorably come in the calling forth according to the lyrics. Somewhere between God and the Devil, amorous lovers are embroiled in slow, delicate motion, in waiting and falling, solicited to 'fall for me' and 'lay me down', amongst cradling guitar caresses and soft breathy vocal melisma. An emotionally reverent and tender atmosphere is created here, implying not the grandiose struggles between good and evil, but love between the figures summoned. A swelling oceanic guitar and a rising and falling vocal melody caught in warm vocal timbre conjoin at the point that language stops and the non-verbal vocal 'ohs' rise and fall, playing with *messa di voce*, controlling the swells of crescendo and diminuendo with a vocal power intermittently comparable with melodramatic Piaf-like chanson and tragic Callasian operatic lower octave range. Wave-like, the spiralling oceanic swirl of sound flows between voice and guitar, increasing in intensity and volume across three refrains and a wide spectrum of emotional dynamics, wherein erotically charged dark jouissance teeters on the edge of blasphemy since the fluid transgressive movements of reverberant bodies blur the subject positions and spaces between God, the Devil, heaven, hell, the addressee and addressed amorous other. All these figures and their movements commingle in the musically orgiastic space of erotically-charged queer desire, where the stasis of moral highs and lows have diminished across multiple layers of interwoven pleasure. Musically, the space between the guitar notes, the space of the sacred resonance of reverberation, establishes a sensitivity which serves ultimately to bind together the movement of distinct instruments so that, whilst the song begins with a heavily reverberant guitar solo, it is not continually solipsistic or ever-dominant but, in fact, opens up to a hushed breathy slow voice which it moves for and with, allowing for a sense of intimate reverence and a time for 'feeling' between sounds. From the outset, this space injects an immediate sensual breath that brings sexual life to the song whilst bringing the listener into closer proximity with a quieter sedate resonance between sounds, drawing the listener into feeling an impression of each development of the guitar phrase, slowly growing in ardency. By the first few chords of the guitar, listeners are drawn into a close intimacy with the physicality of her variation in strumming style, sweep-picking arpeggios and a swirling flow of continuous notes created by circular stroking of the strings. Every now and then, the metallic edge of the strings sounds to cut through the air like blades as the fingers move along the frets in transition. Breathing spaces of dark sonic resonance build through the sonic shadows wrought by the unique singularities of her amp, reverberation effect, guitar and technique, holding the affects of the variation of pace and volume intensity as the listener moves along fleeting, almost simultaneous, signifying encounters with a host of genres: blues, gypsy jazz, rockabilly, flamenco, opera, chanson, rock.

Calvi's individualized strumming style is developed from an intention to create guitar sounds that are like those of orchestral strings or a piano, a style that, she explains, she wanted to create with her hands as opposed to using lots of pedals, preferring, on her debut album at least, to use only reverb and slight distortion (Calvi, cited in Brakes, 2018). Her guitar effects are as a result relatively minimal and yet her hands create a huge, grand enveloping sound evocative of her classical influences and articulated particularly in her circular playing style, creating, in effect, curved lines of sensual bends, rich melodic textures of curves and swirls. Calvi herself points to the difference in trajectory when she reflects on the track 'The Devil', explaining that her intention was to create a middle-section that 'sounds like the strings on a Hitchcock soundtrack. It crescendos towards an explosion, but in a real and honest way. It's not about bravado' (dominorecordco. com). Distancing herself from the cultural stereotype figure of the guitar virtuoso and the contrived trajectory of technical guitar solos, Calvi makes an important distinction between her style and the kinds of guitar 'bravado' that express the dominant logic of phallocentricism through clichéd sonic climaxes that ultimately seek to transgress femininity and the female body. Desire in her sound shapes and is shaped by a different form, displacing the notion of the guitar as a 'phallic instrument' to be stroked up and down according to the motions of male masturbatory pleasure. Her technique makes the guitar sound like 'a piano going up and down' and provokes comments that marvel over 'her distinctive, circular playing style – half picking and half strumming' and remark, 'Someone once told her after a show that it looked as if she was stirring soup, but the motion has more finesse then this; it's closer to the taut strokes a violin bow makes, or even the commands of a conductor's baton' (Richardson Andrews, 2011). With this kind of circular 'finesse' and skill orientated around the shaping of the hands, attention veers directly towards a corporeal relationship with the guitar and a 'difference' that destabilizes the heterosexual, masculinized subject-position of physical-musical-practical modes of 'climax', to introduce queer modes of pleasure that pertain to women's bodies. In Calvi's work across her three albums, there is a constant unfolding and enfolding of what Patricia MacCormack has, following Deleuze and Guattari's 'becoming-woman' and Irigaray's model of 'two-lips' (where a woman touches herself as a condition of her being), posited as a 'becoming-vulva', recognizing the vulva as that which 'privileges fluidity, connectivity, aspectual apprehension, tactility and the other senses' (MacCormack, 2010: 95).

OPEN TO THE DEMONIC

Most importantly, woman touches herself as her condition of being, not as autonomous choice. The phallus rents the two vulva lips apart and penetrates the vagina, shifting woman's relation to herself to one as object for male sexuality and her many folds as quickened into a mournfully empty aperture. Male language forces itself between the mouth lips of women, compelling her to listen and speak only in the language and always flawed. The use of a tool performs two functions. The first is to nomenclature the expressive aspect of the content within a phallic discourse, the second to prevent it acting beyond or without that discourse and especially, acting for itself (which is the self it does not and cares not to 'know', but to think or touch). (MacCormack, 2010: 101)

If the blues-rock electric guitar is seen as an extension of the phallogocentricsm rendering the two lips of the female apart in anticipation of a hole construed as lack, if the guitar and its techniques are tools that situate the primacy of phallic desire in relation to specific movements (in/out) across a time-space posited as linear and orientated towards the survival of heteronormative male subjectivity, his dominance and future, Calvi moves away from these techniques of control. Instead, she rearticulates the guitar within a practice that is becoming-vulva in circular sweeping movements that raise queer desire, the fluidity of the feminine, the materiality of flesh and blood in strokes that reach towards circular temporality, drawing curves of infinity as opposed to lines of linear time with a dubious teleology, a becoming-vulva of the zero – the hole, simultaneously open and closed.

Calvi's becoming-vulva enfolds the demonic within its movements as that which embraces anguished and passionate female sexuality, specifically the historically demonized sexuality that lies outside of the remit of procreation. Within the circular gestures of musical bodies and the transgression of genre wherein blues, flamenco, folk and gypsy jazz touch and fluidly interconnect, the deeper resonance is with the darkening of bodies across time and space in a genealogy of demonization that implicates women, people of colour, homosexuality and the working classes. The sound and style displace the central figure of maleness and introduce a queer desire that refutes and transgresses the fundamental boundaries of heternormativity and binary gender identity. In doing so, her 'womanliness' transgresses the confining social, musical and performative hegemonic boundaries of the construct 'woman' understood through lack and engenders the possibility of multiple unknown femininities, an ongoing play of difference and invention that has desire at its core. 'Maleness' is here not so much banished as rewired in unexpected forms, similarly open to unforeseen potential and able to coexist in change and difference, without dominance and with the becomings of the feminine – blurring genders, feminine, masculine, each into the other, creating new forms of being and desire. We hear and see this blurring of being in the track and music video for 'Don't Beat The Girl Out Of My Boy' (*Hunter*, 2018) in which Calvi raises the constructed nature of gender and the violence of enforcing categories, whilst attempting to articulate the transformative being of being and the right to experimentation and choice. In the video she is featured amongst different types of queered bodies, skin touching skin, moving together in flowing choreography with Calvi at the centre of touching gestures, to then focus on a relationship with an androgynous-looking woman who caresses her in a gesture of passion and sensuality. The move in this video and in the album *Hunter*, is a move towards the utter embodiment of unrepressed wild desire, dark in the sense that it is taboo for a woman to wield such threatening skill and agency and to experiment with a sexuality that is so clearly not tailored to a heteronormative male gaze, orientated way beyond its confines. Queer desire is figured not only through visual representations that accompany music here, but embodied between her voice and her relationship with the guitar. Indeed, Calvi has made this point crystal clear, stating in one interview, 'One person asked me how I felt playing a "phallic instrument". It might be phallic for you! Don't project that onto me! That's not how I see the guitar at all' (Calvi, cited in Smyth, 2018). Far from being a 'lack', Calvi's 'openness' is then an enfolding of the demonic into the becoming-vulva of her guitar technique and vocalizations, whilst also an embrace of bodies and sexualities that are demonized. In effect, Calvi's sound articulates a sensual desire that cannot be contained, regulated or suppressed.

4

The black hole song
of unsounding mothers

We're here protesting and sharing stories, but when everything else is so loud, how do you penetrate through?

(Camae Ayewa aka Moor Mother, cited in Pothast 2019: 37)

In 2003, NASA issued a press release based on a discovery by astronomer Dr Andrew Fabian from the Institute of Astronomy, Cambridge. Using the NASA Chandra X-ray telescope, Fabian's studies of the Perseus Cluster and X-ray images of clouds of gas made observable ripples of sound waves emitting from a black hole, the frequency of which can be interpreted in musical terminology as a B-flat, '57 octaves below middle C or one million, billion times lower than the lowest sound audible to the human ear!' (NASA, 2003) This incredibly low infrasound, inaudible to the human ear and described as the 'deepest note ever detected from an object in the universe', is not least interesting in that it appears to inspire reports that tie together what is so familiarly, in clichéd terms, kept apart by a logic that supposedly distinguishes scientific objective fact from romantic mysticism. In keeping with the excitement of a cosmological discovery where the boundaries between science and mysticism regularly blur, the inaudible (un) soundings of this black hole instigate a scattering of romantic responses, ranging from terms such as 'cosmic performance' and 'cosmic symphonies' to moments that attribute to the black hole a notion of its 'song', whereby this entity of the unknown acquires a specifically vocal emphasis by drawing attention to the 'mouth' of the black hole as it 'sings'. In this, the cosmic inaudible sounding of the black hole is perceived slightly differently than the idea of cosmic sub-bass with no origin that is the 'sound of negation' in space, an 'unsound' discussed by Eugene Thacker in relation to Arthur Schopenhauer's metaphysics (Thacker, 2014: 182–94). Whilst the black hole's *un*sound might be considered to be an expression of emptiness and nothingness, the fact that it is romanticized as a song from a 'mouth', is suggestive of some kind of origin, even agency of sorts, albeit a sound emitting from an undefinable objectless black hole that draws the imagination to the limit of what can be said, sensed, known and imagined.

The cosmic song of the black hole, both 'real' somewhere in space, and 'imaginary' as an audio-image to an inner science fiction literary ear, elaborates on the longstanding symbolic use-value of black holes, whilst significantly disturbing the aeonian silence attributed to them. This chapter interprets a symbolic relationship between the black hole and the mother and, in so doing, the discovery of a 'real' sound emitting from a black hole (romantically positioned as 'song') has a symbolic, material and psychic value for reinterpreting the mother's unsoundings. The mother's unsound might be read as the suppression of her voice via a constructed lack or, considering the definition of unsound, it could be interpreted as the cultural framing of the mother's speaking subjectivity as passive, prone to irrationality and unhinged and therefore not heard or worth hearing to the degree that meaningful sound can be deduced; this alongside the cultural expectation to carry and bear, *no matter what*. The song of the black hole signals however, an opportunity to refigure symbolic equivalences with the mother's body, challenging aeonic lack and silence by placing particular attention on what constitutes the sound of the unsounding maternal. The audio hallucination of the cosmic black hole infrasound sound is then circuited with another audio hallucination, that of the earthly rumbling unsounds of mothers (including 'Mother Earth'), which, as discussed later in this chapter, is a sonic hallucination frequently conjured in sound and music discourse to express the spatial sonority of both the abject and the sublime at the mouth of chaos, oblivion, the abyss and sonic metaphoric black holes. As Julia Kristeva writes, 'the abject is edged with the sublime' (Kristeva, 1982: 11) and this close proximity between the abject and sublime recalls the close symbolic and psychic meaning of black holes and mothers, in that both have been correlated with a sublime and abject unknown as each presents a dark void and the threat of engulfment caught in centripetal spiralling motions causing disorientating dizziness and vertigo. The mouths of the black hole and the mother's body raise fearful risks to the subject, not least, in the case of the black hole, 'spaghettification' and annihilation, but moreover anxiety around the borders of the self and the survival of the 'I'. Kristeva asserts that in order for the self to become autonomous, the child breaks away from and abjects the mother, she is repelled away (1982: 13). And the problems caused by remaining tied to the mother, particularly for daughters, come up in Kristeva's discussion of depression and melancholia in her 'Black Sun' ([1989] 2002), where there are correspondences between the black hole, mothers and suppressed unsoundings of grief.

The unsounding song of a black hole

In the section of Kristeva's volume entitled 'Death-Bearing Woman', the requirement for (psychic) matricide for both men and women is made explicit. For women, however, given the identification with the mother (who is death-bearing and must be killed), and given the introjection of the maternal body into the self, things are, as Kristeva notes, more difficult, in effect meaning that the hatred for the mother who must be abjected and the matricidal drive towards her death might all be stored inside the self, redirected within the self, as opposed to enacted on the mother. In one particular case, Kristeva analyses a woman, Isabel, who had lost her own mother, had desired to become pregnant and who had a child, all during the long-term period of her analysis and treatment. Kristeva compares Isabel's melancholia with a kind of black hole held within herself, a grief that, in being kept 'secret, unnameable, and unspeakable, had turned into a *psychic silence*', a nothingness that takes the place of any wound rather than represses:

> A nothingness that is neither repression nor simply the mark of the affect but condenses into a *black hole* – like invisible, crushing, cosmic anti-matter – the sensory, sexual, fantasy-provoking ill

being of abandonments and disappointments. [...] Isabel needed that 'black hole' of her melancholia in order to construct her living motherhood and activities outside it, just as others organise themselves around repression or splitting. It was her own thing, her own home, the narcissistic center where she foundered as much as she replenished herself. (Kristeva, 2002: 394)

Despondency, 'black moods' and the legacy of womb-based, black-bile female melancholia here whirl into an 'oceanic void' that is the black hole of the inner self, which holds out the promises of nothingness and is the death-bearer within. Such an inner black hole is here regarded as a 'psychic silence', a terrible melancholic unsounding within that internalizes the lost object...and its loss. Taking this idea of the black hole of the inner self, which is the sadness of not being and impossible loss (which, Kristeva suggests in this case, is accompanied by a kind of smugness in sorrow and isolation (2002: 396)), one can imagine a spiralling into the abyss of the self, an abyss that is created by the loss of the mother and expands through the redirection of internalized nothingness. Importantly, this black hole is a 'psychic silence' (replacing the wound of loss and grief) that can be understood as the mother's unsounding (carrying the traces of at least two feminine bodies) which is held both within the self as the black hole, but which also extends into the social and cultural in Isabel's everyday motherhood and activities; her unsounding, what she cannot say, filling the air with the imperceptible sensation of an inaudible low bass drone: the black hole of the (darkened, feminized) self.

As compelling as this idea is (particularly for those who experience depression) and as indispensable to the cartography of the self and the feminine, I would like to propose a counterpoint to the all-consuming psychic silence of black hole and dark deathly nothingness by questioning and raising the value of the black hole, cosmically, terrestrially, psychically, culturally and sonically. By value, I am referring to a complex series of equations that are based on matter and sound, space and time, i.e., dense matter over non-matter or nothingness, song over psychic silence, warped conceptions of spacetime over linear time. Finding value in the black hole, a black hole that *matters*, retains conceptual ties to the mother (and etymological ties between matter, expression, mother, physical substance and importance) and prompts a sense of correspondence with musicians for whom black holes and mothers appear to be important figures in artistic and aesthetic drives towards critical expression, freedom and liberation from personal and/or collective oppression (unsoundings). Björk and Moor Mother are two such figures and both write and produce sound and music that aim to make the matter of black holes materialize, as physical substance in space and as that sound which is ordinarily inaudible, negated and/or silenced: they each invoke the black hole song of the unsounding mother, the inner and outer black hole song between the real and imagined. The liminal space between real and imagined, where the real and imagined blurs, is key to the creative drive of both artists.

For Björk and Moor Mother, the mother is a key figure both implicitly and explicitly (as the name Moor Mother suggests) and both reflect on the maternal and the mother through creating dark spaces and black holes as sonic time travel, as if sound could not only fuse dark unsoundings, but metamorphose the unsoundings of mothers and black holes across the ages into sound, into song, into poetry. These artists do not cut themselves away from the mother, as per the advice, as per the matricides and silencing of psychoanalysis (and some feminist theories); they refuse to be bound by the psychologically and culturally inscribed devaluing of the mother, the terrible fate of mother–daughter melancholy and death-bearing women, but nor do they break away from the mother in order to distance or critique the essentialization of their womanhood – neither artist needs to cut ties from the mother in order to de-binarize their gender or sexuality. On the contrary, the circuitry of their sound is like a metaphysical umbilical cord, hooking up unsoundings between the cosmos, the earth and the mother and instead of reiterating clichés of the mother and the feminine, their refiguration of the mother is also a refiguration of identity, space and time, allowing for both singularity and the multiple to coexist. This is not to say that they are not haunted by loss, as each artist expresses anger and sorrow related to the maternal and the mother; there is in both more than an inkling of the inner black hole through which one 'founders' as well as 'replenishes'. In Moor Mother, the black hole sound might be perceived as the violence and chaos in which the singularity of a protesting voice (understood through the mother) is trying to get through. Nevertheless, the sonic creation of and immersion in the black hole dispenses with the foundations upon which understandings of the unsounding mother are based and proceeds to produce difference, matter and sound where there was absence and silence. And in Björk, the black hole sound might be considered as the struggle to sound when caught in grief and the loss of a partner. Björk's black holes are terrestrial, they create an ecological imaginary that refines a cyborgian-earth-mother-child, contrary to the divides between nature/science/art, whilst Moor Mother's sound places an emphasis on the *blackness* of the black hole and the extraterrestrial, the alien and the cosmological, drawing power from a legacy of black women and mothers's voices in Black Quantum Futurism in order to produce different conceptions of space and time in a practice that serves black lives (inner and outer) and identities.

In order to understand the production of difference in Björk and Moor Mother, its impact, and the potential for change via a refiguration of the mother, it is necessary to discuss and trace some elements of the relationship between the black hole, the mother and her 'unsoundings' in music and sound discourse, where the mother is a figure regularly evoked and where there are traces of attempts to return to, move through, cut from the mother's body: a discourse that exhibits a normative relationship with the mother and the maternal which is darkened as a black hole. Sound discourse and practice are very often caught in the orbit of a black hole of potential, which is the zero of nothing and the generative space of something: oscillating between the void and the womb, destruction and creation, penetration and immersion. Powerful metaphors and mystic language not only circumvent the spiralling curvature of orbit around the black hole, but also orchestrate a gateway into the dark unknown of sound creation and destruction, hovering on an edge that the discourse has created in a supernova explosion of psychoanalysis, theology, ontology, metaphysics and science fiction. Many cosmic sound adventures poised on the precipice of black holes legitimize a sense of sonic adventure by assuming a journey that has the apparent risk of annihilation and engulfment. To borrow Luce Irigaray's language however, the risk courted is often poised on the fake edginess of a 'rigged game', one implicitly based on ensuring the silencing and negation of both female desire and the maternal matter upon which the risk and the potential depend, ensuring the means to realize the survival of his form and her formlessness (Irigaray, [1974] 1985).

When does a mother sound like a black hole/when does a black hole sound like a mother?

By an inaudibly low drone or 'song' sung through the mouth of a black hole, attention is drawn through metaphysical sojourns and an ambiguous ontological status to an 'edginess' and liminal boundary point one might conceive of as an 'event horizon' of thought. A 2017 *Guardian* article entitled 'Edge of Darkness: Looking into the Black Hole at the Heart of the Milky Way', introduces the sublime magnitude of the black unknown by situating the reader's imaginary self at the 'edge of darkness', 'looking into' its unfathomable abyss. Within the weave of metaphors and imagery of the article, the black hole acquires a beguiling impression of agency derived from a 'devouring' nature that beats at the heart of our galaxy:

> At the heart of our galaxy, a vast black hole is devouring matter from the dust clouds that surround it. Little by little, expanses of interstellar material are being swallowed up by this voracious galactic carnivore that, in the process, has reached a mass that is 4m times that of our sun. (McKie, 2017)

As a devouring 'voracious galactic carnivore', the language adopted to describe the black hole recalls psychoanalytical theories and the kinds of cinematic analyses initiated by Barbara Creed, whose work theorizes representations of swirling black holes as signalling the monstrous-feminine with an 'appetite', read through castration anxiety (Creed, 2015). Finding parallels with Creed's 'vagina dentata' theory, Aram Sinnreich, in conversation with Jessa Lingel, insists on the Freudian dimension of black holes and the symbolism that significantly associates black holes with the vagina (the big 'O') in a psychoanalytical context. Referring to Freud's psychoanalysis, he argues that 'the sight of the vagina is sufficient to produce castration anxiety [...]' and this links to the Oedipal phase and the child's desire for the Mother (Lingel et al., 2016: 5690). He writes, 'the black hole as a symbol carries the capacity to trigger profound emotional responses in male adults, such as feelings of inadequacy and guilt associated with the man's sublimated sexual desire for his own mother' (2016: 5690). (The question of what the black hole symbolizes for women is here left open, but, as discussed, Kristeva suggests that the black hole is symbolic of female melancholy, tied to the mother.) Textual and visual representations of black holes draw together psychoanalysis, cosmology and science fiction into a connected network of enquiry that imagines and speculates on origins, connections/disconnections, other worlds and liminal points of no return, caught in an orbit on the edge of darkness, looking in. Following the romanticized discovery of the 'song', the black hole of castration anxiety imagined through images of galactic carnivores collapsed into portals to other worlds begins to elucidate a feminized maternal 'mouth' issuing unsounding song from a fearful unknown void, which is the negation of her lack. Following the logic, this lack is indiscernibly yet affectively manifest in the inaudible low bass sound of the black hole that, significantly, cannot be heard, an unsound that is the metaphysical resonance or ambisonic abyss of dark feminized nothingness, a void. Amplified and visualized (the first picture of a real black hole having been achieved and published in April 2019), an abundance of black hole soundings might be catalogued through cinematic sound design and literary texts, forming a cosmic constellation of highly turbulent encounters with black holes, whirlpools, monstrous sucking holes, hideous cacophonies of swirling dissonant 'noise', sublime orchestras descending into lower-frequency frenzies, endlessly spiralling shepard tones, vocal screams embodied in a dark open mouth, or disembodied acousmatic voices at the edges of what can be seen and comprehended as source.

Dreams of umbilical connections between sound in cinema and the maternal continue from the very beginning of Michel Chion's *Audio-Vision: Sound on Sound* (1994), starting with the foreword, penned by film editor and sound designer Walter Murch, in which he underpins the gendered and sexualized dimensions that accord and distinguish 'powers' across an audiovisual dynamic. Murch's text infers a sort of dark audiovisual consciousness that emerges from a psycho-cinematic logic that (naturally) genders vision as masculine and sound as feminine and an understanding of the mother's voice and the sound world of the womb is crucial to the dark audiovisual consciousness implicit in his text. To support his logic, Murch recalls a universal 'uterine darkness' in which the infant grows and in which hearing develops after around four and a half months in the womb. Floating in an undifferentiated everywhere and nowhere, the unborn baby bathes in the sounds of the mother's body and what he describes as the 'song of our mother's voice'. During this time, 'Sound rules as solitary Queen of our senses […]' and yet, following the birth of the infant, the sense of Sight 'dubs himself King' (Murch, 1994: vii–viii). Thereafter (Murch continues with his regal analogy), the Queen, despite her 'marriage' to Sight in 1927 (i.e., the first synched sound film, *The Jazz Singer*), 'withdraws' her power, or 'self-effaces' whilst being ignored by 'we' the viewers, who only have eyes to notice King Sight. Murch uses this analogy apparently to advocate for the importance of sound in cinema and there is a sense that the 'self-effacing' mystery of sound, alongside the association with the mother's womb, functions to provoke and support the desire of the listener. Indeed, the mystery of sound is essential. In Murch's words: '[…] there will always be something about sound that "bypasses and surprises us," and […] we must never entirely succeed in taming the dancing shadow and the singing soul' (Murch, 1994: xxiv). Despite the suggestion that the post-birth infant separated from the mother always yearns for a former sonic and physical unity, the subject still struggles with the desire *to see* the mother: 'and yet we delight in seeing the face of our mother: the one is the price to be paid for the other' (Murch 1994: xxiii). Journeying further and resonating with the language of Conrad's journey into the 'dark continent', Murch compares Chion's contributions and his attempts to map the features of the 'continent of sound' with that of early explorers 'who have forged their own path through the forests and return with tales of wonderful things seen for the first time' (1994: xxiii–xxiv). So even though Murch (in celebration of Chion's work in *Audio-Vision*) places an emphasis on the importance of sound and critically comments on the dominance of sight, his text is orientated around a gendered and sexualized relationship between sight and sound, based on the heroics that organize the tantalizing *glimpses* of sound. Using an autobiographical example, Murch contends that his own preadolescent experimentation with listening and recording sounds enabled him, with respect to film, 'to see through Sound's handmaidenly self-effacement and catch more than a glimpse of her crown' (1991: xv). Sound *herself* is imagined as elusive, a recluse whose door Chion knocked on with the determination of a 'suitor' and who, through her self-effacement in relation to the dominance of Sight, paradoxically acquires power (Murch, 1994: xv). For those brave explorers who notice her, the 'power' of sound is a source of perpetual fascination and is perceived and referred to through all kinds of sight-obscuring metaphors (veils, shadows) until we reach 'oblivion', voids and ever 'farther backwards' to the 'uterine darkness' of the mother's womb:

> Ever discreet, Sound pulls a veil of oblivion across her reign and withdraws into the shadows, keeping a watchful eye on the braggart Sight. (Murch, 1994: viii)

A curious power dynamic and taboo eroticism is established between Murch's constructed feminized sound (servile, passive, self-effacing), one based on fantasies about the dark and shadowy sound world of the mother and her voice. Sound in these cinematic terms bears mysterious marginal power on the basis of a sound source's hiddenness and obscurity. Gendered characters established, the discourse adopts an odd peeping Tom perspective from a subject position aligned with masculine sight titillated by a feminized, self-effacing sound emerging from the shadows of the cinematic light and darkness beyond the centre stage.

Chion's formulation of the *acousmêtre* makes the relationship between mother, gendered sound (dark) and sight (light) clearer in that, in claiming to raise the sonic powers of the mother, upon closer analysis these powers are subsumed under a masculinist scopic regime, one that attributes powerlessness to lacking female bodies, once the lack is 'discovered'. In *The Voice in Cinema* (1999), influenced by Pythogoras's acousmatics, Chion's conceptualization of the (unseen) disembodied female voice of cinema develops through the notion of the 'acousmêtre', demonstrated best by 'God – or even farther back the Mother' (Chion, 1999: 27). Situated farther back than God and, therefore, inferring the development of the infant in the womb, the mother's voice as primary creator exemplifies the powers of the off-screen voice of the acousmêtre. The acousmêtre's powers are 'usually malevolent, occasionally tutelary', as well as 'ubiquitous, panoptic, omniscient, and omnipotent' (Chion, 1999: 23–7). A figuration of the acousmêtre *par excellence*, the mother's voice is presented by Chion as a way of conceiving the powers of the disembodied voice in relation to a static subject held within a cinematic frame and the acousmêtre 'haunts' at the 'edge of the filmic frame', acquiring a unique, privileged spatial, psychic and temporal dimension in relation to a vulnerable subject. At the edge of the narrative represented within the frame, oscillating somewhere between the diegetic and non-diegetic, the acousmatic voice is loaded with powers that beckon the subject within the frame to transgress the limits of the frame. According to Chion, the acousmêtre loses her powers at the moment the voice of the speaker is lip-synched to the body of the speaker and therefore becomes an *embodied* rather than disembodied voice. He compares this moment of loss, this point in cinema where the mouth of the speaker is revealed and synched to voice, to a female striptease that, for him, is 'the point after which the denial of the absence of the penis is no longer possible'; at this moment where her lack is revealed, the voice is 'de-acousmatized' – all the powers are lost (Chion, 1999: 28). Kaja Silverman's critique of Chion's work pursues the processes by which masculinity is aligned with the cinematic apparatus of Hollywood film and how that apparatus confines female subjectivity, which inevitably emerges as lacking – 'culturally debased and devalued' (Silverman, 1988: 84). Picking up on Chion's comparison with striptease, Silverman suggests that the mouth/voice (when voice is visually located) is 'a major port of entry into her subjectivity, but this is actually, I would argue, the site at which that subjectivity is introduced into her' (1988: 67). She continues to describe the disempowerment of the lip-synched embodied female voice via the woman's mouth, which is now an 'organ hole', a 'yawning chasm of corporeal interiority' (67) – in effect the ultimate signifier of lack: the black hole. Both Murch and Chion's understanding of the relationship between sight and sound in cinema thus rely on gender and specifically the mother's voice, when sight is kept in the dark, so to speak. This opens up a series of fantasies and audio hallucinations that desire the mystery of the mother's body to be maintained, because in order to believe in these sonic powers her lack must be kept out of sight.

The cohabitation of horror and fascination, of the desire for rapturous reunification with the womb coupled with the absolute abject reaction to women's lacking and uncanny bodies, plays itself out in the discourse on sound and music from curiously similar perspectives and often with the same oppositional distinction between dark, comforting, uterine, amniotic soundworlds or horrific, claustrophobic, deathly echoic tunnels and chambers of acousmatic sounds and voices. This kind of relationship is noted by Nathan Wiseman-Trowse who follows a thread from the 'bad son' character of Euchrid Eucrow in Nick Cave's novel *And the Ass Saw the Angel* (here considered in relation to Carl Jung's *puer aeternus* – the personification of the repressed infantile), through to the connection between the unconscious and the maternal and the Great Mother archetype, the manifestation of the unconscious, according to Jung. Wiseman-Trowse writes, that for the main character Euchrid, the womb veers between being a place of comfort ('oh, that snuggery where we would float and float!') and a site of horror ('then all the dead belly's unborn, unmuzzled, did sound') (Wiseman-Trowse, 2008: 160). What may be dubbed 'Queen Sound', the acousmatic mother's voice of cinema, and the dark sound of the Great Mother within the text, is made explicit in sound discourse through the notion of 'wombing' sound, which has a 'dark side'.

Wombing sound

When Joy Press and Simon Reynolds discuss Brian Eno's ambient music, they describe a project that intentionally rebelled against the rebellion of masculinist rock by creating music that is 'wombing rather than wild'. According to their discussion, Eno's approach was predicated on making sound that would be perceived as passive, calm and gentle, inhabiting approaches to working with sound and music from the perspective of connecting with the 'yin' and 'feminine intuition':

> The West's ailment is an excess of yang (masculine reason): it can only learn how 'to stop making sense' by exploring the 'dark continent' (African rhythm, female intuition, yin). [...] If the Rolling Stones' ideal for living was the black bluesman, Eno (always the Stones' antithesis) aspired to be … a Chinese peasant woman placidly tilling a paddy field. (Reynolds and Press, 1996: 207)

Despite the 'emasculation of rock', the sonic desire that creates ambient sound apparently similarly hinges upon a discourse that establishes a stereotyped, clichéd version of a passive, racialized dark feminine sound world. The evolution of the term 'wombing' in Reynolds's work is in itself interesting since it is deployed across a range of styles and develops through notions of sanctuary and alienation and through the seemingly paradoxical simultaneity of containment and vast magnitude – such as, for instance, Ciccone Youth's 'Platoon II', 'recorded in an underground silo; it's an ambient dub-scape, stressed and fatigued metal sounds striated and stretched out to form a wombing vastness' (Reynolds, 1989). In *Blissed Out: The Raptures of Rock* (1990), Reynolds's writing centres around experiences of rock music and its oblivions ('aka jouissance…') and, in the process, he deploys the sonic womb to indicate moments when the parameters of the listening subject are blurred and the listener reconnects with and/or becomes immersed in the Other, momentarily losing one's 'self' to sound. Wombing imagines the jouissance of sound through the original Mother Other so that, for instance, the lullabies of dream pop – such as that of the Cocteau Twins, or the amniotic utopias of oceanic rock in AR Kane – have the propensity to take the listener back towards a blissful feeling of an original connection with the mother's body prior to separation, to a feeling of wholeness before the desire for lost objects, before an awareness of time and space free-floating in amniotic utopias and cradled by a musical feminine body. For Reynolds, in the Cocteau Twins the feminine finds a musical pop counterpart to Hélène Cixous's *écriture feminine*, in that both converge in the maternal song and tongue of the pre-symbolic, pre-Oedipal relationship between mother and child, 'a song that comes before language or grammar' (Reynolds, 1990: 130). On the other hand, the 'dark side' of the sonic womb is evoked in relation to the band Loop, whose apocalyptic themes and romanticization of death materialize in music driving towards ends of sorts, in the drones and repetition of deeper and deeper excavating grooves:

> Listening to Loop you feel wombed (or is it entombed)? […] Loop are a darker, more shuddery backwards fall through the mesh of language […] back back into the primal abjection from which we're shaped. […] Loop are the siren song of the Id. (Reynolds, 1988)

Feeling 'wombed' or 'entombed' infers an ambiguous relationship with sound and noise immersion, either nurturing in dream-like waters or buried in the 'grave-womb' crypt, each drawing through the mother's body. From dream pop to rock, from Eno's ambient music to the visceral knowledge effected by jungle on the dance floor and brutal sub-bass both 'wombing and menacing', the dark sonic womb recurs without being confined necessarily to or by genre. Writing about the sounds at the club AWOL, amniotic fluid returns in thick enveloping low-end frequencies that are 'swimmable' and allow the body to feel 'safe and dangerous': 'Like cruising in a car with a booming system, you're sealed by surround sound while marauding through urban space' (Reynolds, 1996). The black hole song of the mother might therefore be considered an immersive lullaby calling forth dreams or the seductive siren call of the chaotic part of the psyche, the id imagined by Freud through analogies to (another feminized witch brew 'container') 'a cauldron full of seething excitations' (Freud, [1933] 1995: 91).

The idea of a black hole 'song' in particular agitates the psychological dimensions of the dark sides of the self and the hidden, repressed, fears, desires and dreams of the unconscious, because its unsounding song/drone infers a dark unknown alien agency of sorts and a mouth/interiority comparable with uncanny returns to the mother's engulfing body, and to the 'primal uncanny' of nature (Creed, 2005: 84), to holes that lead deep within the earth posing the threat of being buried alive (i.e., the underground) as well as monstrous cosmological blackness. The discovery of the sound(ings) of a black hole and the implication of 'voice', whether characterized by 'song' or, in other instances, 'drone', eclipses the dominance of the apparent idea of cosmological silence that arguably presides over interpretations of black holes. In the collaborative paper, 'Black Holes as Metaphysical Silence', Jessa Lingel provokes her co-authors by questioning the function of black holes in science-fiction literature, suggesting that in such sci-fi narratives, black holes tend to confront space travellers with infinity, death and the unknown, whilst serving to indicate underlying fears of holes, space and endless depth. Lingel suggests that the black holes of science-fiction narrative operate as 'portal[s] of silence and transit' (Lingel et al., 2016: 5685) towards an unimaginable future and to other worlds, noting that the outcomes of travelling through black holes are typically 'dark' and anguished. Soundings of the black hole, however, do nothing to prohibit the idea of a portal to oblivion or other worlds and beings. On the contrary, this black hole exuding infrasound inaudible to the human ear only excites the science plus science-fiction imagination to romanticize the darkness of the cosmos, by imagining a sound that means annihilation (on the brink of imagining our own death – spaghettification) or portal to other worlds in science-fiction (encountering new worlds, spacetime, beings). Both black hole as linked to the maternal and as portal to new futures are explored in the music practice of Björk and Moor Mother.

Life and death bearing Mother Earth

The mother and her womb has been aligned with the dark holes of the earth and its resources, to the environment and nature, and therefore arguably linked through the demand to sustain and feed hungry children as long as she is legitimately penetrated, subdued, expropriated and mined for valuable resources, incurring anger and resentment if the maternal body either withholds or resists what is demanded and expected from it. Whilst nature is generally understood to align with an idea of 'Mother Earth' as a nurturing environment, dark holes in the earth raise the implicit etymological undertones of ecology, which derives from the Greek for 'home', connecting them to the mother's body through Freud's assertion that the mother's genitals are the unequivocal example of that which raises the uncanny as 'entrance to the former home' and moreover to what Creed, following Freud, has discussed as the 'primal uncanny' in her reading of the monstrous in horror film (2005). In turn, the sense of depth created through the understanding of primal origin, is a depth both historical, in terms of geological deep time and eerie, in terms of the uncanny spatiality of holes beneath the earth. Eeriness of the uncanny morphs into the 'grave-womb' in Mikhail Bakhtin's study of the Renaissance writer and scholar François Rabelais, when the former discusses the meaning of degradation through the topography of downward (earth) and upward (heaven):

> 'Downward' is earth, 'upward' is heaven. Earth is an element that devours, swallows up (the grave, the womb) and at the same time an element of birth, of renascence (the maternal breasts). Such is the meaning of 'upward' and 'downward' in

their cosmic aspect, while in their purely bodily aspect, which is not clearly distinct from the cosmic, the upper part is the face or the head and the lower part is the genital organs, the belly, and the buttocks. [...] Degradation here means coming down to earth, the contact with earth as an element that swallows up and gives birth at the same time. To degrade is to bury, to sow, and to kill simultaneously, in order to bring forth something more and better. [...] Degradation digs a bodily grave for a new birth; it has not only a destructive, negative aspect, but also a regenerating one. To degrade an object does not imply merely hurling it into the void of nonexistence, into absolute destruction, but to hurl it down to the reproductive lower stratum, the zone in which conception and a new birth takes place. Grotesque realism knows no other level; it is the fruitful earth and the womb. It is always conceiving. (Bakhtin, 1984: 21)

Bakhtin's understanding of degradation and the grave-womb complicates the black hole beyond the void and its 'destructive, negative aspect', allying it to something that also means rebirth and regeneration. In the grave-womb of the maternal earth, death and killing cohabit with life and rebirth. Such cohabitation between death and rebirth typifies the work of Björk in her approach on the album *Vulnicura* (2015b), an album that embodies the association of earth and the maternal in order to articulate the unsounding of grief and manufacture a healing rebirth following her break up with Matthew Barney, the father of her daughter. What is separated in Bakhtin's topology of the 'upwards' motion to the cosmos and 'downward' motion to the earth, a topology that corresponds with the 'upper' and 'lower' body, is here reunited in the circular, almost centripetal movements of the album that gravitate around and towards a moving centre which is Björk's mouth and voice, reuniting upper and lower strata in motions that sweep across the spaces created in the various orbits of each track. The overarching theme of the album is the creation of space both in the music itself and in the artwork and music videos. In 'Black Lake' (directed by Andrew Thomas Huang, 2015a) – which was a two-screen video installation that featured as part of Björk's retrospective at MoMA (the Museum of Modern Art, New York) in 2015 (Björk, 2015a) as well as a music video – the geological deep time of dark underground caves are analogous with a maternal earth and Björk shifts between a maternal and child-like body: that which gives birth, dies and is also reborn. Rebirths induced in these spaces underground and overground (where Björk is both mother and child) also appear to explicitly reference Björk's vocal style as it fluctuates between mature, strong, open resonance and child-like, fairy-tale playfulness. For mother and child, sorrow and healing in this album are directly linked with the imperative to sing and to return to the home of Björk's birth: Iceland.

Inner and outer black holes: Creating space and bridges

In the video for 'Mouth Mantra' (Kanda, 2015), the unsounding of a black hole looms in a 'negative space' that expresses the torment of losing the voice. The video is filmed both inside Björk's mouth as she sings and outside where, head lifted and intermittently shaking, throat extended, she strains to sing. Referenced here is Björk's discovery of vocal polyps and her subsequent throat surgery that left her silent for weeks. The lyrics of the song underscore the pain of a singer unable to sing, and crucially, her lyrical emphasis is placed on not being heard ('My mouth was sewn up / Banned from making noise / I was not heard'). Desperation and madness emerge through the exaggerated repeated focus on not being heard and on the unsounding of her body, as if she were forced to bear not only her own silence, but the genealogy of feminized nothingness and maternal unsoundings, something underscored in the visual reference to hysterical madness and repression as Björk wears and struggles with a costume that looks like a bandage-bondage straitjacket. In the bridge section, the video switches to another swirling image inside Björk's mouth, where the fleshy pink of her vocal apparatus, as well as her teeth moving in the opening and closing of her jaw, swirl in abstract forms around black holes of the inner voice. Accompanying the image, the lyrics collapse into 'silence' and she imagines the 'negative space' around the mouth imploding into a 'black hole': 'In vow of silence / I explore the negative space / Around my mouth / It implodes, black hole'.

The fifth verse that follows the bridge quite beautifully and lovingly thanks her vocal apparatus, which she describes as a 'tunnel' that has 'enabled thousands of sounds', a 'trunk', a 'noise pipe'. In this credit to her vocal body, an intimate relationship is established that nurtures a compassion for her own voice, bearing in mind that 'Mantra is a Sanskrit word composed of two sounds: man, which means "mind" and tra, which means "to cross over" or "to protect"' (Gannon, 2010: 145). The resonance of the mother–child relationship within, as inner self, works to help imagine the spatiality of the body as sonorous tunnels. Vera Brozzoni's reading of this heartbreak album suggests that 'by associating the impotence in her throat to the helplessness in her love/sex life, she is once again [as in "Black Lake"] symbolically superimposing mouth and vagina' (Brozzoni, 2017: 118). Impotence is here equivalent to an unsounding, an explicit connection with lack. The material similitude between the mouths and channels of the female body with the openings and tunnels of the earth continue specifically in the video for 'Family' and 'Black Lake', and suggest relationships between the vulva and *vulnus* (wound) (Brozzoni, 2017: 116), between love, absence and loss, calling forth an expression of interwoven sexuality and sorrow. There is a strangeness of intimacy between body, voice and dark geological spaces underground, an interconnected touching that Björk's work picks up on and expands through the wounded body and processes of healing. More specifically, her work engages with the (un)sound of culturally darkened and actually dark spaces, drawing relationships between the mother's body and geology in a praxis of approach that elicits the necessity of different terms of engagement that involve the values and practice of deep listening and the identification with and embodiment of voided dark spaces.

In the music video (or what Björk describes as the 'moving album cover') for 'Family' (Huang, 2015b), Björk appears as a fossilized, shiny black metallic tarlike body welded on to rock beneath the earth in a bent backwards posture; she is an immovable hidden sculpture of layers bonded to the caverns beneath the surface of the landscape, part of its dark geology. At some point, a transition is made and the same fossilized figure is now situated in the barren landscape of Iceland, above ground. Although body and nature are educed as inextricably tied, the formulation of the image and its colours do not entirely cohere with the semiotics of 'natural' nature, but instead refigure

THE BLACK HOLE SONG OF UNSOUNDING MOTHERS   125

the bond in a triangulation with technology, so that the elements of nature are changed, enhanced and made dream-like in surreal colours, materials and movements created by digital video software and graphics programming. Underground, we hear the frantic striking of strings, the solo body of a cello cutting with the desperate cried vocal articulations of the preliminary verses at the schism of dissonance, all of which is joined by erratic, deep electronic beats sounding a chaotic, unregulated dark space. Above ground, the sound changes so that strings, electronic sounds and voice begin to slow and attempt to find unison of movement, of pace and flow in the transition to composed order from chaos. This musical motion corresponds with the fluid that begins to pour from the cavernous hole in Björk's chest, thick pink wax that melts hard layers and reveals fleshy pink folds of the body, still nevertheless pinned to the rock. The shape of the vulva is repeated in an outfit that frames her face with the same form, a shape that recurs across the album and hints at its spatial properties and ontology of being. As pink liquid oozes from the wound, Björk, still in posture, begins to acquire some movement and so is able to sew the wound together with a surreal, computer-generated yellow cord, whilst little pearls form healing scabs within the pink fleshy wound. She sings: 'How will I sing us / Out of this sorrow / Build a safe bridge / For the child out of this danger'.

In terms of the 'safe bridge' in the lyrics, her bent spine posture is significant. It recalls a yoga asana commonly called the 'bridge pose' that, amongst other possible sequences, can be found in prenatal yoga, and may be used to open the throat and solar plexus chakras. Here, it is adopted in a context specifically related to the damage and healing of the mother's body as well as her felt responsibility of becoming a bridge for her child's safety. This healing bridge is made of body and sound/song; the lyrics pay heed to the cosmic potential of sound to heal (verse 4). To invoke yoga is, as Sharon Gannon discusses, to recall a practice that works towards realizing sound as the source of creation; of moving with the intent to understand sound and breath, specifically mantra, as that which can destroy and create form, bringing about changes in perception, a 'vibrational shift of consciousness radiating into every cell and tissue of the yogi's body' (2010: 141). The idea of healing from suffering is then understood through achieving harmony with the earth and the source of all manifestation, at one with all vibrational forms through sound and the sacred 'unstruck' sound:

The goal of the hatha yoga practices is to develop a sound body and sound mind in order to become more musical – to be able to hear the nadam. The nadam is the vibrational underlying stream that connects all of life; it is the eternal pulse of the universe, known as the 'inner humming' – the sacred sound of OM. All manifested things, including language, emanate from this primal source. (Gannon, 2010: 141)

From this yoga posture and in the context of sound and music as vibration, a number of correspondent practices and ideas emerge, not least that of Pauline Oliveros's 'Deep Listening' practice which adopts a meditative approach to expanding the awareness and consciousness of environmental sound 'inclusive of all perceptible vibrations (sonic formations)' (2005: xxiv), as well as her focus on breath, specifically the practice of breath regulation helping to 'direct energy to the lower abdomen' (2005:10). This attention to space, and the combination of references to 'nature' and 'technology', continues in 'Black Lake'.

'Black Lake': Rebirth from a grave womb

'Black Lake' orchestrates a return to Iceland as a return to a place of origin necessary for healing from a break-up. Visually, the geological features of her homeland are established through filming in underground caves, open crevices and vast, open volcanic landscapes. The narrative presents a process of healing that charts a rebirth from the spaces below ground to the spaces above. The music video for 'Black Lake' begins with Björk situated within a vagina-esque red and orange lava tunnel, kneeling on her bare knees with skin exposed to the damp, cold, hard surfaces of rocks. Despite the inference of motherland earth womb, this is not a soft, nurturing place but, instead, the threateningly dark and indifferent grave-womb. Her grief is performed in swaying gestures of sadness and desperation; raising her hands to initially place them on her lower abdomen, then up to her chest. Occasionally, she taps her throat and chest, drawing attention to the vulnerability of and damage to her vocal body (a gesture also expressed in 'Mouth Mantra'). The lyrics begin by establishing and underscoring the

THE BLACK HOLE SONG OF UNSOUNDING MOTHERS 127

charged connection between the space within which Björk is contained and the space within her body, 'Our love was my womb, But our love was broken'. On her feet, with hands passing across the surfaces of volcanic rocks, she progresses to wander through craggy ravines of black chalky dust and geological vulvic shapes cut into the landscape. As she walks, Björk beats her hands against herself and rock, her increasingly energetic pulsations and stronger vocals aligning with the deep electronic beats that raise the energy before she emerges into the night from an opening in the rocks, bare-footed and unsteady: her rebirth from the earth. The vulva of body and land is the enfolding mouth that confuses the difference between what she inhabits and what she is inhabited by, confusing interior with exterior by creating a portal transition between human and environment, inside and out. This correspondence between Björk's wounded body and the natural environment of Iceland is made explicit in the trailer for 'Black Lake' where she lies amongst a mass of Icelandic moss, fungi and coral, almost entirely camouflaged, and physically cut by a computer-generated wide ravine that looks as though a supernatural deep crevice has emerged in her body. Along this black hole wound, electric blue magma flows down from her chest, out from between her legs spilling into the cave chambers below. It continues to gloop through dark tunnels in the music video proper, but shifts later into eruptions of volcanic lava energy in moments symbolic of elemental fracture that are aligned with the sublime and mythological powers of nature, more specifically with the sublime of Icelandic geology, volcanic and geothermal energy, as well as the wide-open floor of fields covered in indigenous flora and biota.

In her extensive study of Björk, Nicola Dibben raises the significance of nature and national identity (here, inextricably linked and each reflective of the other) to Björk's music and a wider post-colonial contemporary Icelandic consciousness (Dibben, 2009). She calls Björk's album *Homogenic* (1997) her most 'explicitly nationalist' album to date, demonstrating in both the music video and the final composition mix of the track 'Joga', for instance, an extreme identification with Icelandic landscape (empty of humans and animals) to the point of embodiment, becoming 'subject matter'. 'Patriotic' string arrangements reflect wild, open landscapes and are associated with the 'Icelandic folk song tradition of *tvìsöngur*: the string writing in the verse is characterized by parallel step-wise movements in fifths, which has an empty sound' (Dibben, 2009:46). Dibben describes how both strings and beats are attributed an important mimetic character evocative of the topology and extreme meteorology of the country, with percussive sounds 'mimetic of the geologically active landscape' and what Björk refers to as 'Icelandic techno': distorted, un-pitched filtered beats, eruptive timbres suggestive of powerful movement and tectonic shifts created, for example, by swept filters (Dibben, 2009: 59–60). In 'Black Lake', Björk deploys similar musical devices, aligning emotive vocal embodiment, strings and mimetic beats with Iceland, its underground spaces and overground landscapes. Rather than the epitome of emptiness, dark spaces in the music and the visuals are loaded with the potential of geothermal energy, they are the charged spaces of reproductive potential, of volcanic earth tunnels and ravines that hold within them sensations of rebirth and of mother and child. Space as a 'holding' environment is an important element in the composition and arrangement, specifically the space created between voice and strings in a track that is approximately ten minutes long, has no chorus and consists of a series of verses. In an interview about 'Black Lake', Björk states a rationale for its length:

> It's like, when you're trying to express something and you sort of start, but then nothing comes out. You can maybe utter five words and then you're just stuck in the pain. And the chords in-between, they sort of represent that.[...] We called them 'the freezes,' these moments between the verses. They're longer than the verses, actually. It's just that one emotion when you're stuck. (Björk, cited in Magnússon, 2015)

Between vocal verses, sustained chords Björk refers to as 'freezes' are the means by which musical space is created, providing enough space to bridge between each expressive vocal verse. These effective tonal pauses allow the voice to transition verse by verse, so that the voice audibly grows in clarity, resonance and strength, as if each freeze encouraged a further opening of the vocal body. Initially, there is a sparse, gentle relationship established between strings and voice that contrasts sharply with the indifference of the visual space. Responsive strings coax the voice out of the dark corners of the body (and the cave in the visual narrative), tentatively accompanying and responding to the bare, repetitive, melodic phrasing of a voice that is attempting to say something, to address someone in what could be a desperate soliloquy, were it not for the sympathy of the strings (and production) that carve out breathing space. Arranged as reflective rests between vocal phrases, still, grounded, tonal pauses sound to provide a holding space for the vocal breath to gather itself and recuperate, providing a tempo that acknowledges the pace of her corporeal and visceral mourning. Such space and arrangement push away from survivalist choruses and the anticipation of a song structure that would perhaps deliver on expectations and build towards triumphant recoveries: the song itself hesitates to deliver on the habitual expectations of pop syntax (this push away from the movements of delivery on expectations arguably characterize Björk's later work in general). Provided with such space, Björk's physical gestures of grief and anger (such as when she is on all fours) become more dramatically pronounced, placing attention on the choreography of her body movements and, moreover, the beating and sojourning of her body.

Heartbreak in 'Black Lake' is reconfigured with an almost yogic attention to creating space in sound as it corresponds with the geological open spaces beneath and between the earth's surface; musically the track opens up channels for the vocal breath to synch with the earth's energy, encouraging grounded moments of inhales held by 'freezes' that follow each melodic movement. The motion established between strings and voice is like exhaled gusts of breath or wind moving through a tunnel, gathering up vocal grains then settling to inhale and hold the breath before it moves again as an exhale in the open channels of the music-voice-cave body. Thus, accompanied by the gentle sorrow and spacetime offered by the strings, the vocal body builds in energy and is explicitly libidinized by electronic beats compounded by Björk's pounding of her fists and violent pulsations of her body, until she leaves the cave via a crevice in the rock as a rebirth, joining with the earth outside. Epistemological divisions between geology, biology and technology are made porous and interconnect via the feminized spaces of her music's sonorous body, merging in the audiovisual spaces and narrative of a video shot on location in 'nature', yet replete with computer-generated effects that distort the 'natural'. Björk's intervention then, at the etymological roots of mater/mother, is to deploy technology and voice in such a way as to reimagine its relationship with space and matter, recoding the figuration of the dark maternal and its intimate sonorous spaces across hybrids of nature-technology-myth-science. Björk is renowned for musical innovation that creatively embraces technology, and this umbilical cord of connection is a wiring that allows the bodies that it links (physical and technological, 'real' and 'virtual') to fluctuate and transition between mother and child, origin and creation, effectively forming tracks, albums and music videos that are the becoming hybrids of dark earth Mother mythology, folkloric/pagan genealogy, fairytale child-like fantasies and cyborgian bodies. Within this cycle of sound, the unsoundings and soundings of feminized bodies come together in the origin of creation as a mouthed 'O' that merges the mother-child-cyborg-environment. Soundings of these hybrid beings present a life without the father, or the Father, since a cyborgian earth matriarchy has established the power of creation, healing and procreation by creating bridges and space, ensuring her movement into a future as opposed to stasis.

Post-earth cave birth, and now in dim daylight, Björk, wearing a black dress covered with a strange feather-light soft beige material reminiscent of skin, wanders across a landscape of moss-covered planes surrounded by mountains, where everything appears to be a mass of green biota/moss and black stones. She sings the final verse: 'I am a glowing shiny rocket / Returning home / As I enter the atmosphere / I burn off layer by layer'. Whilst singing these words with an emergent smile, the solo string part now follows instead of waits, its melody tracing the contours of her vocal melody, keeping up with a voice now slightly ahead – an effective reversal of roles. Björk stands with bare feet on a patch of black stone and begins to spin in one direction, whilst the camera spins around her in the opposite direction, creating a dizzying spiralling effect evocative of a whirlpool (recalling also the camera movements of 'Family'). This cyclical spiralling motion appears to effect a transition from earth to air, daylight to night-time; a static Björk floats suspended in the darkness, seemingly asleep or unconscious in an extended seat-like position with head and hair hanging backwards. In accordance with the directive of her lyrics, the layers of skin that are part of her costume fall or 'burn' away. Extended and sustained string tones carry her silence and stillness towards another transitional moment: Björk in daylight once again slows her spinning to a stop and proceeds to walk away from the now static camera and into the vast space of the landscape as the music is stripped back to strings only, strings that now follow Björk's vocal as a child follows a mother's lead. The viewer-listener is left behind, static and without the ability to follow her transitions any further.

What Björk practices and performs on this album, particularly in the audiovisual affect developed via 'Black Lake', is a deep ecology of feminine genesis moving and transitioning through open mouths and tunnels, between spatial correspondences between the mother, the earth, music, technology and vocal body, simultaneously immersive and immersed in their sonorous spaces. She orchestrates a rebirth of the mother, a refiguring of the maternal that embraces and expresses the ultimate taboo of the singularity of a mother's sexual desire and her mourning, as well as her healing. Despite the heterosexuality implied by the cultural figure of the Mother, Björk's cultivation of maternal sexuality within her art frequently focuses on autonomous physical and emotional experiences, such as pregnancy and birth and on the sensuality of the maternal body in, for instance, the act of breastfeeding, recalling affective and sensorial relationships with the child (e.g., 'The Pleasure Is All Mine' from *Medúlla* (Björk, 2004)). Intimacy is at times, an overwhelming offering in Björk's work and it is repeatedly given in the material similitude between mouths and channels of the female body and the openings and tunnels of the earth, converging in the opening and closing of sounding spaces that are embodied in her composition, performance and production. In enmeshing these spaces into the audiovisual fabric of the album, the stability of the notion of 'primal' origin is dispersed across a series of ambiguous inner and outer spaces, in rebirths that make of Björk both child and mother, denaturalized and cyborgian … and this results in the audible compassion for dark spaces, for black holes and renewed ecological imaginaries.

Dark matter and black holes

The triangulation of mother, earth, cave and (un)sound warrants further attention and it does so not least because of the (un) soundings of 'blackness' implicit within the blackness of the black hole, the 'black lake' and the rock sediment itself at the core of the semiotic and geological darkness of, in this case, Iceland (subject to centuries of colonialism). In relation to this blackness, both deep listening and deep time ecology not only imply the unsoundings of earth/environment and mother, but also classed and racialized bodies, since blackness resonates with geopolitics, geology and the echoes of bodies that labour to extract precious minerals and fluids from the earth. The unsoundings of exploited bodies and colonized land are writ into the geological layers of minerals as trapped sound in sediment and spaces that evidence toil: miners and labourers for coal and tin, for diamonds and gold, for oil. In the colonial project, blackness and geological resources are intimately related through a spatiality imagined according to the desire, wealth and power of colonialism. In the case of European colonialism, whiteness aligns itself with agency and technologies of biopolitical and geological surveillance and extraction, whilst aligning blackness with non-human resources and 'property', thereby legitimizing the forcible displacement of people from their land and origins. Kathryn Yusoff in her *A Billion Black Anthropocenes or None* (2018) writes:

> Origins are not solely about geography. They pertain to the question of how matter is understood and organized, as both extractable resource and energy, mobilized through dehumanizing modes of subjection and conjoining the property and properties of matter in such a way that it collapses the body politic of Blackness into the inhuman – wherein a codification in law and labor becomes an epidemiological signature, as Blackness is marked property and Whiteness is marked as freedom. (Yusoff, 2018: 66)

Bearing in mind an historical and culturally naturalized entitlement for white Western people to earth's resources, space and time, the black holes of the earth take many meaningful forms, drawing towards the spectres of the Middle Passage and the 'black hole of humanity' (Weheliye, cited in Yusoff, 2018: 53), the brutalization of black bodies, the silencing of voices in life and death, to the voiding of racialized bodies 'where blackness has no value; it is nothing', a non-life in the negative (Silva, 2017). And this is, in part at least, how one might begin to interpret the black holes of Moor Mother's practice, an artist that listens to the (un)sounding of the transatlantic slave trade and its effects, attempting to raise these sounds and voices into the present, as well as question and propose the past, present and future for the African diaspora and black lives, particularly in America, through her art, her community projects and the collective Black Quantum Futurism (BQF) co-founded by Camae Ayewa (aka Moor Mother) and her partner Rasheedah Phillips. For the BQF collective, linear time is the scaffold that upholds the logic of humanist progression presented as universal, but which actually organizes a Eurocentric worldview that privileges the evolution of white subjectivity from rooted origin in the past to location in the present to advancement into the future, an inheritance particularly of the Enlightenment and conceptions of 'Man's' progress. The advancement of 'Man' is organized through a logic of ideal 'human', from which blackness is excluded in terms of dominant historical narratives and the logic of accumulation, belonging, rights to land (space) and progress. Rather than seek to formulate and argue points of access for 'inclusion', the radical praxis of the BQF aims to change the terms of subjectivity, time and space, moving towards other conceptions of worlds, being and knowing, based on the dissolution of dominant conceptions of Eurocentric space and linear time. Here, space, dark matter and the cosmic black hole are important themes.

In the July 2019 edition of the *Wire*, a Moor Mother feature piece begins with a black hole in anticipation of the release of her album *Analog Fluids of Sonic Black Holes* (2019). In the feature, the sonic equivalent of a black hole is interpreted in conversation with Ayewa as a fluid vortex, trapping sound and screams, a 'nightmare image' that is 'an apt metaphor for the feeling of railing against an unjust system, with its police violence and mass incarceration and political corruption, that's so powerful it drowns out everything you throw at it' (Emily Pothast in conversation with Ayewa, 2019: 37). In this respect, the black hole of Moor Mother's solo work, such as *Fetish Bones* (2016) and *The Motionless Present* (2017) in collobration with Mental Jewelry, (metaphorically) indicates the suppressed and drowned out unsounding of contemporary and historical generational trauma. The black hole occurs with regularity in Moor Mother's sound and discourse. One review described Moor Mother's collaboration with DJ Haram (700 Bliss) and specifically the track 'Cosmic Slop', as that which 'blossoms from inky abstraction into a gravity-warped club-beat, as if it's being pulled from deep within a black hole' (Joyce, 2018). Another describes a Moor Mother performance by conjuring the implicit figure of the witch at the centre of 'an aural brew' of electronic sound 'while vocalising into the microphone' (Battaglia, 2018). Moor Mother herself links her practice and performances to black holes in her 2018 New York exhibition entitled 'Analog Fluids of Sonic Black Holes'. In the exhibition, as well as the dark 'aural brew' stirred from spectral callings and black noise, the sonic dimension of the black hole appears to be represented visually in a piece called 'Synth Altar', which features a (magic) circle of leaves and dried flowers against a black background and, inside the circle, the revered electronic music technologies of Moor Mother and BQF Creative, such as synths, effects pedals, vocoder, drum-machines and other noisemakers, this in addition to a pendant significantly positioned at the centre foreground along with stones/crystals, objects brought together symbolically in a way that articulates a mystical, ritualistic approach to making sound. This black hole of creation collapses the objects of science, music and mythology together in ritual practice, deterritorializing the demarcated zones of science (as opposed to myth) and masculinized music tech domain by foregrounding the creative autonomy, power and tools of a black woman.

In the context of Afrofuturism and BQF collective praxis, the sounding sonic black hole of Moor Mother's practice *also* means something that exceeds the silence of traumatic unsoundings and the cacophony of violence against black people, something that pertains to Afrofuturist spacetime as well as the relationship with and soundings of the mother, from the singularity of a black queer feminist audio and visual artist. Black holes in Moor Mother's practice raise the science fiction possibility that black holes offer portals to other worlds, other spaces and times, as well as an idea of critical black aesthetics that resituate blackness and black lives as that which *matter*. As Denis Ferreira da Silva proposes, dominant humanist equations of value where black lives do not matter are potentially challenged and resisted through 'blackness's disruptive force' and 'creative capacity' by virtue of a resistance against dialectical form wherein blackness 'function[s] as a signifier of violence' and therefore justifies violence against black people. She writes of a 'radical praxis of any refusal to contain blackness in the dialectical form' in order to bring about the dissolution of form, of 1 (matter-life) and 0 (non-life) towards the indeterminacy of blackness as matter:

blackness as *matter* signals [symbol for infinity], another world: namely, that which exists without time and out of space, in the plenum. (Silva, 2017: 10)

This dissolve of the dialectic enabled by the sonic black hole of critical black aesthetics therefore holds out the possibility of resisting the dominant modes and structures by which 'T'ruth is established, the hierarchal binary code itself and all its equations. Thus, the zero non-life of blackness, the form of the empty zero, dissolves into a plenum that is full of matter, an inconceivably dense black hole warping spacetime, where nothing, not even the '1' or white light can escape. Rasheedah Phillips extends the meaning of 'blackness' itself:

> The term 'Black' as used in Black Quantum Futurism is not only referring to skin pigmentation, race, lineage, and cultural identity. The concept of 'Black' in BQF encompasses each of those complicated phenomenon, but it also refers to the Blackness that permeates deep space, what is commonly known as 'dark matter'. `It encompasses the Blackness or darkness that permeates mental space and inner space. It refers to the light absorbing darkness which surpasses that of light by not needing to move at all. (Phillips, 2015: 13)

In the sonic black hole of Moor Mother's Black Quantum Futurist practice, all dominant prior modes of understanding and hermeneutic frameworks cease to be operational, and it is black women and mothers who are the singularities at the centre of these black holes of Afrofuturist praxis. Moor Mother's black hole singularity is the critical and futurist refiguration of space and time, the point at which 'density and gravity become infinite and spacetime curves infinitely, and where the laws of physics as we know them cease to operate' (Physics of the Universe, 2009). This central singularity issues a sounding, a black hole song that curves space and time, made audible, articulate and affective in Moor Mother's 'witch-rap', 'dark rap, blk girl blues', 'slaveship punk', 'southern girl dittys', 'black ghost songs' as they recover the unsoundings of history, the present and the future. She is incredibly prolific, tours and regularly collaborates with other artists and groups, including her ongoing collaboration as part of the free jazz improvisation group

'Irreversible Entanglements' and her electronic music collaboration with DJ Haram (under the name of 700 Bliss); influenced by a huge range of artists and genres such as hip hop, jazz, blues, doo-wop, soul, punk, noise and riot grrrl, Moor Mother's sound cannot be readily defined by one specific genre. However, her solo work is committed to lo-fi aesthetics in terms of her roots in DIY culture and consists of rap, poetry, sung text, non-verbal vocalizations and both composed and improvised collages of textures woven from field recordings and vocal samples, from synths, samplers and drum machines. These are, for Moor Mother, the tools of liberation or 'liberation technologies' (Pothast, 2019). With a particularly DIY aesthetic, she works with 'time capsules' of sound, some derived from samples of spirituals and blues ('Valley of Dry Bones' and 'Chain Gang Quantum Blues', *Fetish Bones*), others such as field recordings of 'wild dogs' (used in 'Creation Myth', *Fetish Bones*), and manipulates these sounds in relation to drum machines, mixers, theremins, synths and live vocal processing, all of which are treated with an approach to music-making that is 'nonlinear', that is cyclical and stirring, with slides, sweeps, rips and bends that facilitate quantum movement in electronic improvisations with science fiction and Afrofuturistic resonance.

Whilst celebrating the possibilities offered by (music) technology ('liberation technologies'), both Ayewa and Phillips are keen to refute the oversimplification of Afrofuturism as 'black people with technology' (Phillips, cited in Love, 2018). In reality, the image of 'high-tech' technology is not one invested in by artists who come from DIY culture and aesthetics, from low-income communities in project housing and who work with specifically low-income communities in their workshops. As part of the BQF collective, Ayewa and Phillips deliver workshops in their community (as well as internationally) with titles such as 'DIY Space Travel' and 'Anthropology of Consciousness' and use a methodology developed from DIY aesthetics that foregrounds accessible, powerful technologies such as language, writing and voice (in awareness of the economic privilege of access to certain technologies, such as the internet) to help envisage futures and deeper relationships to space through the interventions of storytelling, memory, healing and individual/collective agency. This is realized in the community resource space set up by Ayewa and Phillips called the Community Future Labs in North Philadelphia, based on radically positive transformations for the marginalized and where art is reconfigured as activism against the gentrification of the area and, in response to redevelopment, poverty, crime and educational inequality. The labs offer workshops in zine-making, writing, 'memory preservation' and music-making, as well as hosting discussions on specific community-based empowerment, such as talks on housing and tenants' rights, fighting misogynoir and 'black women's lives: states of matter'. The project explores sound improvisation in relation to DIY aesthetics and works to develop imaginative possibilities between BQF and available/accessible tools and resources in order to both reconfigure memory and create together radically different positive futures, shifting the reality of now for black people, focusing particularly on the lives of black women. In sound, music, community workshops, radical pedagogy and theory, Black Quantum Futurism develops a praxis that explores and develops other possible concepts of space and time, with the intent to positively affect oppressed marginalized communities, bodies and identities living in the reality of now, particularly those bodies and identities who connect through the collective black conscious and unconscious trauma of the legacies of the transatlantic slave trade and the displacement of African people. Work made by BQF Collective is made up of integrated and experimental writing, sound, workshops and images, all focused on collapsing spacetime into the potential for new possibilities and transformation, changing the 'dystopian reality' of being black in America by subverting chronological time patterns and opening and entering into acts of transformation that blur past, present and future. Drawing together the collective experiences of reality, BQF creatives and visionaries seek to identify and act at the vital intersecting points of potential for change between quantum physics, the visionary utopias of Afrofuturism, the knowledge of ancestors, and the spirituality and philosophy of ancient Africa, 'its traditions of time, space, and consciousness' (Phillips, 2015: 16).

Moor Mother's deep listening to the unsounding of space

Space (cosmic and terrestrial) and the sonic engagement with space is vital to Moor Mother's practice and poetry as it embodies a deep engagement with the spaces in which she writes and performs, through what could be described as an improvisational and imaginative dexterity in sound and text that corresponds with BQF theory. Her musical/vocal/textual improvisations are spontaneously responsive to space, an ethical and creative strategy that deeply considers performative space in order to write in time, overwrite in spacetime, according to what she feels in and from the space and location of performance and what she is told or has learnt about the space. Moor Mother's improvisation responds to othered voices, stories and sounds by engaging with and through a radically altered conception of spacetime in the context of what Tracey Nicholls has theorized as an 'ethics of improvisation', a socio-aesthetic practice made up of performances that model an ethical commitment and response to community (Nicholls, 2012). *In situ*, she meditates on and responds to what has happened in a given space, in effect building through this engagement a deep time consciousness around the correspondences between place, event, memory, text and sound, so as to articulate unheard/hidden narratives and sounds of space and location. This approach to sound-making heightens an awareness of the potential for time-travel, drawing on the unsounding of future, past, present which entangle in the performative moment of 'now'. For her, engagement with space, and what she refers to as an 'anthropology of consciousness', is particularly relevant to uncovering the truth of the legacies and histories of black women, stories that have been controlled and suppressed:

> 'I'm trying to study every place a black woman has been,' [...] 'I'm finding out it's endless. There's something before being "black" and we're not taught that.' [...] 'Our past has been distorted. Most people think we started with slavery, but we were explorers before that. We have to find that information for ourselves. People say to me at shows, "Thank you, I was losing a sense of my identity before I heard you."' (Moor Mother, cited in Beaumont-Thomas, 2017)

The recurring figures of black women and girls are the continual return of Moor Mother's poetry, spoken word and raps. In her texts, the ghostly echoes of voices are amplified, tuned in like a radio picking up lost voices in space with the aim of transmitting sound. They are brought into the here and now via a sonic visceral power and within

THE BLACK HOLE SONG OF UNSOUNDING MOTHERS 139

the context of politicized black noise that insists on articulating excruciating violence, stories of survival, pain, strength, struggles to stay alive and death. Published in *Fetish Bones* (Aweya, 2016a), 'Eviction Day' is about the individual hardships of the speaker's 'mama' who works to keep the home and food in the kitchen, and who is under the constant threat of poverty and physical violence, an image evoked, the reader assumes, from a daughter's perspective. However, the unique relationship between a specific mother and daughter and their experiences translates into a collective sense of mothers and daughters across time as they connect through the trauma of shared hardship, of enslaved labour and the horror of the transatlantic slave trade: 'I hear mothers singing in the fields, / [...] / the Ethiopian sea is red / must be all them dead bodies / babies clinging to their bloated mommas' (Ayewa, 'Eviction Day', *Fetish Bones*, 2016: 7–8).

Across the written and audio spoken text of Camae Ayewa/Moor Mother's solo work, black women, little girls, sisters, daughters, mamas, mothers, mommas, grandmothers, emerge as bodies under attack in a culture of racism, sexism, domestic and sexual violence, state-sponsored incarceration and economic oppression of black communities and the demolishing of neighbourhoods and communities. Specific cases of police brutality are foregrounded in texts that speak of Sandra Bland and Natasha McKenna, both of whom died in police custody, their voices sampled and painfully scoring the air with images of their life and death, of police brutality, and referenced in lyrics such as 'I'm Sandra Bland returning from the dead with a hatchet' ('By The Light', *Fetish Bones* 2016). In 'Time Distortion', from *The Motionless Present* (2017), meanwhile, Ayewa incorporates harrowing audio samples from the footage of Sandra Bland's 2015 arrest in Texas.

Moor Mother's sonic time-travel of trauma stretches back to the race riots of 1866 and extends up to contemporary instances of police brutality, in all cases highlighting the suffering, rage and overwhelming force of trauma. In her written pieces for volume 2 of *BQF* titled 'The Sights and Sounds of the Passage' (Ayewa 2016b), Ayewa describes the conditions of the slave ships, the treatment and slaughter of men, women and children and dead bodies thrown overboard:

The sound of suffering. Chains heavy screaming and chanting. I recognise these spells. Someone is trying to sink the ship. Another is cursing the captain. I'm not sure who is alive or dead. [...] When the white man declares himself science he is no longer human. The sound of everything at once. The sound of babies screaming for mother and mothers gagging in agony for the return of their babies snatched from the womb. (Ayewa, 2016b: 11)

There are, in Moor Mother's witch rap and spoken word, important transitions between spoken word, cries and screams, that insist on the power of words/voice to re-remember stories in a series of crafted and improvised utterances which conjure to uncover truths whilst raging at its suppression. 'By the Light' (*Fetish Bones* 2016) vocally, affectively inhabits both fearful terror and targeted rage, struggling between the polarities of wresting oneself free from an aggressor, to up-close confrontation with a voice that expectorates the truths of violence, that leaves the listener less and less space to hide from the racism of the past or present by drawing together closer and closer the distances between time and bodies in space to the point of collapse, thereby creating an ambiguity of threat for listeners. For white listeners, this means a frightening encounter with the threat of multiple truths returning from the margins to which they have been kept, in order to maintain (racist) alignment between white subjectivity, science and the morality of light, returning to intersect and interrupt that 'centre' ground of comfort and privilege. A processed and pitch-shifted voice navigates the terror of past and present ('get these chains off me') whilst a vocal body with purposeful muscular low-body physicality wrenches words from the depths to articulate fragments of agonizing bloody narratives, including the moment of the subject's birth, in amongst scarring techno-like industrialized electronic beats, which are themselves caught between a polarity of erratic splices of sound and repetitive beats. 'Of Blood' (*Alpha Serpentis* 2012) furthers the alignment with women's bodies by critically calling to account the misogyny of all the enforced hidings of women, with a track that again refuses to simply inhabit victimhood. Instead, Moor Mother uses vocal processing to articulate a multitude of subjects fragmented and multiplied across trans-gendered and denaturalized voices and migrates across disturbingly gender-ambiguous voices, including the child-like and the seemingly supernatural. The emphasis in 'Of Blood' draws attention to the abjection of menstrual bleeding as symbolic of the feminized social taboo and, through the trope of blood, both music video and track indicate a critical concern with women obliged to 'go into hiding', especially women in domestic abuse situations. Placing the struggles and potential of women and particularly black women, at the centre of her practice, women are for Moor Mother central to the definition of protest music: they are the singers of 'trials and tribulations' and the cultural figures expected to hold, save and nurture, despite feeling like 'a hunk of bones':

> That goes back to the woman—just because you are the creator, you're not everyone's savior. At the end of the day, you've been used and ran through. […] That's what *Fetish Bones* is. Feeling like a hunk of bones. (Moor Mother, cited in Pelly, 2016)

In the title of Moor Mother's album, *Fetish Bones*, a number of criticisms are implied and these are expounded on in various interviews which seek to uncover the ties between racism, sexism and capitalism, all of which imbricate ideologies of dissociation from the maternal and a logic that marginalizes, displaces, brutalizes and exploits black communities and women. Moor Mother wrests the voices and sounds of black identity and culture away from the appropriating forces of capitalism and fetishization, reactivating the political charge of memories, subjectivity and narratives within the blues, gospel, spirituals, rap, free jazz, improvisation and punk. At the centre of this cyclical time travel in sound are black women and the mother, single mothers, the marginalized as BQF creatives, working in and through dark energy, creating transformative colour.

Black hole song singularity: The BQF sorcerer

In Afrofuturist sonic and lyrical witch-rap craft, Moor Mother raises the status and significance of the maternal (Moor Mother) in the form of goddesses and priestesses, 'Grandmothers of Magic' (Ayewa, 2016a), and Mother Africa. She reappropriates the witch as a powerful feminine figure of knowledge, rage, resistance, vision and ritual, formulating an unknown and irrepressible power derived from the reverence of the maternal in relation to ancient beliefs:

I'm always into mysticism and the occult. When it comes to ancient rituals, the woman—the maternal—was very revered in a sense of respect. Not like it is now. (Moor Mother, cited in Spiegel, 2017)

Summoning notions of origin and power through the maternal together with reference to the occult and mysticism, in this context Moor Mother's performative embodiment of sonic mantras and searing electronic beats finds resonance with Joy Kmt's understanding of the 'sorcerer', a figure of black resistance that not only draws from mythology and uses words as tools of power, but who is necessarily inhabited by the mythology so that 'words possess the sorcerer in order for the word – the words – the spell – to be potent' (2015, 52–3). Via such sorcery, Kmt proposes the possibility of stepping into other worlds, other timelines:

They [the sorcerers that move beyond 'cults' and their own gain] turn back to the myth for instruction. They pull the truth of the mythological timeline into reality in word action and deed. […] Indeed the sorcerer is no longer privvy to many challenges, once the mythology is fully integrated into the psyche of the sorcerer and becomes lived truth. Lived truth is the evidence of a new reality. (Kmt, 2015: 53)

As advocates of the entanglements and 'retrocausality' (beginning with the vision of survival and positive future as the end point) of spacetime, this weave of influences emphasizes 'the overlap between ancient African consciousness of time and modern quantum physics', which according to Phillips, means that the BQF collective is able to 'increase the knowability of the future and the past as formally equivalent' (Love, 2018). Ayewa and Phillips are resolutely against the straight-line linear conception of time and promote through their praxis African conceptions of time and consciousness that are cyclical, spiralling, dimensional, where/ when the future enfolds and flows backwards into the present and 'the past and present overlap in an African conception of time, as the present swallows up the future and the past swallows up the present' (Phillips, 2015: 24). Phillips's essay features a diagram of 'event mapping' (which differs to a cause and effect model of linear-thinking event) that has a centre, a focal point of 'now' around which events cluster in a circle and the BQF Creative 'determines the centre of the field, the uniting factor and synchronicity around which certain events will be grouped' (2015: 28). The cyclical dynamic quality of the interaction may be orchestrated by the BQF Creative (or sorcerer) installed at the centre of deep space, able to identify and operate at the nanosecond of the potential for change, altering spacetime through the darkness of the unknown that is both the darkness of trauma and the positive potential for other futures. This cyclical movement traces the orbit around a black hole of the unknown, one that is explicitly politicized as the potential of BQF practical and theoretical activity. In the case of Moor Mother's work, the black hole may be configured explicitly around the gravitational singularity of the black maternal, a mystical Mother Africa connected to black female subjectivity that is the sorcerer BQF at the centre of quantum effects and spacetime curves, forming portals to other ways of being and knowing. The black hole of the unsounding maternal therefore transitions to a song of a future that collapses into now.

5

Becoming-shadow thing

Chelsea Wolfe's heavy mourning dirge in dark times

In the dark times
Will there also be singing?
Yes, there will also be singing
About the dark times.

(BERTOLT BRECHT, [1936–8] 1987: 320)

Will there be singing in dark times?

Dark times can refer to individual or collective experience and the two can converge. The dark in the expression 'dark times' alludes to powerful malevolent forces of oppression, exploitation and violence, as well as to the melancholia, grief, pain and death effected during the historical and cultural specificity of the period loosely or rigidly marked as a 'dark time'. When people talk about dark times, it is 'light' that is hoped for and equated with the morality of goodness and light that is perceived as being under threat, whilst the darkness of dark times accrues momentum via a matrixial weave of media collective consciousness, trauma and threatening experiences, of physically and mentally painful events (individual and shared), of sustained damaging micro- and macro-cultures, and/or the overwhelming sense of an imminent threat to one's own and to others present and future. In an age of mass extinction of life on earth, with depleting land, clean water and food resources, dark times is an increasingly blunt colloquialism. Living during the augmenting awareness of a global climate crisis, ever-rising record-breaking temperatures and the threat of ecocide, the darkness of the ecological imaginary of this current time has arguably deepened beyond a post-apocalyptic world to something that is accelerating towards the absolute black of infinity, of death forever with no survivors. This immense darkness emerges from the blackening of air, soil and water, of fossil fuel emissions, and of burnt scorched earth, all toxically inhaled by a body-mind consciousness that coalesces to form the blackened core at the heart of an ecological imaginary; herein hope is overwhelmed and disperses in a black abyss without edge and immeasurable depth. How does a singer sing *about* these dark times? What words, timbres, melodies and sounds can possibly express such boundless darkness in a performative voicing that is the imperative response to the dark times implied by Bertolt Brecht in the epigraph to this chapter? Doesn't this imperative to voice lose its drive in the face of the current ecocidal psychopathic powers and their relentless forceful push into a colossal black lacuna that exterminates meaning and all life on earth?[1] A singer poised at the edge of utter destruction despairs at the brink of an immense cataclysmic abyss. On the precipice of total annihilation, the singer is arguably compelled to acknowledge that there are no songs to be sung about these dark times, only the cries of horror and grief, the silence of death and the blackened void.

Perhaps, instead of singing 'about the dark times' a more appropriate response might be to listen, to pick up and record the sounds of the darkness in order to reveal something about its temporality, spatiality and non-human character. Recordings of the dark can be produced by using microphones, hydrophones, geophones and other transducers that pick up the sounds of worlds that otherwise elude the human senses. To do this has the potential to introduce active agencies that reach beyond representational logic and any anthropocentric perspective implied in the song sung 'about the dark times'. Moreover, such recordings can change the character of what constitutes understandings of the 'dark', thereby altering human perception and introducing the possibility for change in behaviour and response to the darkness. For example, field recordist and composer Jana Winderen's album *The Listener* (2016) is a 23-minute electroacoustic composition formed from recordings of the ordinarily inaudible or unheard sounds captured by hydrophone recordings of, in this case, underwater insects. Her work captures sounds from the underwater world of the river and its life, decentring the human subject and song by bringing the sounds of insects to the fore, sounds that *say or sound something* about life and death beyond the human, whilst also speaking of human effects given that the recordings can be used to determine the health of the river and provide insights/in-hearings into its ecology. In other words, this album simultaneously articulates both the darkness of humanity's effects and a darkness which extends beyond humanity, elaborating on and even changing what 'we know' about dark ecologies: this is the dark sound of the Anthropocene and the potential to imagine that which exceeds humanity, its excesses and perhaps the anthropocentric character of the epoch itself. Even whilst we may hear the impact of humans on the natural world, can this dark sound also constitute hope and, if so, what is the nature of that hope, despite the audible signs of the destructive and death-bearing activity of humanity?

From a similar field recording perspective, Susanne Pratt, in '"Black-Noise": The Throb of the Anthropocene' (2016), discusses her installation made from recordings that she describes as 'black noise'. In the context of her practice-based research, 'black noise' is read as a continual humming infrasound that is both the actual sound of coal mining and machinery at very low frequencies (in the Hunter Valley, Australia) and a metaphor for the 'blackening of the air'; the vibrations of corrosive capitalist economy energy systems and their material effects on ecologies. For Pratt, the installation 'Black Noise' (2013) was made in response to the 'waves of apathy, disgust, and mourning that I feel daily – the feelings which surge with each news report of increasing fire risks brought on by changes in climate, the blackening of the skies from smog pollution, or stories of toxic tailings that leach into waterways' (Pratt, 2016: 21). Her sound installation offers a refiguration of singing about the dark times that raises an ecological imaginary thick with the affects and vibrations of dark sound and black noise, ambiguously fluctuating between 'real' sounds, affects and metaphor. Here, grief and mourning ('the act of sorrowing') are atomically bound with waves of low frequencies and the real and metaphoric infrasound of industrialization and these are, in turn, woven amongst a range of omnipresent audible and inaudible frequencies of nature as in 'ocean, waterfalls, volcanoes and earthquakes' (Volcler, 2013: 21). Ecological and environmental concerns link the field recordings and transdisciplinary practice of both Winderen and Pratt, however Pratt's impetus for this particular work is significant in that she reveals to her reader that her installation is driven by and derives from the grievous emotions of mourning. In making the emotive components of her work explicit ('waves of apathy, disgust, and mourning') the notion of singing in dark times and questions around the kinds of songs that can be sung about, within and perhaps despite the blackening of the air, emerge once again having acquired the emotive and affective weight of mourning.

The burden of mourning dirge

At the edge of the abyss, the air is thick and blackened smog. Pratt describes the blackening of air in terms of a 'burdening', the 'burden of coal and black noise' as it presses upon her home country. In doing so, she imparts a feeling of powerlessness and something of the heavy force, weight and effects of black noise when it is indicative of immense power and destruction. The burdening of black noise is the impression it makes on bodies and ecologies; it is the mental and physical impression of death that threatens all life, inducing mourning affects that lay heavy on human mind-bodies unable to repress or evade the burden. Such heavy toxicities threaten to crush the stomach, chest and throat of the singer who, drawing breath from blackened air, gasps for the breath to sing a song whilst the weight of this burden depresses their body, leaving impressions that are both 'real' and metaphoric. The burden of black noise and a growing awareness of the dark abyss also impinges on the song itself, suffocating its space, depriving it of words and putting both singer and song under such pressure that there can be no celebrated resilient energy boosts or survivalist escapes to be drawn out by singing in dark times. In such a context, the songs that are most reflective of this blackened air, the songs that become audible and/

or embody the times, are mourning dirges weighted by a dark, blackened amorphous burden that embodies and causes an acute sense of loss. Yet, the process of grieving and the object of that loss cannot be fully grasped by a mourning dirge of these times; one that attempts to mourn the blackened ecology Pratt renders in her combination of inaudible infrasound, the vibrations of capitalist networks and vaporous blackened air and imagined in this chapter to be circulating around the edge of a death chasm that is the threshold of what can be heard, said and comprehended. In fact, one of the deeply disturbing burdens of this mourning dirge is that it cannot grasp or express what has been lost or what will be lost, placing it in a strange liminal place between the already fragile distinction theorized by Sigmund Freud ([1917] 2005), between mourning and melancholia, between mourning over a specific loss that is eventually accomplished when the libido detaches itself from the lost object/other and perpetual melancholia which inspires a sense of indistinct object-less loss, something repressed that cannot be resolved. Immersed in the mourning dirge at the edge of a mass ecocidal abyss, the libido cannot hope to detach itself from such an immense indistinct object-less loss and that which is mourned. Rather, the drive towards pleasure, love, sex and survival gets caught up in a loss in which one's own death is implied, creating a chaos of ego defences, only to be swallowed up by the depressed chasm within oneself in death-drive trajectories, so that the subject gravitates not away from, but towards the abyss in fits of repetitive compulsions and aggression externally directed at the world and internally towards the self in misanthropic and melancholic dirge.

Guided by approaches to dark sound which work from a fundamental premise of listening and capturing that which ordinarily evades human attention or escapes the human senses (Winderen) and by the blackened noise conceptualized by Pratt via an imperative relationship between mourning and ecology in these dark times, this chapter endeavours to listen for parallel correlations of concern that materialize in song. It will propose this correlation via the work of Chelsea Wolfe, whose sound and practice suggests a heavy indwelling of blackened ecological doom in musical styles that cross between metal, gothic-rock, funeral folk, spectral electronica hybrids and which merge to form heavy mourning songs that are about these dark times, without the overstatement or explicit protest that this might imply. Whilst Wolfe's work is not explicitly tagged with the label 'eco-activism' nor regarded in the same way that, for instance, Wolves in the Throne Room are appraised for their eco-black-metal (Morton, 2013), there is nevertheless a comparable resonance with ecological blackening and heavy sound that, for Wolfe, is based on song and music technologies which can affectively articulate the inextricable connections between mourning, environmental crisis and the blackened ecological imaginary. Wolfe's sound proposes that the heavy burden of ecocide mourning dirge cannot be articulated without technology, without machines in that the dirge needs to bear the capacity for black noise (industrialization, oppressive power networks and systems, toxic air, dark ecologies, the human and non-human) and to bring bodies to the extreme threshold of the culturally abjected abyss of the blackened ecological imaginary. Technology here is not so much reified as a tool for liberation or fetishized as a tool of power, as made manifest only out of the darkness of the interconnectedness of machines and bodies, bringing to the fore a blackened ecology out of a bitter, vengeful mourning dirge. In this case, sound extends beyond the signifiers of human capacity and the 'natural', corrupting the circuitry of meaning and affect by connecting machines, nature and culture in song that moves towards death, to the edge of the pit.

There are certain correspondences between these dark circuits in song and what black-metal theorists have conceptualized as 'melancology', a term found in the title of an edited collection of essays dedicated to black-metal theory and which joins melancholy with ecology. Melancholic bleakness in black-metal theory can be considered through investments in negation, Satanism, anti-capitalism, pre-Christian pagan culture, misanthropy and fantasies of death, including suicidal narratives. In the volume mentioned, the authors unpacking the theoretical concept of 'melancology' propose that it is desire that motivates the sonic and cultural movements towards transgression and death, not the gendered conceptions of lack that plague psychoanalytical understandings of melancholy; that black metal is concerned with 'tragic intensity' rather than pining sorrow and is rather in love with death itself, whilst at the same time haunted by 'the spectre of the undead, eternal bleakness of the universe' (Wilson, 2014: 14). In such discussion therefore, the transgressive agenda and carnal desires that drive towards death and the dissolution of the ego, have apparently surpassed gender, or at least migrated towards that which is deemed separable from gender concerns. And yet, as Aspasia Stephanou argues in her paper 'Playing Wolves and Red Riding Hoods in Black Metal', the transgressive act of black-metal's 'lycanthropic entities' and howling wolf-becoming is based on the necessity of father signifiers (Christian God/Satan), so that whilst 'A living incarnation of Satan has taken the place of a dead God' it is also that 'the original father needs to be brought back and recomposed repeatedly for the transgressive act to have meaning' (Stephanou, 2010: 161). Under such terms, the meaning of death fantasies, of evil, of transgressive acts, all have a foundational basis in the topography of grand patriarchs torn between heaven and hell. In her discussion on death metal, Jasmine Shadrack makes a comparable case for the consideration of gender as it bears on understandings of 'extremes' in sound. She argues that the 'extreme' of 'death metal' is effected through the assumption of female passivity and women as victims of extreme physical and sexual brutality so that, alongside timbral assault and 'maximal' noise, the aesthetic representations of violence against women 'manifest their representations of extremity' (Shadrack, 2017: 179). Her argument extends beyond the suggestion that 'heavy' or 'extreme' subcultures tend to attribute cultural and aesthetic weightiness or gravitas to masculinized valuable sonic 'extremes' through the territorialization of technologies that drive 'powernoise' (amps and guitar pedals) and proceeds further to elaborate on the production of 'extreme' as based on the requirement of a passive feminized position. As an abject and passive void, the feminine in this context offers aesthetic value and cultural capital for hetero-masculinity in that male subjectivity is able to sonically and culturally exert its weight on to a pacified object whilst drawing the currency of 'extreme' gravitas from the subjugation of the feminine converted into capital at key moments of dark jouissance, which are the sonic expressions of violent transgression, muddying masculinity between ego and id. Although semiotically and aesthetically close to death, dark and blackened, Wolfe tempers the rhetoric of the necessity for the kinds of 'extremes' expressed in Satanic rebellions and the nihilism held within discourses on noise, black-metal, death-metal, rock and so on, in order to continue to articulate something about the burdening of these dark times in song. Wolfe's mourning dirge raises the repressed shadow of femininity, reintroducing the dark feminine to the chain of associations between melancholy, death and ecology in sound. For Wolfe, a vital part of this circuit is established via the dark feminine as a mythology integral to the heavy mourning dirge of these dark times, a time that has revealed the historical, heavyweight layers of patriarchy as a burden of now, as a force blackening the air all around.

The nightmare weight of patriarchy and the abyss within

Heavy sound in Wolfe's *Hiss Spun* (2017) can be interpreted through the weight and effects of patriarchy and sexual abuse as a burden that makes indelible impressions on oppressed/suppressed bodies. In this album, the performative act of the witch is central to its attempts to exorcise violence insofar as this feminine archetype represents a legacy of persecution, while alluding to the power that comes from combining voice, occult knowledge and language in curses, spells and incantations. The occult power of the dark feminine, channelled through the combination of word, voice and sound, is configured by Wolfe through the use of voice in ritualistic recited formulas of words that produce an effect...and affect. *Hiss Spun* is bound together in short syllable words. As Wolfe describes it, 'flux, hiss, welt, groan, swarm, spun, scrape, [and] strain. They became a sort of guide. Flux represents movement and flow. Hiss is life force and white noise. Welt is the brutality of life, [and] groan represented sensuality and death'(Wolfe, cited in London, 2017). It is an album that ritualizes an exorcism of sexual violence, that menacingly invokes and rages against the historical legacy of violence against women. It does not purge sexuality from the album but, on the contrary, darkens and queers sexuality in the gothic sensuality of, for instance, the track and music video for 'Spun'. Recorded in Salem, Massachusetts, Wolfe draws an explicit comparison between the recording location and the cultural shadow of witchcraft: 'There is a lot of anger on this album for what my female and genderqueer antecessors have had to face, so recording in a town that historically murdered women for being "witches" was fitting' (Wolfe, cited in London, 2017). Along the lines of ancestral legacy, Wolfe forges a weave between the cultural and the personal, past and present moments in American history:

CHELSEA WOLFE'S HEAVY DIRGE IN DARK TIMES 153

There's anger about the election and what's to come from that. There's anger that's directly expressed from the viewpoint of a woman, and thinking about what my foremothers had to go through, and what I had to go through sometimes. (Wolfe, cited in Appleford, 2017)

Whilst personal trauma is imparted in the lyrics for the song 'Scrape', there is a consistent acknowledgement here of a historical burden of violence and threat that is utterly individual whilst also shared across centuries with other darkened bodies. Wolfe's *Birth of Violence* (2019) suggests the progression of her historical interrogation of specifically American history as well as the potential of song to exorcise the effects of violence and assume power. It also establishes a sense of uncanny mourning in tracks like 'American Darkness', which infers a critical disposition to the deep time strata of 'dark' American history, set in resonance with a narrative that tells the story of a war widow who dances with the ghost of her husband. Such layered haunting superimpositions abound in Wolfe's cinematic albums, which draw from the cultural fluidity between the witch and the widow as shadowy feminine figurations. The *Abyss*, released in 2015, also moves backwards (in time) but combines this movement with the notion of falling into the abysmal darkness of oneself via disorientating dream states. In liminal nocturnal states, the album and its artwork intimate a falling or floating subject who is propelled downwards, descending into a fearful abyss and laden with the psychological weight of inherited trauma. Individually and collectively, these three albums produce spectral shadow-things wherein the dark feminine is both the haunted and the haunting apparition. *Abyss* is an intensification of the 'drop' into the darkness of one's haunted and haunting self.

In a press release for *Abyss*, Wolfe writes of the album's sound as 'hazy afterlife...an inverted thunderstorm...the dark backward...the abyss of time ... [It's] meant to have the feeling of when you're dreaming ... and you briefly wake up, but then fall back asleep into the same dream, diving quickly into your own subconscious' (album press release cited in self-titled magazine, 2015). In this respect, the album is orientated towards Ric Allsopp's suggestion that the arts may be seen as 'forms of public dreaming that sit at or traverse the threshold between consciousness and unconsciousness and form a transitional and liminal state'

(2016: 3). At the junctures of transitions in liminal states between consciousness and unconsciousness, the *Abyss* acquires a dreamlike nocturnal temporality and fluidity flowing into 'the deep blue sea' of the last eponymous track. There are recurring words in the lyrics of the tracks that emerge like fragments of vivid meaning in a lucid dream; words such as 'wake up', 'find me', 'end', 'endless', 'lost' and 'night', underscore a feeling of disorientation in a dark world between sleep and awake, between lucidity and the sleep state that Robert Macnish described as 'a temporary metaphysical death' (1845: 2). Wolfe has sited Carl Jung's autobiography *Memories, Dreams, Reflections* (published posthumously in 1962 (1995)) as an important influence stemming from wider research into sleep, insomnia and dreams. In one interview, she reflects on the significance of Jung's dream experimentation and in particular the idea of 'letting oneself drop':

> [In the book] there's a dream Jung recalls experimenting with [and] the first line of the section is "I let myself drop" [...] That became the goal of my writing sessions: to drop into deep parts of myself I'd been avoiding. I was thinking about the mind as an abyss; as something very internal. (Wolfe, cited in Potts, 2016)

Wolfe's interest in Jung derives from personal experiences of sleep paralysis, a condition that varies in the extent of its symptoms, but in general terms, refers to a frightening albeit temporary inability to move, either when waking up or falling asleep. For the sufferer, it can also mean restriction of breath (as though the chest is being crushed), an inability to open the eyes and hallucinations that often feel as if a presence is in the room with harmful intent. Wolfe has described presences in the room as 'shadow figures' that move from the dream state and into a waking disorientating 'reality', causing intense anxiety.

The album's cover, painted by the Norwegian artist Henrik Aarrestad Uldalen, shows Wolfe falling in black space. The image is inspired by Wolfe's interest in the painting 'The Nightmare' by Henry Fuseli (1781), an oil painting that features a woman dressed in a white nightgown laying on her back with her head dangling off the edge of the bed, eyes closed and arms splayed above her head, as if lifeless or unconscious. An incubus sits on her chest and looks out at the viewer, whilst a horse's head with strange white eyes protrudes from behind red velvet curtains. 'The Nightmare', first exhibited at the Royal Academy in 1782, attracted a great deal of attention due to its (shocking) focus on terrifying psychological experiences undergone in deeply vulnerable sleep states and underscored by the sexual and supernatural connotations highly evocative of the witchcraft trials and accusations launched especially at women said to have been sexually seduced by the Devil. Augustine's *De Civitate Dei* refers to the 'incubi' and their 'wicked assault' of women, whilst Heinrich Kramer and Jakob Sprenger's *Malleus Maleficarum* (or *The Hammer of Witches*) ([1487] 2011) details sexual 'copulation' between humans and incubi, women being more vulnerable to these nightmare attacks, more easily seduced and pregnable in body and mind. According to the American writer Max Eastman and his account of a visit in 1926 to Sigmund Freud's apartment in Vienna, 'The Nightmare' was a painting hung on one of Freud's apartment walls and this has been interpreted as a pictorial symbol of Freud's intention to medicalize the supernatural (Thomas, 1992: 70, cited in Adler, 2011: 60). Shelley Adler demonstrates how even the medical and philosophical texts of the Enlightenment and continuing through to the nineteenth century, never fully shed the supernatural aura of the nightmare and were especially prone to describing the 'weight' on the chest of the sleeper during the nightmare attack (2011: 52). This is a weight that infers a legacy of witch accusations woven in time with misogynistic attacks and the interrogation of a darkened female psyche and sexuality, in mind and body.

Performing/inhabiting the witch

The witch as a performative act in Wolfe's practice (which is not necessarily to infer inauthenticity) is vital to the mourning imperative of her material, because the witch embodies the weight of the dark feminine and, as such, signifies the inhabitation of its burden, as well as the potential power of weight redistribution. Inflections of the witch feature in the music video for 'Carrion Flowers' as superimposed electronic 'scribbles' that erratically dart across Wolfe's body and face and as extensions of her gestures, indicating a surreal supernatural agency. Ropes coil around her body (later reflected in affiliation with the movement of the snake), black liquid, smoke and vapour flow backwards, a reverse movement also replicated in the electronic sounds and some of the reverse gestures of Wolfe's body, which is seen to be going backwards, a motion aligned with witches (Williams, 2015: 104). At times she writhes beneath a cocoon made from tight fabric:

> The scribbles and ropes in the video are about my own madness and self-doubt, and costume designer Jenni Hensler made me a human cocoon from this insane fabric – it represents a feeling of claustrophobia, like you just want to scratch your way out of it. And there is anger in this song; it's got a sense of revenge for anyone who has suffered or died because of injustice. (Wolfe, cited in Whelan, 2015)

Encumbered and suffocated with misogynistic fantasies, the witch is a heavy burden to carry and dubiously appropriated for feminist purposes, precisely because it speaks of a historical legacy of persecution and torture, legitimized by the church and the state in the context of the evolution of patriarchal capitalist societies in Europe and America and migrating through the carnage of the witchcraft trials and the horrors of colonialism (Federici, 2014). To inhabit the witch is to inhabit the trauma of women who bore the weight of strategic torture and subjugation, forced to internalize misogynistic baggage, a hatred directed inwardly at the self and externally at other women. At the centre of this active hatred, as Silvia Federici has discussed at length, lies the capacity for the female body to reproduce and to serve the economy at the advent of capitalism; in other words, her capacity to produce value in the form of labour to be bought or sold. There is always, therefore, within the performative act of the witch the propensity for collective mourning. However, given the differences in legacies of trauma and oppression as they intersect across various social categories of identity (race, gender, class, nationality, sexuality), this notion of 'collective mourning' in relation to the figure of the witch, is necessarily problematized by questions about the weight that has been borne (and by whom), its impression, legacy and measurability.

Performing the witch is an act also laden with the dark side of the essentialized connection between women and nature. As a disorderly figure, particularly in the form of post-menopausal 'barren' hag or husband-less widow, the witch is woven from a dense discourse that is chiefly concerned with female sexuality, fertility and infertility. In terms of the widow accused of witchcraft in particular, the concern with fertility and control explicitly extends to the land that she 'inherits' and its potential to produce. In sixteenth-century poems and paintings, the pastoral representation of Woman and nature produces an abundance of earth Mother symbolism which pertains to female fertility, such as naked women laid pliantly amongst blooming flowers (Merchant, [1980] 1990: 1–41). These passive and fertile creatures are aligned with tamed and cultivated pastoral nature: a blooming open garden. In contrast, a legacy of female representation dramatized and popularized in the Middle Ages and also within the art and literature of the sixteenth and seventeenth centuries, conflates wild nature with woman's 'dark' side in terms that oppose gentle virginal passivity with feminized disorder. Representations of feminine chaos – lust, madness and vengefulness – connote in this context the requirement of 'control' by 'civilizing forces'. 'Witches' became embodiments of an association between Woman, death, dangerous sexuality, evil and the disorder aligned with wild nature, predicated on the 'conjunction of Woman as nature'(Mother Earth) alongside the temptress Eve as Mother of Sin (Bronfen, 1992: 66). A witch was thought to castrate, to kill, seduce and could summon and control the extreme forces of nature by creating storms and floods, destroying crops and bringing plague (Merchant, [1980] 1990: 140). In this sense their powers align with the kinds of perceptions, sensations and emotions elicited by the vast magnitude of natural phenomena, ruptures and extreme weather: lightning, volcanoes, thunder, floods, droughts and intense heatwaves, which is to say, forces that create havoc with farming and the means of sustenance. Such phenomena are related to what Felicia Miller Frank suggests are examples in nature of that which provokes sublime feelings and delight predicated upon fear:

> Examples [of the sublime] from nature include volcanoes, lightning, overhanging rocks, waterfalls, the ocean; all must be a source of fear, but not a direct menace, for the emotion of the sublime to occur. Delight arises from the fearful when it does not menace us directly. Instead, it awakens sublime feelings through the mind's ability to stand above nature and be moved, but not crushed by a sense of enormity. (1995: 178).

Miller Frank notes that, in order to delight in the sublime of nature, fear must be present but must not entirely overwhelm the subject of this experience, thereby implying the potential weight of nature's sublime. The sublime phenomena of nature must provoke fear, but not directly menace in order for delight to emerge and to avoid being 'crushed by a sense of enormity'. This is where the potential of witchcraft emerges via its connection with the noise of sublime wild nature inextricably linked to the dark chaotic abyss artificially implanted within women's wombs, sexuality and psyche. Practicing witchcraft both assumes the burden of the darkening of femininity and the ability to redirect some of the weight that has been borne, bringing it to bear on the delights of patriarchy, whether they be derived from romantic distance established in relation to the wild natural sublime, or the heteronormative hypersexualization of youthful 'witches' and the degradation of older women. Wolfe's sound articulates the burden of violence and grief via the witch and a corresponding sonic archive of blackened noise derived from the patriarchal discourse on women's bodies as, via the witch, connected with black bile and the inorganic blackened barren earth. This is an electric atmosphere that charges a circuit between 'black noise', disorderly chaos, low-frequency rumblings, mumbled curses, the shrill cries of feminine madness and the weeping and sighing of female melancholia. Wolfe dredges up the unproductive sounds and turbulence of a blackened, feminized ecological imaginary and brings those sounds to bear on the idealized audiovisual consciousness of the American Dream, which coheres around patriarchal productivity propped up and tooled up by machines, as well as the romanticized images of wild sublime and pastoral landscapes cut by the open road as the principle of 'freedom'. In doing so, Wolfe introduces a blackened toxic interference that is the onset of a claustrophobic nightmare.

The toxification of the American Dream

Dreams of America are navigated and edited together through a shared, cinematic mediated consciousness of America's development and progression; dreamt of in pastoral images of tamed 'wild' lands and evolving through industrialization, whilst at the same time arguably repressing the atrocities on which such understandings of economic and 'civilized' development have depended – such as the colonization of indigenous people's land, slavery and exploitation. That being said, idealized 'development' involves an ideologically shifted emphasis from the power of the natural sublime to the supreme utility and power of the machine which tames and extracts resources from the land. Leo Marx critiques the accuracy of such chronologically navigated development alongside what he calls the 'rhetoric of the technological sublime' ([1964] 2000: 214), arguing that the transition from wild nature to cultivation, or from the brutal savagery of the land to the pastoral and to industrialization, cannot be read simply or as total ([1964] 2000:145–226). Likewise, Wolfe's album is dedicated to highlighting the temporal fluidity between these historical periods of 'development'. Moreover, the album contains within it an apparent contradiction, which is that the power of technology in music practice is used to critique the 'rhetoric of the technological sublime' as it relates to the industrialization of America, as much as her deployments of technology defy the terms of 'nature' and 'natural' sounds. Technology (particularly guitar pedals) is vital to the album's blackened toxic interference, which confuses and conjoins the sounds of nature and technology in a blackening of sound, not least in that some of the sounds of the album are made of dark ecology field recordings, 'thunder, electricity in the ground, and atmosphere'. Her sound corrupts the reified image of the 'wild natural sublime' *and* the 'technological sublime' in moves that darken both, depressing the delights of either. Whilst there is therefore a summoning of forces that are indicative of the sublime (in its wild nature and machinic forms), these forces are corrupted and poisoned in a grievous dirge that dredges the foundational principles of sublime soundings, proceeding to convert them into more abject, abjected affects and aesthetics.

Shot in black and white, the video for 'Carrion Flowers' features desert and deserted landscapes, rocky valleys and abandoned canyon roads. Moving shots of these landscapes underscore familiar images of long open roads that lead all the way to the horizon and the kind of light that is the sunrise and sunset of American cinematic consciousness. However, the intensity of colour that usually saturates these images in vivid blues, yellows and oranges is removed, insisting on the bleaker ramifications of being inbetween places when one is moving through nowhere spaces. Thus, tracking shots of landscape are juxtaposed with static shots of dry arid lakes and the cracked surfaces of earth, appearing to demonstrate all the effects of intense white heat whilst the sun itself and the sun's light are washed out and grey in a surreal perversion of its celebrated energy, unnervingly shifting the perspective of such intense power to the 'unnatural' and/or the nuclear. A series of fragmented shots are edited together into collages of vast desert emptiness from a range of different perspectives and without a discernible narrative, using techniques that also reveal the superimposition of white light 'scribbles' over the image that are the white noise glitches of the media, the phantoms of necromedia. Through the lens we catch glimpses of the 'nothingness' of dried inorganic barren land and yet, these landscapes are not altogether empty. Something in each shot appears to disturb interpretations of the natural sublime and the kinds of calm, silent, geological darkness testified to by Jean Baudrillard in his thoughts on Death Valley:

A silence internal to the Valley itself, the silence of underwater erosion, below the waterline of time, as it is below the level of the sea. No animal movement. Nothing dreams here, nothing talks in its sleep. Each night, the earth plunges into perfectly calm darkness, into the blackness of its alkaline gestation, into the happy depression of its birth. ([1986] 2010: 75–6)

Baudrillard presents the inorganic valley, or rather a desert that 'is beyond the accursed phase of decomposition, this humid phase of the body, this organic phase of nature' (2010: 75). In contrast, although there are parallels with the idea of an inorganic blackness of desert gestation, Wolfe's desert has not been delivered from organic matter as death and rot occurs with regularity in the thorned stalk, the dried out dead twisted trees, the wild plants, the jaw bone and teeth of a dead animal, the black liquid oil bubbling to the surface or running over tree bark, the vultures circling high overhead; all this death and decay means that we have neither been entirely delivered from the organic nor attained an ecology that has surpassed the abject and abjected of nature. Putrefying rotten flesh is underscored by the title of the track 'Carrion Flowers', also known as 'corpse flowers', because they emit an odour reminiscent of rotting meat to attract scavenging insects (as pollinators) and can be overwhelming for human olfactory senses. The overpowering stench of the carrion flower enacts a strategic selective attraction and repellent based on survival and this 'flower' provides a reference point for understanding the collective 'we' distinguished from 'you' in the first verse of the song: 'We learned how on our own / Never needing help from you'. 'We' signifies an identification with the abject and the strategies of the abjected organic stenches of nature that have been harmed and or killed. Later in the song, the lyrics provide an impression that something is eerily focused in its pursuit of the 'you' addressed and it is a something which is possibly in a state of decay and made abject through 'repeated crimes', but which has nevertheless survived and is returning with agency, slowly and relentlessly towards its target.

Identifying with dead/dying abjected forms that return to the perpetrator of violence as abject and vengeful is a morbid music practice that can be interpreted through Wolfe's critique of specific corporation practices and the detrimental harmful impact on water supplies, environment and communities. In an interview posted online in 2012, Wolfe highlights the problematic treatment of people, animals and resources by corporations, causing immense suffering and economic deprivation: 'There's an immense disrespect and disregard for life or nature. People get pushed off their lands; pushed into poverty and have no way out. Evil breeds evil and the cycle causes people to do things for money or food that are deeply saddening' (Wolfe, cited in Brendt, 2012). This dynamic is expanded on in 'Carrion Flowers':

> The visuals in the video allude to the drought in California and frustration about corporations being allowed to pump out all the water, destroying environments and communities, just to sell it back. While writing 'Abyss', I lived near where the water is piped into Los Angeles, but the lakes were dried up and the mountains were burned from fires. During filming we were exploring cracked lake beds and washed out roads – at one point I was laying in the middle of an abandoned canyon road with no chance of a car coming, and it was very surreal and quiet. (Wolfe, cited in Roberts, 2015)

Amongst the collage of images, scratched media and jump cuts, there are discarded remnants of machinery and industrial activity, such as a corroding car and old farm buildings juxtaposed with other sedentary, but hyperactive energy-conducing connective objects: huge pipelines, electricity pylons and power stations. Wolfe's sound here sets up the relationship between power, technology, movement and politics in a way that might be understood through a legacy of industrial music and aesthetics of the machine; we hear the vibrations and materials of industry, its metal, booms, thuds, mechanized and electric sound, in effect, aural manifestations of immense machinic power juxtaposed with redundant retrograde machines. Grave earthbound tempos and heavy textures and timbre make up layers of sound that act anaphonically on the ears, so that listeners might imagine a relationship between the industrial drum beats of the tracks and the workings of a machine that is *doing* something to an object, a body, the earth. This emphasis on a heavy impactful relationship between the organic and machinic is particularly pronounced in the intense contrasts of 'Iron Moon', wherein a critical disposition to the nightmarish developments of capitalism and state controls transmutes into a heavy mourning dirge.

Mourning song for bodies made machinic

'Iron Moon' begins with dense sludge metal that suddenly transitions into an utterly different, quieter sound and intimate space with very reserved, softly sung vocals accompanied by Wolfe's delicately strummed guitar. Before the sharp shift in atmosphere, the introduction to Wolfe's 'Iron Moon' invokes the power and metallic elements of the machine by virtue of a heavy, doom-laden riff comprised of minor chords: Dm, Em, Am (its 'doom motif'), played through distorted guitar effects repeated in what is established as a slow, yet relentless dirge-like tempo. Drum cymbals fill the top end frequency space with crashing elemental metal, setting up a demanding consistency of pace and providing the momentum of the drawn-out crescendo of doom. Bass, bass guitar and bass drum sounds are accentuated as dominant tones in the mix, accompanied by the presence of amplification buzz that becomes an enhanced electronic sonic residue. From the low, slow-moving propulsion in time, the shift to Wolfe's singing effects a transition in atmosphere to close-miked, intimate vocal delivery that exaggerates the audibility of breath and tone and a solo electric guitar that sounds as if it comes from a bedroom amp. In the verse, the guitar chords shift from the doom motif to C/E, Em/B, Bm/D, A/Csharp (guitar tuned down to D), accompanying the vocal melodic phrase before this chord pattern is repeated in the chorus. Together, the quiet, gentle, breathy vocal delivery of the verse and the isolated electric guitar (produced to create a sense of small space) dramatically change the perception of spatial dynamics and diminish the effect and all-consuming power of the objects that produced the opening heavy sound. Lyrically, the words sung are saturated in loss (and being lost) and they evoke a terrible emptiness that is elaborated on by the gothic romance of a heart in contact with death: 'my heart is a tomb / my heart is an empty room'. The lyrics of the verses refer to pale sickness in identification with bodies that bear no fruit, no life. Later, the sickly death-bearing 'we' shifts into shadow beings internal and external to a subject: 'I go to him in paths of dreams / in bed awake with shadow beings / they crawl inside and wait with me / the creatures here become machines'. Drawing together the shadows that haunt a deathly subject, the nightmarish phantasmagoria created by the song explicitly antagonizes a sonic crisis by creating an image of creatures (sickly and shadowy) becoming machines.

The lyrics of 'Iron Moon' are inspired by the poetry of Xu Lizhi, a twenty-four-year-old migrant employee who killed himself by jumping from the window of a residential dormitory owned by his employers, Foxconn. His dorm was owned by the owners of the electronics factory where he worked, based in the southern Chinese city of Shenzhen. Lizhi's poems (all of which are translated via Nao's blog 2014) speak of the demands on the minds and bodies of workers, of the hardships of working-class existence, the effects of exposure to dangerous chemicals on skin and of the impossibility of loving human relationships in circumstances where the body is so suppressed it cannot express love or even tears under the force of an industrialized, relentless pace. In the original poem 'I Swallowed a Moon Made of Iron' (2013), all the industrial materials and machinic factory floor detritus are forcibly swallowed by the worker who is, in this case, typically representative of a populace subordinated to the machine, one of those who die young choking on 'nails' and 'industrial sewage' to the point that it spills out of their mouth onto the land of their ancestors and into the text of the poem. The act of swallowing and the choking on iron that ensues is as important as the 'Iron Moon' itself (symbolizing mechanization and exploitation), a moon directly compared in the poem with the head of a nail. In swallowing and choking, the breath and voice are inhibited in moves that prevent speech or crying out and, moreover, threaten life: the body is not only subjected to the machine, but infiltrated by it and its toxic materiality in a terrifying image of a helpless body overwhelmed and becoming-machinic. The emphasis on vocal inhibition and voicelessness is present in other Xu Lizhi poems that write, for instance, of silent distress signals sent out in the darkness of the night, only to return as echoes of desperation ('My Life's Journey Is Still Far from Complete'). Iron is a recurring chemical element in his poems: in assembly lines people stand like iron; a screw falls to the ground 'lightly clinking', failing to attract attention and, in 'The Last Graveyard' (2011), stomachs are 'forged of iron, Full of thick acid, sulphuric and nitric'. The properties of iron are repeatedly described in relation to an infiltration of the human body, which, accordingly, deteriorates under the toxic effects of this industrialized chemical metal. Combining 'iron' with 'moon' forges an unnerving image capturing the ominous effects of the machine by drawing on a legacy of powerful romantic poetic imagery; the moon, suggestive of romance and night as 'free time', is here overwhelmed and corroded by the orange glow of iron rust and polluted bodies. Images of machinic bodies, technological sublimes and dreams of industrial progress are thoroughly evacuated of any romance, divulged of utopian, consumerist, gleaming advertisements and demonstrated as objects of torture and oppression driven by globalization and capitalism. Wolfe's 'Iron Moon' is an attempt to respond to a silenced voice by engaging with the visceral impression of desperation and frustration within Lizhi's text and his story and thereby evacuating the rhetoric of the technological sublime and shifting perspective on heavy metal power. Melancholic attachments to shadow bodies are here the mourning spectral voices of metalized bodies under erasure.

Wolfe's heavy mourning dirge mourns an individual in the context of these current dark times, where the threat of ecocide looms ever greater behind the state-sponsored capitalist consumer facades that protect the imaginary from compassion, empathy and fear of the destruction of the planet. In such times, witchcraft is positioned by Wolfe as assuming the burden and (perverse) powers of the dark feminine and her losses in order to corrupt the terms of the sublime and suffocate the space inserted between the subject and a blackened ecological imaginary on the verge of the abyss. Delight and distance evacuated, witchcraft in sound summons the onset of an overwhelming mourning that immerses all in the grief of absolute irretrievable loss, loss that has already occurred as well as that which is yet to occur, in effect pulverizing subjectivity. Witchcraft moves to corrode all that shields the subject's imaginary from death and present it with the sheer colossal scale of ecocide's enormity, whilst it works to toxify the 'natural' of nature with poison and black bile leaked from within the essentialized heart of nature and woman, inducing inorganic barrenness and bringing into being the already dead – so that there is no recognizable 'natural' life to return to. Wolfe's practice demonstrates that sound is an integral part of that craft, specifically in terms of realizing the heavy burden of Pratt's conception of 'black noise' and the dark feminine; its weight and impact culminating in a heavy mourning dirge. This strategic crafted dirge is the practice of bearing within sound the paradoxes of contemporary grief as it reaches out to find its object and finds both nothing and everything. There is here then a fundamental paradox, namely that the weight of the abyss in sound is testimony to an incredibly dense mass, as well as an intangible melancholic shadow-like weightlessness. How can sound bear the paradox of burden and mourning in these dark times wherein shadows weigh heavy?

Becoming shadow-thing: The echoes of witches and widows

Even though it doesn't affix itself sonically and musically to a specific genre identity, in stylistic terms, Wolfe's *Abyss* can be generally understood as a 'heavy' album, with each song offering and effecting transitions between styles such as heavy metal, rock, doom, industrial, post-punk goth, American gothic folk, and indie electro pop. Ultimately, though, it is perhaps better to think of *Abyss* in layers of textures and the dynamic interplay of contrasts between the minimal and maximal, the intensely intimate quiet of breathy vocals and acoustic instruments contrasted with pounding beats and abrasive, heavy guitar-driven fuzz and distortion, commingling soft and brutal affects. Further, the sound field that encompasses and encourages this interplay is often a huge reverberant space in which programmed sounds, digital reverbs and electronic effects, generated by pedals and reamping, push the limits of the space with dense material resonance, gargantuan doom beats and highly charged electronic sonic harpies that spiral upwards and reverse in backwards-descending movements at varying disorientating paces. Equipment such as the Minimoog Model D used for bass synth, ('Earthquaker') guitar pedals and reamping are fundamental to this 'heavy' and 'raw' sound, producing distortion, overdrive, delay and reverb to effect tonality and texture. Often the sound works to suspend the notion of progress via slow dragging tempos and bass-resonant beats, so that the body is arrested by a feeling of oppressive doom. This archetypally 'heavy' sound is contrasted with the spectre-like behaviour of electronic sounds which transpose and invert, attack and decay, finding perhaps more resonance with electroacoustic sensibilities and spectromorphologies (Smalley, 1997). Tracks like 'Dragged Out', with complex noise textures and swooshing decays, establish a place of inchoate phantom apparitions, congruent with the lyrical narrative of a subject who is mentally disturbed, 'dragged out in the weather / dragged out in the madness /dragged out in your loneliness', and who is brought to the edge of a precipice on the brink of 'losing myself' out of an inability to sustain resilience against the forces that drag the subject away from libidinal energy (of rock music): 'I'm so tired, I'm so tired'.

In contradistinction to full-bodied power vocals, Wolfe's breathy voice in particular frequently suggests degrees of weight on the subject which, under pressure, proceeds to fragment and destabilize the subject's coherence amidst heavy and spectral sonic disturbance. 'Maw', for example, begins with delicate whispered vocals, establishes reverberant melodic contours that facilitate the emphasis of vowel-sounds and proceeds to engender (via lyrics and the space created by production) melancholic searching for another ('where are you?') in a sustained ethereal vocal style that elevates away from the material body. In this track, the voice suggests it has lost someone and is also itself lost in a space replete with sonic shadows detached from physical corporeality. Wolfe's vocals are often highly echoic and reverberant, particularly in explicit mourning songs as heard in her cover of Roky Erickson's 'Night of the Vampire', a dedication to

Erickson and his influence on her following his death in May 2019. Her thin, wraithlike and echoic vocal persona, attached to mourning and melancholic affects, is elaborated on through black gothic performance attire and, earlier in her career at least, the adoption of a black Victorian mourning veil which served as a coping mechanism for stage fright. In the video for 'Mer' (*Apokalypsis*, 2011) broad references are made to earlier periods, the 1800s and the burgeoning of the industrial age in America by virtue of period features and underscored by the crude painted cardboard waves that mechanically move in front of her, recalling props from an old proscenium arch theatre and cinematography that hints at portraiture style and colour saturation of daguerreotypes. Shadows flicker on the wall behind candelabras made from twisted branches like small supernatural trees growing from the wall and bearing candles. In this room of supernatural resonance, Wolfe's shadow is unusually pronounced and looms over Wolfe herself, her face covered by a black silk-lace mantilla in an image that situates and associates mourning widows, eroticized religious modesty (associated with Catholicism), mysticism and witchcraft in the becoming shadow of her performance. These are associations that are deliberately equivocal and morph throughout the shrouded mysticism of Wolfe's work, so that her performative figure ambiguously fluctuates between the supernatural energies of nature, mourner/widow and witch, thus creating an ambiguous static in the overwrought shadows. The black mourning veil of the widow points to a broader concern with, in Elisabeth Bronfen's terms, the aesthetic relationship between death and femininity (1992). This is highlighted as a performative act inscribed on the feminine body by Wolfe via a tattoo that features a line from Sylvia Plath's poem 'Widow', which reads 'Death is the dress she wears' (Plath, [1961] 1981).

To her audience, the widow, as a dark feminine figure dressed in black, not only casts the shadow of death in the world of the living, but is the shadow-thing itself, a liminal figure between life and death. Wolfe's reverberant voice, performative gestures and electronic wraith sounds establish this ghostly liminality and move to bring the listener into a closer proximity with death and mourning. The congruence between widow, shadow and echo is picked up in Plath's poem and is suggestive of a deathly absence and negation which rotates around the void of the vowel sound 'O', itself contained within the 'dead syllable':

168   DARK SOUND

Widow. The dead syllable, with its shadow
Of an echo, [...]
Death is the dress she wears, her hat and collar.
[....]
Widow, the compassionate trees bend in,
The trees of loneliness, the trees of mourning.
They stand like shadows about the green landscape —-
Or even like black holes cut out of it.
A widow resembles them, a shadow-thing.

(Plath, [1961] 1981: 164)

An archetypal mourning widow of the kind evoked in Sylvia Plath's poem 'Widow' cuts the image of a feminine figure in close proximity to death via a mourning loss that is illustrated through evocative imagery of the blackened abyss of evacuated landscapes and witch-like form, alienated from God. She is also indicative of what Jacques Derrida referred to as the 'rhetoric of mourning' in terms of the participation in the rites and codes of death genres. Derrida wrote many eulogies following the death of friends and colleagues and in many of them he (necessarily) explicitly admits the 'aporia of mourning' and the limits of language as it encounters the unthinkable, unspeakable death of a friend – when there are no words to say or songs to sing (Derrida, 2003). Despite the limit, he is called by a duty to speak of the dead, to both acknowledge their irredeemable absence and to say something about the unique singularity of the dead other in ways that endeavour to be faithful to the friend, to maintain fidelity to who they were in life (Brault and Naas, 2003: 1–30). This, for Derrida, means a 'politics of mourning' that avoids the temptation of egotistical self-pity and narcissistic 'personal testimony', which 'tends towards re-appropriation and always risks giving in to an indecent way of saying "we", or worse, "me"' (2003: 225). Being haunted is, in a sense, part of the responsibility to the other, in that whilst acknowledging their infinite alterity, the language adopted in mourning is inhabited by the interiorization of them 'in me': 'Ghosts: the concept of the other in the same, [...] the completely other, dead, living in me' (Derrida, 2003: 41–2).

Sylvia Plath's 'Widow' is haunted in such a way by the dead other: her dead spouse or the dead other 'living in me'. However, this poem goes beyond an internalized death and calls attention to the gendered politics of the 'politics of mourning', the ideologies and values of a ritual, rite and genre so often assumed as that, which, in death, surpasses gender, and induces a democracy of mourning. 'Widow' reminds the reader that the widow's relationship to the aporia of mourning and its politics cannot be considered without the gendered relationship to language, to absence, to loss, to mourning and melancholia in the wider context of patriarchy. Her dedicated eulogy to a friend, to a husband, has no necessary platform, and is always already based on a culturally-inscribed lack, always already aligned with weeping, sighs and silences as opposed to the agency of the voice that speaks the self (the 'I') in the symbolic realm of language such that, what Derrida warns against, the reappropriation and narcissism of a personal testimony, isn't necessarily available to her. Isn't this what the tone of the poem suggests that there is a necessity of intimacy brought forth in the text that allows us to hear what would otherwise elude ears, or that which would be received as only a shadow of an echo of a former (married and therefore 'whole') self? Plath's text facilitates a close encounter with the widow, providing intimate insights into her haunting interiorization of the dead other and her mourning. The widow poem reminds the reader that the feminine is always removed from the ideological substance of life, its agency, its 'I' form. 'Dressed in death', in a state of mourning, the widow becomes what Plath calls a 'shadow-thing', describing, thereby, a gloomy, recondite figure caught in the residues of life, somewhere between body and spectre, name and anonymity, vows and nullity. She is looked upon as a woman who is visually, vocally and gesturally linked to absence, to the loss of life and stasis of the corpse she mourns and in whose shadow she must remain. The widow's recovery is always already based on a surreptitious cultural ruse, in that she has not only interiorized the ghost of the other but has been spectralized herself, bound to interiorize the absence of her 'self', her inferior-ness and the implicit desire for her erasure under the violence and pressure of misogyny. Plath's shadow-thing draws on archetypal correspondences between the witch and the widow, both bound to bent, withered mourning trees and the 'black holes' cut from green landscapes: to absence and emptiness. Through the becoming shadow-thing of widow and witch, the notion of articulating and voicing sorrow is raised as a painful difficulty, if not an impossibility, since the vocal palette of both are so aligned with hysterical disorder and inarticulate weeping. This in turn alludes to the gendered politics of mourning and a feminized aporia that is the dark spectral absence of the constructed feminine that foregrounds a gendered relationship to loss and moreover an inability to express, to vocalize and articulate loss. Inarticulate 'noise' and dissonance conjoin the witch with the unregulated and unproductive effects of melancholia, the most extreme cases of which, so Robert Burton argues in his *Anatomy of Melancholy* (first published in 1621 (Burton, [1621] 2001)), are to be found in 'maids, nuns, and widows', i.e., women without a husband (phallus-less and without male presence). Such an understanding of inarticulate voices (the voice that cannot be comprehended) is essentially aligned with female bodies and sexuality, link the legacies of witchfinder discourse with psychoanalysis and its attempts to construe and investigate the dark unknown empty space imagined within the female body.

Although psychoanalysis posits a primary loss for both boys and girls in the lost connection with the Mother, the relationship to that loss and to the discovery of castration is significantly different. Luce Irigaray argues that the little girl, on entering the Oedipal phase, discovers that both herself and her mother have been deemed lacking, castrated and are ultimately culturally and socially devalued, internally and externally. As such, the 'fall in self-esteem' suffered by the little girl on the discovery of her 'castration' (and that of her mother) is immense and her understanding of her devaluation (according to Freud) accords with the moments she 'acknowledges the fact of her castration and with it, too, the superiority of the male and her own inferiority' (Freud, cited in Irigaray, [1974] 1985: 67). Irigaray links Freud's theories on the little girl's libidinal economy and her 'castration' with Freud's work on melancholia, suggesting that the little girl's castration corresponds with an inability to complete the work of mourning; she has no consciousness of what she has 'lost': 'it is really a question for her of a "loss" that radically escapes any representation. Whence the impossibility of mourning it' (Irigaray, [1974] 1985: 68). In this respect, Irigaray seems to suggest that there is no recourse for the little girl other than melancholy, since her primary attachment and identification is with her (lacking) mother who has also 'lost' *something*. Importantly, however, even melancholy isn't wholly available to her insofar as, for Irigaray, the little girl has barely enough reserves of narcissism to become melancholic and has no ability to express (her) loss in the signifying economy, to which she is prevented access (Schiesari, 1992: 64–8).

Drawing on Irigaray, Juliana Schiesari considers the inaccessibility of the signifying economy for women alongside the historical and cultural devaluation of women's mourning. With a daughter's identification with the (lacking/lost) mother in mind, she notes the consistency with which women find themselves at a loss to express loss as she has introjected the devaluation of her mother, women and herself (Schiesari, 1992: 76). To challenge this sense of enduring and enforced struggle to express, Schiesari formulates an argument which contends that women's public mourning rites have been devalued (1992: 162–3) whilst the canon of melancholic art has placed great value on male sorrow in a cultural system that devalues and appropriates women's losses (1992: 166). In critical response to the historical privileging of male-authored melancholia and the devalued status of women's mourning rites, Schiesari proposes a radical refiguring of female mourning that is collective and aims to establish a feminine symbolic in opposition to patriarchal and structural devaluation of women's sorrow/grief:

> The loss that is mourned is, thus, not merely the mother's absence, nor simply the daughter's devalued sense of self, but also and more generally the structured denial of privilege for *all* women within patriarchal societies. As such, the individual and apparently contingent case of the depressed woman finds it correlative in the traditional and *communal* practice of women's mourning. But this is, then, also to pinpoint a locus of women's resistance. (1992: 77)

By way of dealing with the devaluation of the weight of depression suffered by women in patriarchal societies, Schiesari thus suggests a communal practice of mourning. An example of this practice might be found in the adoption of the red robes and white bonnets of the handmaidens described in Margaret Atwood's dystopian novel *The Handmaid's Tale* by women's rights activist groups. In the novel, the coded dress of the 'handmaids' signifies their subjugation and servitude to a commander with whom they must conceive and for whom they must bear a child (for the Master and his infertile wife) before being reassigned. Drawing from the signification of these costumes, certain women's rights activist groups protest together in subdued silence, heads bowed as if in mourning for the contextual synergy between the fictional oppression within the narrative and the current real life attack on women's reproductive rights and Planned Parenthood in America: this is mourning as an act of resistance. Collective resistant mourning might also be discerned in the political activism action of 'die-ins', in which protesters lie on the floor and pretend to be dead, in key strategically chosen locations, or for the mourning ceremonies held for melted glaciers. In each case, rebellious mourning protests rely on the contextual resonance of their action (place and audience) in correspondence with the collective performance which adheres to funeral-like silence because it produces subversive meaning within the context and, moreover, implies the internalization of the already dead state of the living. Although silent, this mourning nevertheless sings about these dark times by identifying with the already dead.[2]

Although a solo artist, Wolfe's identification with the widow and witch forms a symbolic communal practice of women's mourning that is the becoming shadow-thing of her albums *Abyss* and *Hiss Spun*. Echoes and reverberation are here sonic shadows expressive of a legacy of the darkened feminine, female melancholia and mourning. Instead of moving away from the melancholic loss at the centre of the dark feminine, Wolfe 'let's herself' drop into its abyss whilst simultaneously sonically articulating the heavy amorphous abyss itself, the dense mass of its presence in life – the already dead and gone. Voice, image, performance, gesture, all combine to produce an intensely gothic dark feminine that, in terms of Wolfe's vocals particularly, can be read in correspondence with what Rebecca Munford has called, in her reading of gothic literature, 'spectral femininity'. As Munford writes: 'Owing to its cultural associations with the territories of irrationality, otherness and corporeal excess, femininity has been particularly and peculiarly susceptible to "'spectralisation". [...] the gothic brings into view the troubling movements of wraithlike women' (Munford, 2016: 120). These 'troubling movements' are indicative of the gothic preoccupation with liminal thresholds between life and death and specify the feminized liminality which is cultivated in Wolfe's gothicism via a spectralized voice. Inhabited by a plurality of vocal ghosts, her echoic voice mourns an indistinct loss and is itself spectral. She who mourns is also she who is mourned, always already shadow-thing. In this respect, the widow of Plath's poem and Wolfe's sound epitomizes the cultural spectralization of femininity, as neither being nor non-being, caught in liminality and as such endowed with the ability to produce haunting affects and an uncanny gothic potential to transgress the thresholds between life and death. To inhabit a 'being' with ghosts is to inhabit an unresolved continuous mourning that bears the material and psychological traces of gendered mourning and melancholia, the traces of fragile connections/disconnections and irredeemable lack and negation. The melancholic 'echo' of Plath's 'shadow-thing' appeals to the losses of women in a culture that has designated their being as lacking, as though culturally encouraged to become a sonic shadow of a subject caught in the dissolution of a material body and bound to the non-semantic register of the cursed nymph, Echo. By reactivating the historical magnitude of the cultural association between women, negation, blackened ecologies and death, the widow recharges an occulted feminized abyss that is the phantom negation that has always already haunted her being, a death she carries in life. The shadow realm of the dark feminine is invoked by Wolfe in voice as echo and reverb, echo here being the sonic shadow of a legacy of the dark feminine in resonance with mourning and women's losses. As Mark M. Smith suggests, echoes invoke a sense of an original sound as well as a historical past. Smith writes 'An echo is nothing if not historical. To varying degrees, it is a faded facsimile of an original sound, a reflection of time passed' (Smith, 2015: 55). Echo as a faded reflection of time passed, in Wolfe's work, is an invocation of the dark feminine as shadow-thing, echoes that bear the history of women's negation and darkening and therefore bear a paradoxical weight that is the burden of the dark feminine, both weighty and weightless: the 'heavy' sound of becoming shadow-thing. Wolfe brings the witch-widow-spectre shadow-thing to the edge of a blackened ecological imaginary where the 'originary sound' is lost amongst an uncanny cacophony of spectral shadow-things.

Reappropriating the abyss: Femmeheavy sound

In her analysis of the musical representation of witches, melancholics and the mad in music for the seventeenth-century English stage, the penultimate chapter of Amanda Winkler's book *O Let Us Howle Some Heavy Note: Music for Witches, the Melancholic, and the*

Mad on the Seventeenth-Century English Stage (2006) focuses on a scene from John Webster's *The Duchess of Malfi* (1614), a play in which a duchess is imprisoned as punishment by her brothers for an 'inappropriate' marriage, having been widowed from her first marriage. One of the brothers sends 'madmen' to torture her and, on entering her prison, one of them sings 'O Let Us Howle Some Heavy Note': the Duchess is to be tortured by the affective discord of aural madness, sending her further into despair, as if the sound itself were the instrument of her torture, combined, of course, with the relentless physical threat of an absolute male power to incarcerate and inflict violence and pain. Winkler's analysis migrates through four versions of the score and she notes a progression from the 'literal' bestial mimetic howl of the first version, to the 'ornamentation on insignificant words', to a further abstraction moving away from the visceral (2006: 126–8). In each case, the 'mental disorder' of the howling and heavy masculinized sound is meant to infect the psyche and to do violence to the duchess, but Winkler notes an ineffectiveness:

> In fact, she embraces the disorderly sounds: 'Nothing but noise and folly/Can keep me in my right wits, whereas reason/And silence make me stark mad' [IV.ii.5–7]. In a world run mad, the Duchess tells us, discord is the only appropriate music – the only music that can adequately give voice to her torment. (2006: 125)

In this respect and according to Winkler's interpretation, the Duchess's embrace of the madman's noise and his howling heavy notes does not necessarily express her resilience in any simple way. She has not defied her melancholy, nor is there a way out of her situation. In fact, she ends up being strangled to death, along with her two children. However, in acknowledging this heavy mad noise as a noise that allows her to keep her wits about her, a noise in opposition to 'reason' and enforced silence, she reappropriates the psychic domain of the dark feminine and reforms a purposeful alliance with singing and howling heavy notes, making her torturers the ventriloquists of her torment, thereby averting all out madness. The stroke of morbid brilliance witnessed here thus resides in her ability to combine rationality and irrationality and to draw on sound to occupy a liminal space between melancholy and mourning, life and death, proposing within that liminality an acute articulation of

CHELSEA WOLFE'S HEAVY DIRGE IN DARK TIMES 175

her suffering. Despite the patriarchal power and territorialization of mad articulation, the Duchess demonstrates a reappropriation of heavy howling noise that enables a voicing otherwise suppressed by patriarchal and linguistic structures.

Howling (wolves and the lunacy of werewolves) and heavy sounds are typically territorialized and appropriated by masculinized music, heavy/death/black metal being obvious references, but also many genres that identify through 'bass heavy' sound, distortion, noise and the styles affixed to 'dark sound' when it speaks to and of, alienated male bodies struggling to reterritorialize internal and external space via the power tools of music technology. Given her engagement with genres so deeply territorialized by white heterosexual male identity, Wolfe's heaviness arguably assumes some of the howls and intensities of powerful men of war, men of metal, lords, kings, emperors or wolves, as they apparently drive towards death only to be reborn yet more complexly powerful, authentically melancholy and 'extreme'. In doing so and in drawing on vivid evocations of blackened ecology, Wolfe raises the spectre of a complicity with the undertones of white male power and the nostalgias of eco-fascism (in these music discourses and cultures), both of which are related and might be considered through the contradictions between returning to/or preserving an idealized past and the entitlement to extract capital from the earth and abyssal othered bodies (black holes). As Joseph Dodds discusses, Melanie Klein's theories of object relations elucidate on fantasies and desires that coalesce around this contradiction in the figure of 'Mother Earth' and phantasies of:

> an infinitely giving earth breast we feel entitled to suck on with ever increasing intensity without limit. [...] The infant generally does not always take kindly to weaning, or to mother's explanations, but often responds instead with rage, envy, hatred and destructiveness. (2011: 58)

Wolfe's heaviness works strategically from within this complicity with violence in a way comparable to the Duchess's appropriation of the heavy howl. The albums *Abyss* (2015) and *Hiss Spun* (2017) work to rearticulate 'heavy' sound as a voicing of torment that, in these dark times, reveals the inseparability of the blackened ecological imaginary and the dark feminine, the abyss of ecocide and the abyss in one's darkened self. She uses the figure of the witch and the widow as visually and sonically indicative of the deep time strata of violence against women and the earth and as a grievous contemplation in practice on the darkened and feminized abyss within. This is not to cement an essential association, but to release the association from its repression by rearticulating heavy sound. To inhabit the witch and the widow is to carry a cultural legacy of violence and mourning that is a feminized burden, but it is also to in some way recognize a complicity with misogyny, racism and the intensity of demands from one's 'holding environment' to provide, as directed inwardly and outwardly in violence and demands without limits. Nevertheless, her voice amidst heavy sound draws from a tormented abyssal melancholy in a huge reverberant reappropriation of the dark space of the abyss and, in doing so, she shifts the weight of patriarchy and establishes a link with other darkened bodies. What happens in this crafty shifting of heavyweight sound is not the pathos release from mourning, but rather a voicing of mourning and torment that links the shadow of the self with the shadow of others. This stroke of radical morbid brilliance introduces the possibility of an unusual narcissism that accrues in the blackened shadows. Unusual in that it loves and grieves for an object that exceeds the self and introduces, into heavy sound, compassion for the dark spaces within and without.

6

Abject virtuosa, darkened virtuosity

Diamanda Galás and swarms of power

To figure the generative source of effects as a swarm is to see human intentions as always in competition and confederation with many other strivings, for an intention is like a pebble thrown into a pond … it vibrates and merges with other currents, to affect and be affected.

(Jane Bennett, 2010: 32)

Once and for all, enough of this closed, egoistic and personal art.

(Antonin Artaud, [1938] 1974: 764)

Virtuosity means great technical skill. It is a term frequently applied in the fine arts, most typically in reference to music. Virtuosos are the composers, performers and musicians who possess and apply virtuosic skill and ability, and who 'master' their art. In other words, virtuosos craft and articulate something that is felt, heard and seen to be qualitatively distinguished from the norm, pushing the limits of human ability and the artform itself through an exceptional efficacy and 'technical' skill. Etymologically, virtuosity has developed through the meaning of 'virtue' and tracing this evolution discloses some of the historical ideological substance of virtuosity. The term has developed from the Latin 'vir', meaning 'man', to 'virtutem': 'moral strength, high character, goodness; manliness; valour, bravery, courage (in war); excellence, worth'. A 'virtuoso' acquires skill and exceptional worth, virtuousness, 'manly qualities' and 'mastery of the mechanical parts of the art'. Drawing links between virtues, morality, reason and God, Marc Pincherle, in his book *The World of the Virtuoso* (1964), explores the etymology of 'virtuoso' as defined in Sebastian de Brossard's *Dictionnaire de Musique* (1703): '*Virtu* means, in Italian, not only the propensity of the soul which renders us agreeable to God and makes us act according to the rules of right reason; but also that superiority of talent, skill, or ability which makes us excel.' Further, 'virtuoso' is the name most commonly attributed to those musicians who 'apply themselves to the theory or to the composition of music' (Pincherle, 1964: 16). Connections between qualities agreeable to God and superiority of talent culminate here in the application of music theory and the ability to write/apply/articulate, to make musical expression intelligible via a skilled understanding of technical qualities. To this extent, the virtuoso can be understood through a strongly established sense of individual agency capable of wielding complex techniques and making intelligible an intention through inordinate skill and knowledge; the virtuoso is then far less disposed to notions such as the 'swarm of effects' conceptualized in the epigraph above.

The evolution of the discourse of virtuosity is one that travels along a spectrum of ideological light (when light means soul, goodness, morality) only to reach a point when its virtues and ideals become so utterly transparent as to become invisible, radically dispersed and untraceable effluence. That is to say, the power and gendered legacy of virtuosity discourse is occulted by an objective neutrality that naturalizes its assumptions so that the construction of value disappears, its history obliterated, its contemporary currency obscured and infinitesimally fragmented. Virtuosity is embroiled in the patriarchal strategies that occult the power of language whilst retaining an insidious grip on the reins of this technology (and language is a technology), one that can curse as much as it can elevate and charm its subject and, as such, virtuosity is one of many execrations that have either calculated or inadvertently excommunicated on the basis of identities.[1] Should excommunicated identities (those without 'manly qualities') display and seem to possess virtuosic skill, certain strategies of containment and curtailment would flood the system, erratically eradicating forces that work to insinuate a lack of training, diva vanity, demonic possession (or selling one's soul at the crossroads) and which connote the inability of an excommunicated individual to *fully* learn, acquire, harness, control and master the craft with complete agency. This is the cumulative doubt woven between intersecting misogyny, sexism, racism, ageism, homophobia and ableism that holds fast to a faith in the heteronormative bourgeois white able maleness at the core of true masterpieces and normative modes of virtuosity. Virtuosity is a word and an ideology now so thoroughly entrenched in music discourse that it does not need to be explicitly uttered in order for it to exert power: an occulted word legitimately available to the maestros of the brotherhood, their entitlement.

This chapter discusses the music practice of composer-singer-pianist Diamanda Galás, whose work draws from the legacies of virtuosity whilst at the same time destabilizing its stability by re-wiring connections with all that virtuoso ideology has outcasted and finds revolting, with its repressed abject. Galás brings different vocal modes and techniques together, displacing the dominant ideological links between virtuosity and its ties to God, Man and Reason, as well as its implicit ties to reverent musical ineffability, defying containment and introducing into that circuit what has always been opposed in the chain of virtuoso hierarchy: demonic, woman, racialized Other, irrational. In 1979, Galás made her professional vocal debut in Vinko Globokar's opera *Un Jour Comme Un Autre* (Festival d'Avignon, 1979), a vocally demanding role based on the arrest and torture of a Turkish woman (documented by Amnesty International). Also, in the early 1980s, she performed the premiere of Iannis Xenakis's 'N'shima'. This, alongside her debut album *Litanies of Satan* in 1982 featuring Galás's terrifying electronic vocal rendition of the poem 'Litanies of Satan' by Charles Baudelaire, itself renowned for a 'blasphemous' treatment of liturgy from his *Les Fleurs du Mal* (The Flowers of Evil, 1857), drew an impression that combined virtuosic 'devilish' technical difficulty with the explicitly satanic.[2] Her music and performance, abominable amalgamations of maelstroms of shrill caterwauls, clamorous squalls, operatic trills, tongue lashing ululations, raging beating piano keys and electronic noise, form amongst assemblages of abject and abjection; encouraging the swarming of power, summoning violence, threats, sickening affects, revolting fluids, whilst seeking out opportunities to exploit the porosity of agency at the threshold of the inside and outside of bodies. Galás's voice and repertoire begin with 'mandatory virtuosity', drawing from different vocal styles and cultures that invariably situate women at the centre of the capacity to express intense sorrow, to mourn and cross the boundaries between life and death as primary communicators with the dead. Her extreme sound is focused through a targeted intention to raise from historical obscurity specific horrendous events and bodies that have been tortured and killed, that have suffered from the violence and erasures of oppressive ideological cultures and histories that would prefer to obliterate them and their memory. In sonic and textual vortices, Galás creates the summons and repulsion of the 'abject', the repugnant bodily fluids, excommunicated and corpses 'I thrust aside in order to live [...] at the border of my condition as a living being' (Kristeva, 1982: 3). This requires a strength of voice, technique and expressive skill, as much as it does an unparalleled ability to evoke and embody the abject; the abject in Galás's practice is aligned with truth, the truth of suffering and unspeakable horror. What follows is an attempt to track Galás's darkening of virtuosity through the ways in which she engages with power and swarms of effects via the dark feminine and the abject.

The behaviour of power

Making a virtue of manly qualities (and at the same time contributing to the construction of the meaning of 'masculinity'), virtuosity is emboldened by the accrual of value across a spectrum of words that especially includes application to technical detail as it shows up in 'mastery', a term which etymologically both implicitly and explicitly adopts man as the referent of 'master', who is an authority, in control, eminently skilled, knowledgeable, great and powerful ('master race' being the most ominous and violent of these assumptions). Alongside and related to the definition of mastery, the meaning of 'technique' evolves through art, skill, craft and 'formal' practical details of artistic expression. All this meaning, accrued in the language and legacies of virtuosity across centuries, establishes power and privilege based on a heavily gendered and ideological foundation. To this extent, there is an obvious relationship between virtuosity and the exclusion of women from technical mastery, artistic genius and canons of musical greatness, which have been explored in detail by many, including Christine Battersby (1989), Susan McClary ([1991] 2002) and Marcia J. Citron ([1993] 2000). It is less obvious perhaps how virtuosity and its ideologies continue to perpetuate, however subtly, in contemporary music discourse, despite what is arguably a reluctance to specifically deploy and attribute the word 'virtuoso/virtuosity' in music (sub)cultures that may wish to distance themselves from the formality, virtues and classicism of the terms and yet surreptitiously maintain the privilege and (occult) power accorded to the chain of associations that circumvents the adoration of a (virtuosic) individual: skill, mastery, wizardry, technique, manliness, contextually driven virtues, bravery and excellence. Here, whilst the individual male musician (writer, painter, poet, philosopher, cook, gardener) may still be reified, the source or origin of stealth maintenance that rearticulates and strengthens the discourse of male musicianship, excellence and superiority, is impossible to pinpoint given it is distributed across such a vast network of human and non-human agents, or what Deleuze and Guattari refer to as a 'rhizome', which has no locatable central organizing system. On the one hand, this understanding of network possibly endorses a dismissal of individual responsibility, in that an individual cannot be held specifically responsible for the exertion of power, the spell cast, the ritual performed, or in this case, the legacy of virtuosity they inherit. Agents themselves may be oblivious to their participation in the exertion of this power and the ideologies of gendered virtuosity, or uphold a sense of passive ignorance, or radically deny that they participate in the network and its benefits: the latter agents are always 'elsewhere'.

Jane Bennett discusses these issues of power, intentionality, responsibility and agency in terms of, following Deleuze and Guattari, 'assemblages'. These being a grouping of affects and bodies, of human and non-human agencies that are, in Bennett's words:

ad hoc groupings of diverse elements, of vibrant materials of all sorts. [...] Assemblages are not governed by any central head: no one materiality or type of material has sufficient competence to determine consistently the trajectory or impact of the group. (2010: 23–4)

Thinking of assemblages in this way means that power is distributed unequally and as part of the effectivity of the grouping, what Bennett calls 'the agency of the assemblage' and this, as she discusses, prompts a problematic and critical consideration of responsibility given the limitations of any one agent's intentionality and the emphasis on the collective of both human and non-human agents:

> To figure the generative source of effects as a swarm is to see human intentions as always in competition and confederation with many other strivings, for an intention is like a pebble thrown into a pond, or an electrical current sent through a wire or neural network: it vibrates and merges with other currents, to affect and be affected. This understanding of agency does not deny the existence of that thrust called intentionally, but it does see it as less definitive of its outcomes. It loosens the connections between efficacy and the moral subject, bringing efficacy closer to the idea of the power to make a difference that calls for response. And this power, I contend along with Spinoza and others, is a power possessed by nonhuman bodies too. (Bennett, 2010: 32)

This human–non-human assemblage shifts the agency from a willing intentional subject to an 'agentic swarm' of intersecting efficacy, causality, intention. Does this understanding of assemblage therefore suggest that no one individual can be made accountable, responsible for an exertion of power that oppresses, harms, privileges and is unjust? Bennett's work attempts to complicate the operations and interconnectedness of power through an understanding of 'vibrant matter', meaning that whilst an individual can exert agency as part of an assemblage, they cannot be *fully responsible for their effects* in something such as an electricity power blackout, which is the example Bennett uses. The ethical focus then becomes more a questioning of one's responsibility and exertions in a 'world of distributed agency' (Bennet, 2010: 38) and one's 'response to the assemblages in which one finds oneself participating' (Bennett, 2010: 37). An 'agentic swarm' complicates power and accountability beyond the single culprit or agent and attempts to account for both human and non-human effects and this is a useful way to broaden the scope on how power operates and what it means to be politically responsible. It is also pertinent to the questions of political accountability, power, ideology and gendered virtuosity, as they intersect through the repertoire and performances of Galás whose work raises powers that draw from the actions and operations of state, religion, patriarchy and institutions. Or, in Louis Althusser's terms, her opponents derive from both the repressive and ideological state apparatuses, with a particular emphasis on the church, asylums and armed state forces. Over the course of her career, from the late 1970s to date (writing in 2019), Galás's ability to embody and demonstrate power and affect in voice, music and sound makes her one of the most important artists of the late twentieth and early twenty-first century, jolting political consciousness through an affective sonic materiality and text.

The operations of power and agency within Galás's practice are complex and comparable to Bennett's agentic swarm of human and non-human effects. Her musical, sonic, vocal and textual 'assemblage of agency' raises the language of judgement, prohibition and law, in painful frequencies, ritual and mourning lament, calling forth a swarm of forces that are the inordinate connections between power and its effects. Nevertheless, despite the swarm, she holds power to account, tracks it to multiple origins across a network of intersections and assemblages. In short, her work is based on unspeakable suffering and horror: on rape, sexual trauma and revenge ('Wild Women with Steak Knives' from *The Litanies of Satan*, 1989); on the abjection of homosexuality and the suffering of individuals with HIV and AIDS (*Plague Mass*, 1991); on torture and genocide (*Defixiones: Will and Testament*, 2003); on mental illness, torture (by drug/chemical experiment) and incarceration (*Vena Cava*, 1993; *Schrei X*, 1996b; *Das Fieberspital*, 2017). Galás's specificity can be derived from the extreme extent to which her albums and performances effectively seek to embody pain, mental illness, disease, torture, violence, as distinguished from any work that describes an event: 'Most pop music is descriptive; it's *about* the thing, not the thing *itself*. Whereas my work is the thing itself, it *is* the sound of the plague' (Galás, cited in Juno and

Vale, 1991: 14). The difference between music as description (as it tells a story about the thing, represents the thing) and music as the *thing itself* (an embodiment of the thing) is deeply considered and reflected in a repertoire that, from her first solo release in the 1980s onwards, has been politically concerned with the suffering of bodies, the limits of language and the ideological force of powerful states and institutions. To realize this level of power, affect and violence in sound and practice, in composition and in song, demands what Galás has described as a 'mandatory technique', a virtuosic skill that is compulsory to realize the work. In other words, there is a strong suggestion in the discourse about Galás and the ways that she talks about her abilities and vocal prowess that suggest, or rather insist, on the kind of agency, mastery and control indicative of the virtuoso, with its attendant underpinning masculine qualities. And this kind of individuality is at odds not only with the agentic swarm encountered by any musician *'always in competition and confederation with many other strivings'*, but, more specifically, with the swarms of power in Galás's sound that form assemblages of human and non-human, with a multitude of voices that mourn and accompany the dead and that sound 'possessed'.

Mandatory technique

Galás's practice is arguably committed to unravelling the occulted power of patriarchy and language, so her relationship with virtuosity creates interesting tensions between, on the one hand, engaging with this discourse, claiming virtuosity and, on the other, appearing to destabilize and undermine its ideological foundations. Concomitant tensions abound, such as that between the ego and its dissolution, individual agency and the swarm of effects, the unitary and fragmented, producing a masterpiece whilst destroying the 'masterpiece'; and underlying these tensions the logic of binary gender: heteronormative masculinity and femininity. Indeed, it could be argued that Galás's skill, her insistence on differentiation from 'performance art', from 'amateurs', whilst expounding in interviews on technical virtuosity, is not just an account of her work, but a strategy to deal with sexist assumptions that assume an 'amateur' untrained status and the biologically essential 'intuitiveness' and undirected 'emotional' output of female performers and artists, denied access to the value of inherently masculine rationality:

> Well it is generally thought that we women create intuitively rather than rationally. If a man creates a piece of work which is emotional or even zany, many conclude that he chose to do that. With a woman, it would appear to be a gynaecological imperative instead. (Galás, cited in Chare and Ferrett, 2007: 69)

Learning vocal technique in practice is presented by Galás as essential to the themes, composition, improvisations and performances she wanted to create and develop. An accomplished pianist from a very young age, performing in the San Diego Symphony Orchestra, a church choir (led by her father), a jazz band and active in the improvisation scene, Galás began studying the voice in her twenties, developing an extraordinary three and a half octave vocal range and a vocal musculature based in classical vocal training, particularly bel canto, so as to develop and maintain technique, stamina, strength and range. Galás draws parallels between her vocal technique and the demands Wagner placed on singers. She discusses a necessary ability to sustain long phrases with changing timbres and her bel canto technique which, as Wagner understood, is necessary for singers to 'cut through that huge orchestral sound'. This attention to the physiological prowess of the voice almost invariably reoccurs throughout her interviews whenever she is asked about her vocal technique, promoting her power, ability to improvise, as well as legitimating, in part, her virtuosity and the longevity of her vocal abilities. When asked about the sustainability of her voice, sensing the zeal for a diva's fatal vocal malady (the point at which the singer's voice ages, weakens, cracks), Galás switches the focus from physical vulnerability to that of an imminent threat posed by a voice capable of wounding, saying that she wields a voice with a 'hard edge' that 'cuts like a knife': a lyric spinto soprano whose 'keening tongue is razor sharp' (Chare, 2007: 57). Despite frequent references to her 'scream' – and it is difficult to find words other than scream to describe the horrendous intensity of her high-pitched, lacerating keening – Galás notes that she really isn't screaming, as to do so would damage the vocal chords (Galás, cited in Oldham, 1999).[3] Rather, her vocal technique sings the scream, bel canto, in techniques and timbre that move 'through the bone structure of the skull, all through the skull, the resonance of the skull' (Galás, cited in Oldham, 1999). In technical terms, then, Galás is aligned more with opera, blues, chanson and jazz than with something that might fall under the rubric of performance art, and this is an important distinction for her that speaks to the context of her musical background, love of songs, technique and training. She sings technically difficult vocal compositions with an extensive vocal range across Greek, Middle Eastern, classical, blues, French chanson, German cabaret, jazz and gospel styles (influenced by many including Maria Callas, Oum Kalsoum, Edith Piaf, Chet Baker, Ray Charles, The Supremes, Jimi Hendrix, Jacques Brel) and it is this transgressive versatility that develops a unique voice, capable of reinterpretation and extraordinary vocal feats. In sum, Galás's incredible vocal range, the timbral, textural, microtonal forensic detail and frequency intensities of her sound, particularly when it is combined with reverberation, tape delay, ring modulation and other forms of electronic processing, live desk and studio manipulation, question what can be physically sustained and tolerated by both her own body and those of her listeners. Technology and the non-human effects of her performances are key to the development of multiple voicings, to range, timbre, pitch, duration, space, aesthetic and to the impact of extreme sonic affects.

Central perhaps to an understanding of Galás's virtuosity, its combination of composition and improvisation, is the notion of technique and the play between control and its loss and/or deliberate relinquishment, the tension between *tekhne* (will to mastery, control) and *tukhe* ('chance, fortune, luck, the whims of the gods or that which "just happens"' (Kilroy and Swiboda, 2007: 4)). Galás's vocal improvisations draw from movement between these apparent oppositions, whilst being dependent on highly skilled virtuosity and an extended technique enabling a vocal versatility that is, according to Galás, mandatory, in order to develop an absolute accuracy of detail alongside moves towards the theoretically impossible.[4] With voice as the most 'direct' and 'sophisticated' instrument, Galás establishes a specific singular virtuosity through a uniquely developed technical approach and ability that *exceeds* 'simple vocal virtuosity':

the *absolute accuracy*, the *absolute detail* I am referring to requires a virtuosity, a versatility with the instrument that has not yet been approached. The most minimal or the most maximal increment of *timbral* change over the smallest unit of time is required and, in many ways, resembles what is attempted in subtractive synthesis of white noise, wherein highly specified pitch/timbre bands may be heard suddenly alone, in quick succession, or simultaneously. The question here is not one of simplistic development of vocal virtuosity. Rather, it involves a redefinition of a *most accurate* sonic representation of thought via the most accessible, direct, and sophisticated music-making apparatus. (Galás, 1996a: 3)

Focusing on accuracy, on detailed changes pertaining particularly to pitch, timbre and duration, Galás's account of her vocal versatility and vocal composition claims that her vocal technique has exceeded 'simple vocal' virtuosity and necessarily so, since she must have the ability to realize extreme mental and sentient states, both composed and immediate. Such excessive virtuosity transgresses the organized demarcations and ideologies of the 'virtuoso' or musical 'genius' and the assignments of these labels, to a canon of male composers/ musicians and introduces an unnerving interference emergent from a dark feminine sounding, in that her 'screams' and high frequency keening are acutely associated with the historical chain of associations between madwomen, hysteria (wombs) and witches.

More specifically however, Galás's 'excessive' classical singing styles engage with her cultural background and the Greek tradition of female moirologists, professional mourners who are expert vocal lamenters capable of expressing extreme grief. Moirologists are women who have the role of singing laments, especially during times of death in the community. Further to these mourning lamentations, Galás interprets the 'blood language' of the Mother through the melodies of *amanes*, a word that refers to 'mana', or mother, in Greek. Galás incorporates Armenian '*dromoi/makams* scales' and the melodies of *amanes* shared across Greek and Anatolian cultures between Greeks, Armenians, Kurds, Jews, Arabs and Assyrians, cultures that, Galás claims, shared verses and sang to 'a god invented by despair' in the historical context of the displacement of Asia Minor peoples which occurred during and after the Turko–Greek War of 1914–23 and then again during the German Nazi occupation of the 1940s (Galás, cited in Gottschalk, 2008). The *amanes* is musically and culturally associated with the *moiroloyia*

188 DARK SOUND

as feminine and/or female-led 'excessively' emotional vocalization, again a highly demanding melismatic vocal style of Asia Minor music that was sung in the cafés aman. In her online paper '*Amanes*: The Legacy of the Oriental Mother', Gail Holst-Warhaft argues that 'sorrow' is articulated by an *amanes*, and that the 'pain' and 'grief' expressed by this style plays a significant role in the formation of Greek identities, the nationalist myths of Greekness and in the collective consciousness of the diaspora where the *amanes* came to be associated with the female voice, the mother, the oriental, femininity, darkness, emotional intensity and nostalgia for homeland/origins. According to Holst-Warhaft, 'close not only in spirit but in verse to the traditional *moiroloyia*', *amanedhes* are a tradition of vocal improvisation often concerned with the loss of male kin who have died or gone abroad and typically display the impressive vocal skills of the singer (Holst-Warhaft, 2000). Galás deploys these technically demanding vocalizations and improvisations in bitter militant mourning, as despairing cries for a mother in terrible moments of suffering, for revenge, cries of grief and unbearable sorrow, drawing on a combination of female cultural roles and dark feminine mythologies in the performance of vocally-testing death laments.

A Greek-American with a 'Mikrasian background', Galás's death laments should be understood in the context of a politicized unspeakable, attempting to raise, in sound and text, a testimony to the voices of the dead and their suffering. *Defixiones: Will and Testament* (2003) is a double album that draws together texts from poets Siamanto, Adonis, Pasolini, Vallejo, Celan, Michaux, alongside writers Bet-Oraham and Soteriou, as well as work published anonymously. Sung in eight different languages, each text speaks of the horror and violence of persecution as they relate to specific historical genocidal atrocities such as the torture and burning of Armenian women in 'The Dance', and of the mourning for the destroyed homelands of Assyria and the forced exile of its people in 'The Eagle of Tkhuma':

> *Defixiones* refers to the warnings engraved in lead which were placed on the graves of the dead in Greece, Asia Minor and elsewhere in the Middle East. They cautioned against moving or desecrating the corpses under the threat of extreme harm. Will and Testament refers to the last wishes of the dead who have been

DIAMANDA GALÁS AND SWARMS OF POWER

taken to their graves under unnatural circumstances. [...] It is an album dedicated to the forgotten and erased of the Armenian, Assyrian, and Greek genocide that occurred in Asia Minor, Pontos, and Thrace between 1914 and 1923. (diamandaGalás. com, 2017)

The album mixes its vocal styles, between *amanes*, blues and spirituals of the Deep South, whilst the text of each song shifts through disorientating subject positions that speak with 'orders from the dead', as if the living were called upon to do the bidding of the dead and to bear witness to the horror of unbearable torture, despair, pain and massacre witnessed by those now dead during the moments 'when the world went up in flames'. Multiple speakers, culminating in a textual 'us', are required to embody voices which, after death, refute the erasure of their name and insist on the memory of the circumstances of their murder. And so the text addresses the massacre, the witnesses and the would-be erasers of the crimes of torture and genocide. Meaning develops through a violent narrative that tells of abominable crimes so that, for example, in 'Orders from the Dead', featuring a text written by Galás with excerpts from *Farewell Anatolia* by Dido Soteriou, there develops a narrative of the tortuous destruction of families and of the burning of Smyrna, told in language that oscillates between English and Greek.[5] Galás's virtuosity in this respect is a foundational requirement for engaging with the utterly abject in order to counter the forces that seek to erase the traces of violent deaths, existence and obliterate accountability. This is not the steadfast individualism of the virtuoso and there is no place here for adoration of the individual. There is rather a necessary giving over of the 'I' in a practice that requires an array of techniques to survive the subject and swarm of effects the sound seeks to connect with and embody. A combination of dark feminine mythologies and virtuosic technique morphs in the keening rituals of death laments, the moiroloyia, the blues and spirituals (with underscored links to African-American spiritual practices). Through a vocal cacophony of bloodcurdling shrieks, operatic bel canto, the moiroloyia, blues and spirituals, Galás is drawn into a diversity of cultures and ritual practices that have 'taken the role of shaman' in so far as women and their voices have been believed to be the ultimate conduit between life and death, embodiments of the 'spiritual' qualities that makes women into ideal mourners. Mani is an area of southern Greece to which Galás is related through her mother. Galás's practice engages in this relation through the traditional laments and performative mourning of the Maniot women, whose voices and gestures preside and dominate at funerals; these women, dressed in black, cry, ululate and tear their hair in mourning practices that Cynthia Carr conceives of as a journey through death comparable to Galás's 'Saint of the Pit': 'The women sing directly to the dead. In a sense, they accompany the dead. That is the journey made in *Saint of the Pit*' (Carr, 1993: 190).

'Guilty' witch-cyborg mutations

A mezzo with the capacity for soprano and contralto range, Galás's extreme vocal soundings incrementally shift in timbre and flit between very low and extraordinarily high pitches, between comprehensible words, non-verbal sounds and 'speaking in tongues'. These multiple voices are developed and made all the more extreme through electronic processing such as reverb and delay, hooked up to the cultural inscription of feminine madness, female mourning and spiritual/demonic spirit possession. Many commentators on Galás, such as Carr, have heard in Galás's voices the hellish sounds of 'possession': 'Chanted harangues, wordless croaks, eerie screeches and whispers – it sounds like the voice of one possessed. Galás stands in the fire and brimstone and outburns it' (Carr, 1993: 189). Joy Press and Simon Reynolds suggest that Galás (and Lydia Lunch) extracts from the political potential of appropriating the cultural signs that have produced and designated what constitutes the delirium of women, their demonic possession and rambling madness. Galás, they write, has both aligned herself with the 'persecuted and demonized women' and 'resurrected the witch as a terrorist against patriarchy' – and this is a political strategy (Reynolds and Press, 1996: 278). Furthermore, the alignment with the demonic does not so much specify solely women, but rather expands beyond that category of being to trans-women, gay men and those targeted, tortured and inscribed as 'demonic'. To underscore the alliance further and to critique the processes of 'naturalization', her practice places particular emphasis on the processed material relations between technology and bodies comparable to the 'cyborg' Donna Haraway proposed – a body where 'humanity' or the 'organism' is always already compromised by technological dependence and complex information systems which prevent a body's claim to the innocence of being 'natural' (Haraway, 1991: 163).

Galás is keenly aware of the regulatory norms and acts that constitute gender, both by the ways in which the body *shows* itself, the terms of display and the various complex translations of these processes and acts in music and the voice (to which Susan McClary pays particular attention in *Feminine Endings* when she discusses operatic 'madness' and Galás). She is also deeply attentive to the social *punishments* for deviating from these gender norms and how the force of those punishments are assumed and redirected in practice, as a means of survival and protest. Her relationship to femininity and to 'Woman' is thus complicated, since she both engages with gender and femininity (albeit as an 'unnatural' performative act) and also seems to evoke the gender abolitionism of xenofeminism which recognizes '*innumerable* genders' as 'only a first step in the refusal to accept *any* gender as a basis of stable signification' (Hester, 2018: 31). As with Helen Hester's provocation and interpretation of xenofeminism's technomaterialist, anti-naturalist, gender abolitionist feminism, an area of contentious focus emerges in Galás's practice at the site of those bodies capable of becoming impregnated and with the capacity to grow a foetus, i.e., the focus on a biological relationship with reproduction and the social hegemony of reproductive futurism as it specifies 'Woman' and the norms for her body and that of the 'family' structure. Her practice offers interesting tensions between the all-out abolition of gender, the production of multiple difference and the power derived from the appropriation of feminine mythologies such as the witch, augmented here as 'cyborgian witch'.

'Wild Women with Steak Knives (The Homicidal Love Song for Solo Scream)', performed live, is a multi-microphone piece that Galás says is inspired by a Greek funeral tradition where women preside over funerals by carrying large knives as signs of revenge in a ritual for those killed. Revenge in this track however should be heard as mobilization against rapists, of castration vigilante groups (Black Leather Beavers). The knife that cuts is manic, murderous and bloody ('sirens in a never-ending bloody bliss'), symbolic of the harm done: 'I commend myself to a death of no importance, / Wild women with veins slashed and wombs spread, Singing songs of the death instinct / In voices yet unheard' (Galás, 'Wild Women with Steak Knives' [1992] in *The Shit of God*, 1996a).

The line 'veins slashed and wombs spread' picks up on a theme common in interviews and writings where Galás specifically points to the obscenity of childbirth and an anti-breeding critique. Put together, these textual slashes may in turn account, in part at least, for the contradictory labels that have been applied to her as an artist, both 'radical feminist' and 'misogynist' and a number of articles have featured a quotation in which Galás says that most of her favourite writers are/were misogynistic. She isn't particularly invested in feminism and is irritated by the confines of the label 'Woman' as an unnecessary limit, preferring instead to focus political intention through a multiplicity of hybrids and mythic creatures that include Sirens, witches, transvestites, vampires and snakes:

> From the Greeks onward, the voice has always been a political instrument as well as a vehicle for transmission of occult knowledge or power. It's always been tied to witches and the shamanistic experience – the witch as transvestite/transsexual having the power of both male and female. (Galás, cited in Juno and Vale, 1991: 10–11)

Galás has said that she 'learns a lot about being a woman' from drag queens with whom she lived, worked and sang on the street and that it was through the encouragement of these 'tough' drag queen 'broads' that she discovered her propensity to sing. In doing so, she de-essentializes and trans-sexualizes her own 'femininity', as well as the roles of strong nurturing 'mothers', something that is significant in terms of her vocal soundings, pushing beyond biological determinism. In 'Wild Women with Steak Knifes', 'Woman' and 'Man' are traceable as variable markers of gender, but are, in Galás' terms, 'trans-sexualized' to the extent that the heteronormative gender binary is understood through the sexualized pitch and timbral markers of the voice: infected, expanded, multiplied beyond the binary. Given the range of her voice, Galás can blur between sounding feminine, masculine and non-binary and this is enacted most obviously when she sings through octave units that shift the pitch of her voice into 'excessive' and 'abnormal' ranges, tones and timbres. Early in the development of 'Wild Women with Steak Knives', a 'trans' voice occurs, disturbingly slow and pitch shifted to a lower octave voice. It is 'masculine' to an extent, or rather something that bears traces of both feminine and masculine, but is moreover hideously machined in such a way as to invoke the non-human or indeed the anti-human demonic voice, the malice of which drags the human pulse out of time, accompanied by a dreadful slow drum beat. This is a satanic voice to the extent that our ears have become accustomed to recognizing the 'demonic' in cacophonies of possessed cries and via queered excessive and technologically-processed voices that are perceived as 'extreme' and/or unnatural…or supernatural.[6] Swarms of excessively high and low voices occur in rasping, heaving timbres and ululations delivered in rapid succession and irregular rhythms, as if trapped and entangled in highly reverberant space. At certain points, the buzz contracts into a focus on one key monstrous vocal around which the horde of vocals gather and shadow in the background, until the moment when the grouping expands and inflates, dispersing across the sound field to become a crazed insectile swarm once again within a contained space: this is the frenzied electronic crowding that provides the sensation of demonic-cyborgian schizophrenia, multiple and yet unique to Galás's sound.

The listener suspects (as directed) that all these layered voices originate from Galás's body, but has no definite way of confirming her body as source since the multi-layered, multiple, voices exorcised through different microphones have utterly *processed* the referential gendered body: voices morph into sounds, beats, noises, both drawing and exceeding the limit of 'Woman' and even 'human' by exceeding the sound of the 'voice'. Or perhaps, to borrow the terms of Judith Butler's understanding of performative gender norms, it would be more appropriate to describe what Galás does as *stretching* the limit of 'Woman' and 'Man', as she seems to make audible the oppressive and painful reiteration of gender norms and the strength of force required to make them resignify by dehumanizing the voice, subjecting it to the mutations of Others, the rabble. Galás takes this logic to the extreme and disarticulates the body organized and ordained across gender and sexuality, 'humanity'. This is not to underplay the importance of dark feminine mythologies and the notion of 'Woman' in her work, however, for these are significant markers of power and transgression within her practice, as is noted by commentators who, in discussing her work, make frequent reference to mythological figures such as the Sirens and Medusa and bestow titles upon her such as 'Queen of the Damned', 'Demon Diva', 'Diva of the Dispossessed' or 'Goth's High Priestess'. In Galás's practice, the dark drag feminine as it links with demonic creatures, chthonic grotesques, tragic heroines, vocal seducers and mourners, are performed and processed through electronic composition via which they acquire further supernatural extensions. The voice is made multiple, flitting between the feminine and the masculine, destabilizing the norms upon which they are based, creating machinic-animal-non-human-queer-trans-feminine-demonic-mythic mutants. Nevertheless, mythologies of the feminine, as they mutate with the frequently oscine, serpentine creatures of female vocal grotesques (Medusa, Sirens, Harpies) and electronic technology, are key to understanding the rites of mourning, her vocal genealogy and saying something about bodies that have suffered the inhumane: vital therefore to understanding *how she harnesses power* and darkens virtuosity with demonized and abjected forms of non-binary gender, tabooed sexualities and non-human effects.

Galás first performed *1984 – End of the Epidemic* at the Cathedral of St. John, New York in 1990, where it was recorded live and released in 1991. The work is based on the social dispossession of people with AIDS and their suffering. The performance was, according to Galás, received as a mass, indicating the appropriateness of the context of the church, which she has elsewhere described as the best acoustic environment for her work. Extensive church-like reverberation draws attention to power as it bears contextual resonance with a connection to God, sacrifice (of the Son) and the intensity of the symbolization of blood with respect to Christ's body. In *Plague Mass* Galás chants 'Hoc est signum corpus meum' (This is my body) and 'Hoc est signum sangre meum' (This is my blood) whilst she covers herself with ceremonial blood in the reverberant space of the divine, holy ground. She stands naked to the waist covered in blood with multiple taped voices echoing the words of the consecration. Blood and gesture here symbolize the sacrifice of people with AIDS, whom she regards as modern day saints, as well as homosexual bodies that have been made abject

DIAMANDA GALÁS AND SWARMS OF POWER

and abjected. Leviticus, a book from the Old Testament, designates the 'filth' of the human, places prohibitions on sexual behaviour and bodily fluids (blood) that it deems 'polluting', 'unclean' and thereby punishable. Much light is shed on this scene by Julia Kristeva who, in her volume *Powers of Horror*, studies the book of Leviticus and what she calls the 'semiotics of biblical abomination', drawing particular attention to the 'flows' of impurity as defilements of the body, especially blood, the very flows in which Galás is covered, in a sacrificial gesture (Kristeva, 1982: 102). Punishment, read through Leviticus and the 'Law of Holiness', will be inflicted on those 'guilty' of defying 'sexual prohibitions', which, among other 'violations of nature' such as incest and bestiality, includes male homosexuality (see Leviticus, Chapters 15–18). The 'country will vomit out', literally dispossess the guilty and sexually excessive and as God promises, he will punish unholy, unclean bodies: any who commit such crimes can indeed 'be certain of the Devil' (*Plague Mass*, 1991). *Plague Mass* begins with the threat of this *certainty*, which is why the 'Devil' is invoked by Galás as the signifier of punishment for guilty polluted bodies as well as revenge. In *Plague Mass*, Galás delivers horrendous and repelling vocal attacks in hideous hybrids of bel canto/screams/shrieks/growls such as heard in 'Sono L'Antichristo':

Sono le feci dal Signore.	I am the shit of God.
Sono lo segno	I am the sign
Sono la pestilenza	I am the plague
Sono il Antichristo.	I am the Antichrist.

Between phrases, Galás expels a most diabolical scorching screech-growl that only a unique and developed extended vocal technique could utter without severely damaging the vocal chords in the terrible grate and grind of that horrific writhing of the voice and its pained physiology. The body that hears it squirms, sweats and quivers, hearing all at once, pain, horror, rage, infliction, accusation and immense grief. This 'offertory' part of the mass is addressed to those unjust judges whom she accuses through the heavyweight power of a body it has already judged as diabolical and in part, this is a power bestowed by those to whom she addresses since it speaks of the revolting diabolism that has been attributed to 'unclean' bodies.

Galás retains the sacred and ritualistic in performance even whilst introducing the 'guilt', 'uncleanliness' and desperation of those deemed unfit to approach the greatness of God. In this respect, notwithstanding the facile charges of Satanism and blasphemy, Galás's relationship to the idea of God and theology is more complex than simple opposition. She retains 'faith' in the affective technologies that are liturgies, prayers, poems: affective text. In contrast to the notion of transcending language via reverberant unintelligible angelic cries and what is too great to be uttered, she retains faith in words and language through her own writing and that of others such as the French poet Charles Baudelaire, whose writing, for her, melds the dichotomies of good/evil, heaven/hell into a concept of 'compassion'; and others such as Siamanto, an Armenian poet who wrote about the burning of Armenian women in the desert by Turkish soldiers; and Romanian-Jewish (German-speaking) poet Paul Celan, writer of 'Todesfuge' (Death Fugue), a poem which demonstrates to Galás a cathartic writing of trauma and shock, but also refers to the isolating horror that remains in the brain – what can never be said.[7] Affective text in this sense counters the ideologies and silences of the church and that which ineffability seeks to keep silent with a politicized 'unspeakable' horror. Galás composes her own liturgies, consecrations and lamentations, often drawing extracts from sacred texts such as the Old Testament, (Psalm 22 and Psalm 88 in *The Divine Punishment and Saint of the Pit*) and combines this with the writing of poets (such as Charles Baudelaire, Edgar Allan Poe and Gérard de Nerval in *Masque of the Red Death*) 'who, living or deceased, incantationally discuss a more iconoclastic opinion of a spiritual or physical fighter during a time in which the gates of the city have been closed to him'(Galás, cited in Chare and Ferrett, 2007: 72). In the broad context of her work, Galás is referring to those spiritual and physical fighters persecuted, tortured and imprisoned by imperial or state powers. Richard Smith hears Galás's incantation as the attribution of a saintly image to a gay man with AIDS through an appropriation of the Old Testament in *The Divine Punishment* by which she directly opposes the morality and hatred conducted through specific segments of the Christian Bible and other patrons of prejudice and religious ideologies (Smith, 1995: 88).

It would be too simplistic to merely state that Galás's practice is anti-theological when it dedicates itself so vigorously to the interpretation of biblical texts and cultivates a residing respect for *faith* as it has provided the means for survival and hope for the suffering – a faith she has often summarized as: 'Prayers to a God invented by despair.' That respect is audible in her practice as it moves between different church musics and Greek/Maniot mourning practices – ritual laments integrated into the Greek Orthodox Church – and the dedicated techniques with which she creates her own liturgies from the sacred rites and texts of various churches and the poets she reads as physical fighters and spiritual warriors who have been made into outcasts by society (Gehr, 1989: 117). Thus, the biblical texts that she extracts are used, Gehr writes, as an 'emotionally charged political weapon' against those lawmakers who have accused and who have designated the damned. Galás studies how her enemies accuse, how bodies have been judged and written. The voices she unleashes against the accusers harness their own force of judgement – and what the powerful have rendered demonic. Galás understands Satan as a 'rebellious angel' and notes that, as an outcast and enemy of society, the satanic figure possesses power that can be harnessed to embody the dispossessed, those who are really 'modern day saints' (Galás, cited in Carr, 1993: 189) The voices of the abject dispossessed are the multiple mutations that Galás seeks to make intelligible in her practice through a combination of voice, text, mythology, machine: human and non-human assemblages that darken virtuosity.

High voice, technically articulate

What Galás renders intelligible is significant with respect to the attention placed on her vocal range, specifically the attributions of virtuosity that tend to focus on the intensities of her high voice in much the same way as the lead soprano in opera is celebrated and accorded virtuosity for her *coloratura* and sustained, incredibly high notes. Such a voice is at the core of opera's logic in that the singer's extravagant unearthly cries are the much-anticipated moments of an exquisite experience of simultaneous ecstasy and emotional pain, an operatic bliss that is the jouissance anticipated and desired by an audience. Michel Poizat reads the moment of the high cry as the outcome of the 'logic of jouissance' in opera, which always already anticipates '*coloratura* delirium' as the definitive moment of unintelligible femininity (1992: 145). The unintelligibility of the pure cry is comprehended as an unrepresentable climactic vocal moment at the limit of human vocal ability, a moment of jouissance that is farthest away from speech and produced in the high frequency feminized 'zone of unintelligibility'. An ability to hit the high notes, way above standard singing ranges, have over time accrued a sort of paradox in the thickening of the discourse on virtuosic female singers in that they are celebrated as virtuosos to an extent (although the 'diva' discourse serves as a strategy that tempers this celebration), but on the basis of a vocal regarded as the epitome of vocal unintelligibility, implying virtuosic skill perhaps in relation to the voice, but not the technical skill aligned with language and the ability to structure, communicate, render intelligible or even meaningful. This relationship between the female singer and unintelligibility is articulated by Jacques Lacan who uses singers (Poizat comments in the notes, Lacan 'intuitively uses the female form, *la chanteuse*'), specifically sopranos, to express the antithesis of intelligible speech. In his seminar, Lacan makes a direct connection between the soprano female singing voice and a barking dog, foregrounding the absence of occlusives (or stops) which allows for the speech sound of consonants:

> this absence of occlusives in my dog's speech is precisely what she has in common with a speaking activity with which you are quite familiar and which is called singing. If it so happens that you often do not understand what the singer is jabbering on about, it is precisely because one cannot sing the occlusives […]; in short my dog sings. Perhaps this is why (conversely) some sopranos are said to bark or yelp! (Lacan [1961], cited in Poizat, 1992: 43–4)

The soprano singer offers the ultimate opportunity to collapse the distinction between humanity and animality, as well as the distinction between female/dog, feminine singing voice/dog yelping, in other words, such a singer cannot articulate (cannot 'speak') since her voice lacks the sonic formulation to make language intelligible. This formulation not only conflates femininity and animality but, in focusing on the voice, recalls the notion of female hysterical babble, nonsense and the kinds of soprano roles accorded to operatic 'madwomen'.

DIAMANDA GALÁS AND SWARMS OF POWER 199

Susan McClary explicitly compares Galás's high voice *coloratura* with the renowned vocal difficulty and demands of the vocal composition for Mozart's 'Queen of the Night', alongside the virtuosity of female singers capable of singing the 'unsingable'. Her explicit connection comes from listening to *Plague Mass* and specifically Galás's version of the spiritual 'Swing Low, Sweet Chariot' when Galás sings 'entirely in the range above the staff' and in so doing appeals to 'the signs of crazed virtuosity usually associated with figures such as the Queen of the Night or Lucia'. McClary continues to suggest that Galás's unique take on 'crazed virtuosity' 'comments on the conventional link between the *coloratura* range and madness' whilst maintaining a politics of 'searing protest', despite the risk of reaffirming the conventional mythological chain of associations connecting the *excessive* high vocal acrobatics of the operatic female soprano with the constructed associations between music, femininity, sexuality and madness. Writing in the early 1990s, McClary points to a 'defilement' and 'dispensing with conventional framing devices' and a Galásian performance that 'heralds a new moment in the history of musical representation' ([1991] 2002: 111). In hindsight, this can be interpreted as a transition towards affect studies, a move necessitated by Galás's work explicitly by her differentiation between representation and the 'sound of the thing itself' – something that is picked up on by Marie Thompson in her assessment of the 'affective capacities' of Galás's vocals, specifically the 'scream' (Thompson, 2013: 297–311). The meaningful friction is then between the *coloratura* cry, the scream... and what can be made intelligible and/or meaningful. Here, Galás changes the terms of intelligibility from representation to affect, turning the force of judgement and the violence of abjection back onto the listener, so that violence and punishment are a cruelty that affects both audience and performer. By means of their bodies, her audiences apprehend meaning as it shifts through the flesh.

Schrei X is an example of this apprehension, especially in that the voice is produced through combinations of ring-modulation, changing delay times, other kinds of signal processing and vocal techniques that create 'a lot of noise' and give you 'a sound that no longer sounds vocal'(Galás, cited in Flinn, 1996).[8] In performance, Galás manipulates the spatial conditions of the performance using complete darkness and quadraphonic sound to encage and attack the animalistic nervous system of human organisms – to infiltrate the boundaries of the human species with fearful shrieks, hisses and ululation that are everywhere in the dark – breaching and replacing, in those thirty-five minutes of *Schrei X,* humanism and 'civilized' composure. She kindles the shrillness of her sound as much as possible, to the degradation of other frequencies so as to fry the 'I' in scorching vocal delirium. In the *Angry Women* interview, Galás describes how in some of her performances and with the volume set as loud as possible, she chooses to bypass mid and low frequencies, 'thus accentuating the higher registers – in other words, my sound is very shrill...I have to feel it, I fry under that sound' (Galás, cited in Juno and Vale, 1991: 10). In this, Galás's intense frequencies press upon and work to diminish the boundaries that maintain a sense of coherent self. In the horrendous voices that affect the bodies 'encaged' in a cacophony of voices and sounds, Galás's body becomes both part-executioner (of voices) and executed (by voices). Erratically she becomes both punisher and punished – but always 'condemned'. She inflicts this sonic cruelty on the bodies of her audience, to which she herself is subjected. With this obsessional attention to sonic cruelty both sadistic and masochistic, come 'shared' and 'unshared' pleasures:

> During the performance, I endeavour to move elastically through many different 'states of severe concentration' or 'trance states' with complete obedience to the rigor of each state, and simultaneously attend to the temporal demands of the macrostructure of the piece [...] endeavours and concerns which reflect an obsession with the shared and unshared pleasures of both flagellant and flagellee. (Galás, 1996a: 60)

Because of the association between the scream and pain, between excessive high soprano vocal *coloratura* and mad women, death cries and divas, with shrill feminine nagging and diabolical witch-like shrieks, attention on her affect frequently focuses on her high vocal frequencies as the signifier of feminized abjection which are excessively extended by Galás beyond 'natural' vocal technique and processed through cyborgian intensity. Power and its execution therefore oscillate in Galás's discourse between notions of control/ virtuosity/technique and loss of control and the 'hysteria' that has formed the madwoman discourse.

Whilst much has been made of Galás's immense vocal power, with particular focus on her extended technique, vocal range and high voice or 'scream', Galás does not solely operate by drawing from the 'crazed virtuosity' of the semiotic and trans-verbal or the diabolical unintelligible cries of spirit possession exacerbated by cyborgian electronics, but rather establishes the significance of language (as technology) by articulating an affective text, compelling encounters at the threshold of the unintelligible and intelligible. Coursing through her repertoire are words, languages and text that find parallels with the impressions of language felt by poet and philosopher Denise Riley, who offers a sense of the force, affect and physicality of words in a way that resonates with Galás's bloody 'Intravenal Song': 'There is a forcible affect of language which courses like blood through its speakers' (Riley 2005: 1). Both musician and writer admit the 'bloodiness' of language as it pumps through the veins of a body, and both have a technical interest in 'malediction' that seems to endorse belief in the occult powers of hateful words with evil intentions. As mysterious as this initially sounds, Riley writes of a pragmatic approach:

The conception of an affect soaked power of language itself can be demonstrated quite pragmatically. If the affective quality of music can be granted to exist irrespective of its hearers' sensibilities and their quirks, then why not accord a similar relative independence to language's emotionality? There is a tangible affect in language which stands somewhat apart from the expressive intentions of an individual speaker; so language can work outside of its official content. The speaking of language is far more than its resonances, timbres, its insinuations, its persuasive cadences, or its spontaneous wit. It can kill. The magical thought of linguistic voodoo has been recorded to work. I will die simply because the death sentence through the bone of sorcery was pointed at me; named as the one due to die, I will wither away. Here my belief is necessary, but what I believe is the animated word's power. (2005: 5)

Riley's preoccupation in her first chapter, entitled 'Malediction' (a word that resonates forcefully with Galás's album *Malediction and Prayer*, 1998) is with something she describes as 'far darker' than 'righteous anger' spouted in harmful words. Instead, she focuses on the extreme 'sustained hostility of unremitting verbal violence, like the linguistic voodoo which can induce the fading away of its target' (2005: 10). Her writing is laboured with an acute awareness of the 'violently emotional materiality' of 'bad words' as they injure through verbal attacks that may well last far beyond the event of the attack itself and well after the attacker has become indifferent to the attacked or indeed died. She proposes a kind of 'indwelling' of malediction and 'affective words' that lodge in the accused, but are impersonal to the extent that they reverberate with power distinct from the speaker's intention, and certainly not 'mastered' by the speaker. Indeed, the furious accusers themselves are 'forcibly spoken' by a 'supremely indifferent' language: 'The rhetoric of rage speaks him mechanically and remorselessly. However much the accuser feels himself to triumph in the moment of his pronouncement, he is prey to echo' (Riley, 2005: 17). This is not however to diminish the affect on the accused. Malevolent affective words settle in the accused ('you are a bad person') and it is this indwelling of affective execrations and the violently emotional materiality of language that Galás's sound makes audible whilst it is nevertheless a power that defies individual/human mastery, settling in both the accused and the accuser.

Virtuosity: A necessity of performing the abject

Virtuosity in music is not a perceivable enemy in Galás's accounts of her practice; it is not something she wishes to utterly diminish; on the contrary, virtuosity implies a skill required in order to 'tell the story', to realize the song and to engage with the un-representable. Her work must exceed and move beyond the individualistic in order to bear the besetment of abjection in sound and practice and out of a deep and residing respect for the song, for music and what it can make intelligible in terms of power and its effects:

> Some people hear it as technique, because they can't hear anything but technique, so they think, 'Oh, its about virtuoso singing.' Are they mad? Why do they think a person would be a virtuoso? So they can tell the story properly! Why else? (Galás, cited in Oldham, 1999)

Galás raises the cultural figures and figurations of musical virtuosity whilst antagonizing the parameters of what virtuosity means, when it is assumed and to whom the term is applied. Her music breathes life into the notion of virtuosity and, at the same time, performs a critical autopsy of its ideological and predominantly gendered basis, corrupting and darkening its soundness by making audible a swarm of power, intention and agency that is both human and non-human. Abject and objectionable sounds, fluids, bodies, all of that which is ordinarily cast out of individual and social life and which does not usually substantiate the praise heaped upon the virtuoso, are here relished as vital forces of affect that blur the boundaries between subject and Other. This abominable series of amalgamations includes the immense capacities of dark feminine soundings, as they vitally hook up and connect abjected bodies, technologies and mythologies, to affect and be affected. Galás's vocal technique puts the signifiers of the dark feminine to work, mutating them into affects as an amendment of virtuosity that undermines the binary logic on which male genius is based, weaving together the rational with the irrational, the intelligible with that which has been culturally and socially rendered unintelligible. In the bleed between bodies, technology, sound and text, Galás's 'intravenal song' gets under the skin and into the bloodstream of the individualism, morality, gender binary and ideologies at the core of 'virtuosity', infecting it with the abject and establishing a porosity that invites other and Othered forces into the being of the 'Virtuoso'. In effect, her work forms an assemblage of power and agency that is human and non-human, complicating relationships of power, intentionality and agency in sound, in swarm.

Of these intelligibilities, multiple mutations of hybridized bodies pulsate and vibrate as currents in a network of virtuosos/virtuosity, mutations within her practice that seem to darken and subsume this network (distributive of value and virtues), undermine its terms of communication and identification, whilst simultaneously drawing power from it and making claims to it. In coming into contact with outcast mutations, the network of virtuosity itself is subjected to a virus that infects its virtues, techniques and values with the poisonous, impure emanations of the abject and all that has been abjected. Consequently, virtuosity is darkened by that which moves in the dark and moves in on the light, a pure virtuosity perverted and corrupted with impurities from which it distinguishes itself. These manoeuvres in the shadows of virtuosic limelight are themselves indicative of technique and skill in excess of virtuosity, and of a practice that is able to develop a broad enough perspective on power, from outside and within, that it can create a swarm of intentionality and strivings, conjoining forces. Whereas simple power structures might be thought of as relations between oppressor and oppressed, perpetrator and victim, Galás's practice appears to understand itself as part of an assemblage, to submerge and emerge within assemblages of power and violence, accruing the capacity to exert as much intentionality as possible and broadening the range of places to look for the sources of violence and harm, rather than pinpointing a single source (Bennett, 2010: 37). In this respect, 'patriarchy' is not so much let off the hook as interrogated more deeply, whilst binary gender itself is corrupted through the abject and a darkened virtuosity: a virtuosity not so much dismissed, but appropriated and infected with the abject and the antithesis of its qualities so that there is a cohabitation with the abject forced on to the legacy of virtuosity. Darkness is relished in Galás's composition and performance as that which is synonymous with the abject and, in contrast with the ideologies of light, immanently vital to the intelligibility of truth claims that states the fact: this happened. Her voices bid the listener to bear witness to the unsayable of dark abject truths.

Conclusion

Of the refrain – Is the future dark?

The future is dark, which is the best thing the future can be, I think.

(Virginia Woolf, [1915] 1981)

Relatively recently, perhaps since 2012, I have become more and more aware of the growing significance of the 'dark' in music and sound, and in correspondence with wider perceptions of the zeitgeist of these times. Dark threads in music and other cultural activities and artefacts produce a matrixial weave of consciousness, individual and shared, drawing together perceptions of mortality, uncertain threatening futures, war, refugee crises, climate change and ecocide in a 'now' haunted future that seems increasingly doomed to fail to materialize, 'to remain spectral' (Fisher, 2014: 107). In such haunted circumstances, 'light' it seems is perceived as being threatened with extinction, whilst the dark accrues momentum though a growing preoccupation with dark themes, dark art and dark times. Based on the speeches and political activism of movements such as The Women's March for example, there is a perceptible correlation between the subject of texts such as Hannah Arendt's *Men in Dark Times* ([1951] 2014) and Rebecca

Solnit's *Hope in the Dark* ([2005] 2016) and the current times as they, in this case, present a threat to women and people of colour; this 'dark' threat encompasses reinvigorated and emboldened extreme right ideological movements which seek to distinguish from and subjugate the Others it has created, whilst strategically monopolizing economic, social and political power. In her Women's March speech delivered on 21 February 2017 in Washington DC, Angela Davis extends the identities of the marchers beyond that of 'women' in an address to: 'women, trans-people, men and youth' who 'unify against racism and hetero-patriarchy' (Davis, 2017). She establishes a sense of the longevity, historical legacy and future purpose of the march through reference to struggles for social justice and environmental causes and to the potential of an inclusive intersectional feminism, consciously responsive to difference and privilege and collectively unified against the darkness: 'This is a women's march. And this women's march represents the promise of feminism as against the pernicious powers of state violence … an inclusive and intersectional feminism that calls upon all of us to join the resistance to racism, Islamophobia, to anti-Semitism, to misogyny, to capitalist exploitation […] we dedicate ourselves to collective resistance' (Davis, 2017). Unifying against these dark forces means, to some extent, forming a collective that shares an understanding of the threat and there is therefore a tension here between differences in experience, outlook and identity that Davis acknowledges through 'intersectional feminism', whilst nevertheless appealing for the necessity of unity and collective resistance. To this degree, light, implicitly or explicitly, provides a useful unifying radiance translated as hope and strength against dark powers. Nevertheless and perhaps rather counterintuitively, this book, guided by listening to dark sound, treats the darkness as vital to resistance, imagination, and to new forms of being and knowing in a context where darkness is threatened with extinction.

Darkness under threat

A dystopian 'vision' of a world without darkness is reflected in the concerns of an article titled 'Fear of the Light: Why We Need Darkness' (Petrusich, 2016), in which writer Amanda Petrusich discusses light pollution as it conceals 80 per cent of the North

American and European night sky. Excessive industrial artificial light prevents the experience of darkness through a combination of invasive lighting, air pollution and 'fracking'; a practice that involves energy companies rigging up 'colossal, stadium-style spotlights' and burning off 'excess gas in open pits or through steel pipes, in a process known as flaring' (Petrusich, 2016). The international dark sky association argues that the effects of light pollution 'overpower the darkness' and points to a growing body of evidence that links the atrophy of the darkness and the brightening of the night with detrimental effects on the ecosystem, wildlife and human health, as well as the more obvious links to the impact of energy consumption on the environment. Petrusich's article questions the effects of light pollution and the value of darkness in conversation with dark sky activist Susan Harder, historian A. Roger Ekirch and Matt Stanley (a specialist in astronomy, physics, history of science and religion). What emerges in their conversations and across a shared investment in preserving the dark skies, is the enormity of the challenge in changing attitudes towards the dark given that fear of the dark is linked to perceptions of intrinsic evil, of the dark as the antithesis of light, morality, truth and the light of God (God as the bearer of all light in Christian ideology), alongside the notion that darkness and the night-time is the harbinger and milieu of crime. Each of those interviewed attempts to bring about an appreciation of the colossal loss to humanity brought about by losing the dark and the ability to see the stars, something that, across the course of human development over millennia of different cultures, has provided a sense of the liminal space between the known and the unknown. Darkness therefore is linked to the very catalyst for thought itself as the human mind, inspired by the night-sky, attempts to conceive of the sublime, the beyond, the spiritual, the transcendental and the infinite. The contemporary relevance of light pollution is elaborated on by Ekirch in his *At Day's Close: A History of Nighttime* (2006) in his discussion about the growing visibility of the night in relation to broader enlightenment-related ideologies and principles, including particularly a critical study of enlightenment's disenchantment of the night. His study points to the implications of ever-increasing illumination and the obscuring glare of light pollution so that: 'Only in remote spots can one still glimpse the grandeur of the Milky Way' (Ekirch, 2006: 339). Ekirch's concluding comments bespeak a concern with the atrophy of the dream world (effected by losing segmented sleep) and with it, a loss of a deeper understanding of the inner self. The decrease in sleep and the dazzling illumination of the night emerges from the demands of capitalism and neoliberal economies; the combination takes its toll on the human psyche, the body, wildlife and ecological systems:

> The residual beauty of the night sky, alternating cycles of darkness and light, and regular respites from the daily round of sights and sounds – all will be impaired by enhanced illumination. Ecological systems, with their own patterns of nocturnal life, will suffer immeasurably. With darkness diminished, opportunities for privacy, intimacy, and self-reflection will grow more scarce. Should that luminous day arrive, we stand to lose a vital element of our humanity – one as precious as it is timeless. That, in the depths of the dark night, should be a bracing prospect for any spent soul to contemplate. (Ekirch, 2006: 339)

Such emphasis on the vitality of the dark and the necessity of a break from the 'luminous day', its sights, sounds and demands, suggests a critical disposition to illumination and the constant requirement to be on, available, responsive, to be visual and present. From this critical disposition and given the importance of 'going dark' to creativity, intimacy, dreaming, rest, the 'inner self' and nocturnal life, not only then should darkness be valued, the practice of going dark practiced, but, moreover, an understanding developed on how dark time and space are territorialized in the interests of neoliberalism, capitalism and 'dark forces' – this in order to 'reclaim the night'.

As Matthew Beaumont's *Nightwalking: A Nocturnal History of London* (2016) demonstrates, the territorialization of the night has a long history that speaks specifically of gender, class, race and ethnicity. His historical and cultural study of the night offers enthralling detailed insights into nightlife, the movement of city dwellers at night, and perceptions of night as they emerge in and through literature, paintings and historical documents in England during the period from the Middle Ages up until the mid-1800s. Beaumont focuses on London, a city that, following Paris, Lille, Amsterdam, Turin and Berlin, first acquired oil lamp street lighting in 1684, a date that roughly coincides with the first recorded instance of the verb 'to enlighten' acquiring a sense of 'imparting intellectual light' (Beaumont, 2016: 118). Paradoxically perhaps, this moment of illumination corresponds with both the

OF THE REFRAIN – IS THE FUTURE DARK? 209

disenchantment of the dark during the Enlightenment period as well as a re-enchantment of the streets at night effected by street lamps that light up theatrical territories for social actors who become the commingling classes of performers and spectators of the city (Beaumont, 2016: 120). At night, the lit city itself becomes different and the ways in which one moves through and behaves in urban space also differs in terms of interactions with other social actors, moving through a theatrical shadowy urban space and a temporality associated with sexual pleasure, intoxication, risk and lawlessness. In London during the 1700s, 'no-go areas' consisted of labyrinths of dark alleyways and unlit streets, mostly found in poorer districts that were without lighting. These were the 'pitch black' places most associated with lawlessness and the heightened (hidden) activity of vagabonds, drunks, criminals and prostitutes; as Beaumont writes: 'Like enlightenment, illumination was the privilege of the middle and upper classes'. (2016: 124) Class and gender are particularly relevant in accounts of night-time street movements in the metropolis and the laws that pertained to night-time pedestrians who consisted of gentrified 'nightwalkers' and the 'noctambulants' from the upper, ruling social classes, whereas the poor, 'noctivagants', were made up of the unemployed, the destitute, part-time workers, the aged and 'poorest of the immigrant Irish and Jews' (Beaumont, 2016: 136–40). Any women caught 'wandering' the street at night were automatically assumed to be prostitutes by the self-appointed male night patrollers and, as Beaumont discusses, the accounts related to 'female night walkers' demonstrate misogyny and misanthropy converging in what he refers to as the 'moral topography of the eighteenth century' (2016:137). Noctambulants appointed themselves the spiritual guardians and police of the night-time and were motivated by a curious blend of desires: to socialize, moralize and fantasize about and within the 'foreign territory' of the nocturnal streets. Beaumont's observations from these accounts are important; he writes:

> They [the noctambulants] made excursions into the nocturnal streets because they had chosen to do so, not because they had been exiled there by circumstance. They were on the side of illumination and socialisation, even if this meant something quite different in the cases of a dissolute nobleman and a puritanical preacher. They were colonizers of the night. (2016: 136)

This notion of night-time excursions by a privileged class, on the side of illumination, in relation to a set of identities and bodies associated with the dark (especially in reference to 'wandering' feminine sexuality) is highly significant because of its resonance with charged associations between the Other and the dark, an association that ripples through narratives which feature the figurative travelling bourgeois male subjects who, on the side of light and reason, carry out excursions into darkness and colonize the night. This book has aimed to demonstrate how the journeying into the night and into the dark inherited from the patriarchal, classed, Eurocentric, Enlightenment psyche permeates the discourse on sound and music, as well as the music itself, and the repercussions of this journey for understandings of the dark feminine in music and sound discourse. As such, I question the degree to which hope and optimism can be invested in 'light' and its synonyms, particularly given the complicity between ideologies of light and the neo-fascist and 'corporate cannibal' (Jones, 2008) world-eating machines. The works featured here sound an understanding of the threat to and the value of darkness as intrinsic to politicized practice, critical aesthetics and the dynamism between creation and destruction. In effect, dark sound critically agitates the rhetoric of optimism and the privilege and powers of the territories of light.

The crucial significance of dark space and night-time, made explicit by both Ekirch and Beaumont, is directly relevant to musicians and their spacetime. There is an energy derived from going into hiding that is not only useful to music makers, but is perceived in many ways as vitally productive in opposition to the unbearable glare of the public domain. Of this light, philosopher Martin Heidegger wrote, 'the light of the public obscures everything' (Heidegger, cited in Villa, 1999: 77), meaning that the public world is the 'locus of inauthenticity' and its light 'covers over the fundamental human existence as groundless, finite, and radically open or atelic' (Villa, 1999: 77). Taken as an obscuring force, contemporary parallels with this light can be drawn through the evolution of surveillance culture and social media. In the 'real' public realm, surveillance eyes with modified abilities reach across territorial boundaries of institutions and corporations to quietly infiltrate 'private' life more and more through strange data management systems that reach under the skin and into the head. In an online public world, anonymity appears to be a naive dream, given the

OF THE REFRAIN – IS THE FUTURE DARK? 211

relentless requirement for and storage of personal data and in such well-lit glaring worlds, the practice of 'going dark' accrues a greater and greater significance. Greater because 'going dark', however romantically perceived, poses the prospect of resistance to the permanent and ongoing visualization of the everyday (and night). In his book *Babbling Corpse: Vaporwave and the Commodification of Ghosts* (2016), Grafton Tanner discusses the commodification of music and the 'formless cloud' of music album evaluations, opinions and reviews 'that infiltrates our everyday' on countless media sites. Tanner's criticism is that this writing both declares and hideously parrots an album's value across 'mainstream music outlets' and social media, inducing a terrible fatigue that buries any enjoyment as well as differing critical opinion and, in doing so, encourages those tired of the 'too much' to 'go dark' in the unplugging sense: to try to rest the eyes from PR hype machines and the kind of online music writing 'where anything can be referenced and hyperlinked', the '"retero-historicism," "historical list-making," and "influence fishing"' (Tanner, 2016: 66). Broadly speaking, Tanner's argument raises the suggestion that the contemporary mainstream music industry has not just eradicated the 'body' but rather closed off meaning with unobtrusive, feel-good music. It has found a way to respond to the context of fear and a desire to return to the 'way things were', (specifically prior to 9/11), by selling sound coded with a (painful) nostalgic sense of the past. Unrestrained capitalistic music means 'the tendrils of capital have snaked their way into our nostalgia. Now even our desire to escape and retreat into the past is commodified' (Tanner, 2016: 59). And yet, the artists featured here suggest trajectories that challenge this conception through a different relationship with time (nostalgia being redundant) and the very idea (and practice) of 'going dark' in music and sound.

In general, it could be argued that despite attempts to eradicate darkness and meaning, perhaps even driven by the attempt to wash out all darkness with the proliferation of light, music emerges from impermeant dark audiotopias, the spacetimes formed out of the vicissitudes of dark sound and those that must evade the intolerable glare of the everyday. Night-time and dark spaces are territories familiar to music makers who disappear into basements, bedrooms, cellars, rehearsal rooms, squats, studios, garages, warehouses and places not ordinarily considered hospitable in domestic terms: rooms without windows, spaces underground without natural light, or 'in the box' with a pair of headphones capable of enabling and signalling a 'cutting off' from the outside. Musicians who make 'dark sound' understand that they will inevitably return to the space and time of gloaming, to the territories of the dark (real and metaphoric), to venues that come alive at night, to subterranean 'undergrounds' and to the non-places haunted by touring musicians and their vehicles in movements that reach an apotheosis between twilight and dawn: these times and spaces are vitally linked to identity and creative (and/or destructive) practice. In terms of space and location, music discourse and practice makes use of and actively develops the meaningful partnership between the 'underground' and 'darkness'. The very word 'underground', when it refers to music-based subcultures, conjures images of dark subterranean places undulating beneath the mainstream world in low bass vibrations. However, drawing from Beaumont's description of the noctambulants, even in these dark places, self-appointed colonizers of the night pervade 'on the side of illumination and socialisation' and in relation to the territories of designated 'dark' Others. The gendered, racialized and sexualized dimensions of the territorialization of the night and the dark spaces of music are challenged by the dark sound artists discussed in this book, not just in terms of the deterritorialization or reterritorialization of dark places, but through a practice that indicates a radically different space altogether: not a demarcated dark territory regained by dark Others, but boundless darkness that is the space of the future. Space not territory.

The tools of optimism

Darkness is generally defined in the negative, its literal meaning is 'the absence of light'. The dark does not receive, reflect or transmit radiant light and is particularly associated with night, with 'evil' and the 'unenlightened'. Concerned with the appeal of and attraction to dark themes and subjects, in an article featured in the *Times Higher Education*, academic Robert Zaretsky poses the question 'Why are students drawn to horror?', with a sub-heading that reads: 'Fascination with "dark studies" needs to be countered by studies of the Enlightenment' (2016). In the article, Zaretsky expresses his 'prosaic dread' that a course entitled 'Enlightenment

OF THE REFRAIN – IS THE FUTURE DARK? 213

Stories', 'devoted to the brightest and best of the 18th century', would fail to attract enough students to legitimize its survival. He proceeds to critically question what appears, to him, to be a current and worrying trend of student preference for 'dark' subject matters, and, moreover, classes 'devoted to "moral horror stories"' such as 'The Final Solution and Genocide' – which were 'perennial favourites'. Offering parallels between darkness and the study of 'self-identity', he writes that, 'alongside gender, queer, Jewish, women's and African American studies, we might consider adding "dark studies"'. Zaretsky rationalizes the draw of the 'Abyss' for students who lived and studied in time periods closer to that of the horror of Auschwitz and Hiroshima, and those 'living under the quotidian terror of nuclear conflagration' and asks whether it is any different for his own students, of whom he writes:

> They may well suspect that the Enlightenment, with its emphasis on the powers of human reason and the prospect of social progress and political justice, does not have much traction in the 21st century. Optimism – not just the cockeyed sort mocked by Voltaire in *Candide*, but the more reasonable kinds championed by, say, the American Founding Fathers – is *so* last year. Recent events, from Paris and San Bernardino to the various forms of hate-filled populism sweeping across Europe and the US, all seem to suggest that the forces of darkism, and not optimism, are in the ascendant. This reaction is understandable, but also regrettable. That we need to study the Abyss goes without saying. But it should be no less self-evident that this is best done by way of the tools, and hopes, given to us by the 18th century. (Zaretsky, 2016)

Zaretsky's suggestion that the 'forces of darkism' are ascending corresponds with the rise of populism, neo-fascism and white supremacy referred to also in the resistance discourse of The Women's March. In calling for the necessity of optimism, the article parallels many of the march's speakers' references to the necessity of optimism and the requirement for hope. However, the underside of Zaretsky's desire for optimist studies is less inclined towards an affinity with the chain of critical discourses he identifies and to which he links 'dark studies' in opposition with the study of human reason, social progress and the Enlightenment. Moreover, the disciplines he lists ('gender, queer, Jewish, women's and African American studies' and its added extra, 'dark studies'), invested as they are in questions of identity, might well reveal that the study of darkness (here broadly imagined as hate, violence and horror) is inextricably bound to Enlightenment stories. Furthermore, such disciplines problematize the desire to reconnect with optimism on the basis of the 'Founding Fathers', as if such reunification were naturally opposed to the current forces of 'darkism' in ascendance to which the author refers, as if this reunification were naturally predisposed to a greater, more hopeful 'light' and principles of 'justice'. The wider implication of the voices of 'founding fathers' in a patriarchal society that is less and less inclined to conceal misogyny, racism, homophobia and any of its pathological fears, cannot be detached from the study of the 'abyss', as I hope I have shown in my tracing of the essentialized and mythologized association between women and the dark and specifically between femininity, singing, sound, music and the dark.

Once the 'tools' of enlightenment and optimism have been problematized, the very idea of being in pursuit of knowledge and of 'shining a light' on an object is in itself open to critical scrutiny. Notwithstanding an atypical fear of the dark (epically attuned to the structure of Western thought and its fear of the 'unknown'), to be 'kept in the dark' is a terrible fate that, in Enlightenment terms, means not only to be denied knowledge and its intellectual apprehension, but also to become more vulnerable to the dark's synonymy with the primitive and uncivilized matter of the world lodged in the 'dark ages'. Knowledge and what it means to have knowledge, is guided by a logic situated between seeing (allowing for the cultivation of belief as 'I see it with my own eyes') and visual occlusion (where I am prevented from seeing and more readily predisposed to uncertainty). So accustomed are Western thinkers to the moral connotations of light and the light of knowledge that it is difficult to imagine the pursuit of truth, or the discoveries of learning, to be organized around a trajectory towards the dark, or linked to anything other than 'founding fathers'. Before and after the period known as the 'Enlightenment' and across centuries of Western discourses, the shifting meanings of the dark echo across oceans of colonial, scientific, literary and religious texts that have worked to attach darkness to bodies, times and places as they delimit the 'unknown' and the 'unknowable'. These bodies are feminized, racially and sexually encoded and designated as the dark 'Other' consigned to metaphorical regions imagined as 'dark' territories. Self-anointed 'brave' travellers navigate journeys of discovery throughout these regions via a cultural understanding of their own subjectivity, the centrality of (Eurocentric) location and their own irrevocable 'light'. History, knowledge and music discourse are made up of the traces of these voyages, which depend upon mythologies of the feminized, racialized dark in order to define a superior self over the other, the legitimacy of colonization and territorialization and also to draw capital from convincing one's privileged group of the risk of the journey: this is the constructed danger that defines masculine engagement with the dark.

Emerging in the concerns of Zaretsky's article is this very logic of distinction from the dark that orchestrates my critical suspicion of the 'tools, and hopes, given to us by the 18th century', and calls to mind the words of Audre Lorde who argues that using the 'master's tools' will ultimately narrow and limit the possibility for change with respect to feminist, anti-racist and anti-homophobic activism. Using the master's tools might well offer a temporary win ('beat him at his own game'), but ultimately the question Lorde poses is 'What does it mean when the tools of a racist patriarchy are used to examine the fruits of that same patriarchy?' (Lorde, [1979] 2007: 110–11) Working from this point, in a similar mode of questioning, one might ask what it means to use the tools and hope of the Enlightenment to study the dark as the culturally-assigned realm of the feminine and 'exotic' Others? Further still, what is the nature of the hope to be derived from these stories and what kinds of powers are served by this optimism? Even optimism has a dark side that hides behind presentations of state-sponsored joyousness and this is raised and countered by writers such as Andrew Culp who, in *Dark Deleuze* (2016), draws from the darkness he discerns in a dark Deleuzian philosophy, proposing a 'revolutionary negativity in a world characterized by compulsory happiness, decentralized control, and overexposure' (Culp, 2016: 2). Robyn James's critique of Western capitalism's 'resilience discourse' similarly adopts the darkness of melancholic song as that which counters and corrodes the hegemonic common sense of neoliberalism, which invests in resilience, 'health' and 'bouncing back' from adversity in an industrious recuperation of the capital of damage (James, 2015). And, more recently, the environmental activist Greta Thunberg's statement to the World Economic Forum (WEF) in Davos (2019) explicitly defied the rhetoric of optimism by calling for a response to the climate crisis commensurate to the threat, one that demands not hope but panic in order to initiate action and shock out of complacency.

In correspondence with these critical approaches to light/ optimism, the artists herein make sound that, in various ways, values darkness and its equations with negativity, anti-resilient melancholy, taboo eroticism, shocks of rage and jolts of panic. They make music and sound formed from agglomerations of the 'monstrous power of the scream' (Culp, 2016) and the immense physicality and materiality of the singing voice and instrumental voicing as it tears at the fabric of language at the threshold of the unspeakable. Their assemblages of technology, the human and the non-human, work at this threshold between communication and non-communication in blood-curdling affective text, haunting spectral sound, electronic beats, painful abrasive noise, all woven into the fabric of song. Each of the artists discussed in this book develops a unique singularity that recalls the value of darkness and the suppressed powers of the dark feminine. The forgotten powers of the Sirens are particularly pertinent in this regard in that their dark song speaks not of seduction but of 'an uncanny ability to raise the voices of the dead, to bring the past to life in the present' (Engh, 1996: 134) in song that tells of all that is, has and will happen on earth: this is the cyclical bending of time in Moor Mother's BQF practice or the embodiment of unspeakable suffering and genocidal horror in a work by Diamanda Galás such as *Defixiones*. Their dark menacing awakening moves through sonic affects, demanding that the listener hears and feels the wreckage of catastrophe and its truths in the imagery and assonance between the forces, rhythms and intensities of sound. Their work demonstrates that darkness is not inimical to truth, but the condition for the rethinking of being, time and knowledge.

Dark futures

Writing during the unprecedented scale of destruction that unfolded across the period of the First World War, Virginia Woolf wrote in her journal, 'The future is dark, which is the best thing the future can be, I think' (Woolf, [1915] 1981). Her words stick because they suggest an atypical relationship with the dark. How, during such

OF THE REFRAIN – IS THE FUTURE DARK? 217

unbearably 'dark times', could a writer find hope in speculating on the darkness of the future? Whilst it seems from this excerpt that hope emerges from the unpredictability and uncertainty of a 'dark future', we cannot be sure whether Woolf is writing about a personal or collective future, the future of her own life or that of the world. Either way, there is, for her, some comfort to be drawn from the dark when it means the unknown, the unforeseen. Gilles Deleuze and Félix Guattari begin their plateau '1837: Of the Refrain' with the comfort derived from singing in the dark:

> A child in the dark, gripped with fear, comforts himself by singing under his breath. He walks and halts to his song. Lost, he takes shelter, or orients himself with his little song as best he can. The song is like a rough sketch of a calming and stabilizing, calm and stable, center in the heart of chaos. (Deleuze and Guattari, [1987] 2003: 311)

Singing his little song, the child sketches a moving calm and stable centre that, although vulnerable, establishes the beginnings of order as a thread of orientation through the darkness of chaos. Lyrics, rhythm and harmony, forces of organization within the song, might launch into an improvization 'on the thread of a tune', leaving the territory. Humming to summon strength, singing to oneself in the face of adversity, radios playing, the sound of a television set, these are the sonorous building blocks for walls that mark territories against the forces of chaos and destruction, which mark 'home' and 'one's space' (Deleuze and Guattari, [1987] 2003: 311). When the territorial circle opens, it is not necessarily to rejoin the forces of chaos, but on the side of newness, to join with the potential of 'cosmic forces': chaos, terrestrial and cosmic forces 'all of these confront each other and converge in the territorial refrain' (Deleuze and Guattari, [1987] 2003: 312). Deleuze and Guattari write that the three movements of the 'Refrain', are found in horror stories, fairy tales and lieder, and this is considered by the philosophers in relation to a black hole:

> Sometimes chaos is an immense black hole in which one endeavours to fix a fragile point as a centre. Sometimes one organizes around that point a calm and stable 'pace' (rather than form): the black hole has become a home. Sometimes one grafts

onto that pace a breakaway from the black hole. (Deleuze and Guattari, [1987] 2003: 312)

Singing to orientate oneself in the darkness, singing to mark a territory, can be interpreted as survival in dark times, despite the fragility of that sketched centre and impermanent defences, permeable always to chaos, 'dark times' and 'dark forces'. I have argued that the meaning of darkness in relation to light is based on hierarchal binary logic and, often occulted, ideological attributions of value that have gendered dimensions. I am therefore interested in the black hole set up by Deleuze and Guattari and its relationship to darkness, chaos, singing and sound, particularly the suggestion that 'the black hole has become a home'.

To the degree that a black hole is comprehended as metaphorically and metaphysically silent, uncanny engulfment, utter negation, abject matter, sublime 'edge', and/or the ultimate unknown, it corresponds with an understanding of women's (uncanny, homely, unhomely) bodies based on lack (in psychoanalytical terms) and the construction of notions that the 'mouths' of a woman's body lead to a 'dark continent' at the edge of language, knowability and intelligible rationality. The alliance therefore between light, knowledge, language and Man has afforded a movement that allows him to venture into the dark to return to the knowledgeable status and privileges of the light with the increased value of the dark's cultural capital, whereas, arguably the black hole is always already Woman's 'home' where she remains static in relation to Man's movement, his journey. Her relationship therefore to the forces of darkness, the pace with which one organizes around a centre and even what constitutes a calm centre, potentially differ from that of standard perceptions of what constitutes fear in the dark or how territories are sketched in song and with sound. For example, Deleuze and Guattari, as one of the examples of sonic 'home' delineation, refer very briefly to a 'housewife' who sings to herself to establish order against the forces of chaos: 'A housewife sings to herself, or listens to the radio, as she marshals the antichaos forces of her work' (2003: 311). However, the housewife's singing, or whatever she is listening to on the radio, might just as well be the deliberate summoning of the forces of chaos so as to formulate a breakaway from the calm static centre of 'home', to form an astral duplication of herself or to commit a sonic shadow that ventures further into the darkness, as refuge from antichaos and as the potential for the unknown in opposition to the order of the known. Her breakaway is not therefore necessarily away from the black hole, but further into it, through a desire to meld with the darkness beyond the territorialized predesignated 'home' which has made the black hole, darkness and women's bodies synonymous with all that is fearful and in opposition to the light, towards newness and unknown beings and futures. This future is dark. Through her song, the cosmic housewife, like science fiction, draws as yet unimagined futures from travelling through black holes as portals to other worlds, exciting imagination and possibilities for new being, time and space, beyond her static terrestrial self. This is a political move that cannot be distinguished from the 'dark times' in which one finds or loses oneself.

I have interpreted therefore, in the dark sound of the artists featured here, a movement further into the dark. Their movement into the dark is a resistance strategy that seeks to destabilize and obliterate binary logic and the hierarchal privilege that aligns maleness, whiteness, knowledge, light and movement, but it is more than resistance: their practice moves beyond reactions against misogyny and patriarchy. A future conceived as dark is about moving further into the darkness through which femininity has been constructed and with which the 'darkness' of the feminine has been aligned. As such, the future is not orientated around endeavours to establish a place in the limelight or the journey forward that assumes and privileges bodies aligned with the light. Light is not 'home' for the dark feminine. Instead of a paradigm in which from the blackness and from the shadows, darkened and marginalized bodies seek the limelight of a privileged centre, these artists move further into the shadows, antagonizing the light, but also moving outwards farther into unknown space/time that elicits desire and opens up the feminine to countless becomings and unbecomings. This is a subversive movement, but it is an operation beyond subversive challenges and resistance, one that tends towards the cosmic darkness of the unknown, connecting with a strange desire that imagines both a self and that which radically exceeds the self. Such artists are much more interested in the ability to formulate connections than they are the binary logic of this or that. These are artists whose practice of connections privilege the 'and' of the shadows. This is the movement of dark sound as it gathers momentum through the dark feminine, neither mainstream or underground, but of and from the darkness. The future is dark.

NOTES

Introduction

1   For an extensive study of the relationship between music and the occult, mysticism and magic in avant-garde, experimental and pop music, see John Zorn's edited collection of essays in *Arcana V* (2010).

2   Stephen Heath (a translator for Roland Barthes's work) notes the difficulty in translating the full meaning of 'jouissance' and Barthes's deployment of it. 'The American translation of *Le Plaisir du texte* (*The Pleasure of the Text*, New York, 1995) uses the word "bliss" for *jouissance*; […] it also brings with it connotations of religious and social contentment ("heavenly bliss", "blissfully happy") which damagingly weaken the force of the original French term.' Stephen Heath, 'Translator's Note' (Heath, in Barthes, 1977: 9). And further, 'The problem [of translation] would be less acute were it not that *jouissance* is specifically contrasted to *plaisir* by Barthes in his *Le Plaisir du texte*: on the one hand a pleasure (*plaisir*) linked to cultural enjoyment and identity, to the cultural enjoyment of identity, to a homogenizing movement of the ego; on the other a radically violent pleasure (*jouissance*) which shatters – dissipates, loses – that cultural identity.' Stephen Heath, 'Translator's Note' (Heath, in Barthes, 1977: 9).

Chapter 1

1   There are many aspects of Benjamin's 'The Storyteller' that compare with Piaf's song and the greatness of her storytelling. Benjamin writes of the storyteller's 'sage-like' abilities: 'For he [the storyteller] is granted the ability to reach back through a whole lifetime (a life, incidentally, that comprises not only his own experience but much of the hearsay of others, what the storyteller knows from hearsay is added to what is most his own). His gift is the ability to relate his life; his distinction, to be able to relate his *entire* life.' Benjamin

NOTES

also draws attention to the 'sensory aspect' of storytelling, meaning that it is not only the voice deployed in telling a story, but other gestures of the body such as 'the work-seasoned gestures of the hand' – gestures for which Piaf herself was famous. See Benjamin, W. (1969), 'The Storyteller', in *Illuminations*, New York: Schocken Books, 162.

Chapter 2

1   Barthes in his essay, 'The Grain of the Voice' credits the development of the 'genosong' and the 'phenosong' to Julia Kristeva's understanding of the production of meaning. Kristeva writes of :'The signifying process [that] therefore includes both the genotext and the phenotext; indeed it could not do otherwise. For it is in language that a theoretical approach may attempt to perceive that operation. In our view, the process we have just described accounts for the way all signifying practices are generated' (Kristeva, [1974] 2002: 54). Barthes elaborates on the genosong as the space in which signification germinates 'from within the language and in its very materiality; it forms a signifying play having nothing to do with communication, representation (of feelings), expression; it is that apex (or that depth) of production where the melody really works at the language – not at what it says, but the voluptuousness of its sounds- signifiers, of its letters – where melody explores how the language works and identifies with that work' (Barthes, 1977: 182).

Chapter 3

1   Carolyn Muessig uses the account of Lutgard's singing as an example of the perception of the female singer as a vessel for 'divine' harmony and spiritual teachings. She quotes from an account of Lutgard's singing: 'When Lutgard sang the liturgy of the day it seemed to him that "Christ, with the outward appearance of a lamb, was positioning Himself on her breast in such a manner that one foot was on her right shoulder and the other on the left. He would place his mouth on her mouth and be thus sucking, would draw out from her breast a melody of wondrous mellowness."' (Muessig, 1998: 152–3). See also Bruce Holsinger's discussion of Hildegard Von Bingen and her vocal compositions. Holsinger

attributes an 'openness' to Hildegard's 'melodic gestures' in that her compositions 'open the musical body to the touch of divinity, expressing Hildegard's awareness of women's flesh as a site of erotic exchange with the divine' (Holsinger, 2001: 115). This 'erotic' exchange is informed by a type of sadomasochistic violence combining pain, violence and pleasure, insofar as, according to Holsinger, Hildegard's compositions dictated extraordinary and excessive demands on the female bodies which were to sing them, and, further, these demands had perhaps a *'punitive purpose'* that deliberately foregrounded the *'disabilities'* of the nuns, rather than celebrating the wonder of their vocal *abilities* (Holsinger, 2001: 113).

2 Muessig writes that the 'genius' of women at this time 'was understood to be solely the result of divinely infused knowledge'. However, she states the important point that: 'This understanding created a platform upon which women could discuss theological lessons while not appearing to do so' (Muessig, 1998: 153).

3 It is pertinent here to mention that 'The End' was used in Francis Ford Coppola's *Apocalypse Now* (1979), both at the beginning and the end of the film, a film based on Joseph Conrad's novel *Heart of Darkness* in which a white man travels down the mouth of a river and into an unknown land imagined as the 'dark continent' of Africa (see Introduction).

Chapter 5

1 See George Monbiot's article 'The big polluter's masterstroke was to blame the climate crisis on you and me' (The *Guardian*, 9 October 2019) where he argues that the term 'Sixth Great Extinction' should be replaced by the 'first great extermination'.

2 See Cindy Milstein's edited collection of essays for extended discussions on the practice of rebellious mourning: (2017) *Rebellious Mourning: The Collective Work of Grief*. Chico, CA and Edinburgh: AK Press.

Chapter 6

1 For an extended discussion on 'technology as a language of action' and its gendered dimensions, see Lowe Benston, Margaret (1988), 'Women's Voices/Men's Voices: Technology as Language', in Cheris

NOTES
223

Kramarae (ed.). *Technology and Women's Voices: Keeping in Touch.* London and New York: Routledge.

2   After a performance of *Plague Mass* in Rome, Galás was accused of being 'anti-Christian' and 'more blasphemous than Madonna'. A quick glance at some of her track and album titles would look to confirm the reactionary charges: *The Litanies of Satan* (1982), *You Must Be Certain of the Devil* (1988), *The Divine Punishment and Saint of the Pit* (1989) and on the offending performance in this case *Plague Mass 1984 – End of the Epidemic* (1991) and with titles that include: 'I Wake Up and I See the Face of The Devil', 'Consecration' and 'Sono L'Antichristo'. Having been questioned on her reaction to such Christian criticisms and accusations, Galás ('with laughter') exclaims: 'I just say "Go with God" [...] If I were to spend time explaining to imbeciles why my music isn't blasphemous, I wouldn't have time to make more blasphemous music' (Galás, cited in Gottschalk, 2008: 27).

3   'You know, singers try to imitate what I do and they tell me, "I tried to do that last night, and then I couldn't sing for a week." And I say, "Well, that's not my fault, is it? I respect you for trying, but it's a craft like anything else. I'm not just screaming. Really I'm not." So if a person approaches it as screaming, they get the rewards of screaming. They won't be able to sing for a week!' (Galás, cited in Oldham, 1999).

4   'It's mandatory if you want to extend the voice, doing the kind of work I do, to know what you're doing technically. [...] But also later on I was studying, because what I was trying to do was theoretically impossible, in many ways. It was an attempt to be able to do a lot of what horn players do with circular breathing – but voices, we don't have circular breathing' (Galás, cited in Payne, 2008: 41).

5   Dido Soteriou was a journalist and novelist who wrote and published *Bloody Earth* in 1962 and the English edition *Farewell Anatolia* was published in 1996.

6   In 1992, Francis Ford Coppola hired Galás to provide demonic sound effects for his film *Bram Stoker's Dracula*.

7   See Felstiner, John. (ed.) (2001), *Selected Poems and Prose of Paul Celan.* London: Norton; Baer, Ulrich. (2000), *Remnants of Song: Trauma and the Experience of Modernity in Charles Baudelaire and Paul Celan.* Stanford: Stanford University Press.

8   Galás attributes some of her inspiration for these experiments with no longer vocal (yet vocal sounds) to the treatment of sounding material in Pierre Henry and Pierre Schaeffer's tape concrete experiments and their spatial manipulations of sound. '[Pierre Henry] did a record called *A Door and a Sigh*. And he'd have the closing of a door and the sigh, and that would be it. And he would

have to manipulate those two signals alone, over a period of twenty minutes. And he made that so incredibly effective, with the tape manipulation and with spatial manipulation. And I heard that, and I said "you know … yeah!" I mean, he's not using a voice, but it's irrelevant what material you're using' (Galás, cited in Flinn, 1996).

REFERENCES

Adler, Shelley R. (2011), *Sleep Paralysis: Night-Mares, Nocebos, and the Mind-Body Connection*, New Brunswick, New Jersey and London: Rutgers University Press.

Adorno, Theodor W. (1990), 'The Curves of the Needle', *October*, 55: 49–55.

Allsopp, Ric. (2016), 'On Sleep', *Performance Research*, 21 (1): 1–5.

Appleford, Steve. (2017), 'Chelsea Wolfe: In Search of Brutal Honesty', *Revolver*, 31 August. Available online: https://www.revolvermag.com/music/chelsea-wolfe-search-brutal-honesty (accessed 10 September 2017).

Arendt, Hannah. ([1951] 2014), *Men in Dark Times*, Altrincham: Stellar Books.

Artaud, Antonin. ([1938] 1974), 'No More Masterpieces', in Bernard F. Dukore (ed.), *Dramatic Theory and Criticism: Greeks to Grotowski*, 760–6, New York: Jovanovich College Publishers.

Attali, Jacques. (1985), *Noise: The Political Economy of Music*, Manchester: Manchester University Press.

Ayewa, Camae. (2016a), *Fetish Bones*, Philadelphia: Afrofuturist Affair/House of Future Sciences Books.

Ayewa, Camae. (2016b), 'Sights and Sounds of the Passage', in Rasheedah Phillips (ed.), *Black Quantum Futurism Space-Time Collapse I: From the Congo to the Carolinas*, 9–13, Philadelphia: Afrofuturist Affair/House of Future Sciences Books.

Bakhtin, Mikhail. (1984), *Rabelais and His World*, Bloomington: Indiana University Press.

Bangs, Lester. (1971), 'Nico: A Kind of Frozen Purity', *Fusion*, 12 November. Available online: https://www.rocksbackpages.com/Library/Article/nico-a-kind-of-frozen-purity (accessed 27 July 2017).

Bangs, Lester. ([1983] 2003), 'Your Shadow Is Scared of You: An Attempt Not to Be Frightened by Nico', in John Morthland (ed.), *Mainlines, Blood Feasts, and Bad Taste: A Lester Bangs Reader*, 205–13, New York: Random House.

Barthes, Roland. ([1967] 1977), 'The Death of the Author', in Roland Barthes, *Image-Music-Text*, 142–8, London: Fontana Press.

Barthes, Roland. ([1972] 1977), 'The Grain of the Voice', in Roland Barthes, *Image-Music-Text*, 179–89, London: Fontana Press.

Barthes, Roland. ([1975] 1991), 'Rasch', in Roland Barthes, *The Responsibility of Forms: Critical Essays on Music, Art, and Representation*, 299–312, Berkeley and Los Angeles: University of California Press.

Barthes, Roland. ([1976] 1991), 'The Romantic Song', in Roland Barthes, *The Responsibility of Forms: Critical Essays on Music, Art, and Representation*, 286–92, Berkeley and Los Angeles: University of California Press.

Barthes, Roland. ([1977] 1990), *A Lover's Discourse: Fragments*, London: Penguin.

Barthes, Roland. ([1977] 1991), 'Music, Voice, Language', in Roland Barthes, *The Responsibility of Forms: Critical Essays on Music, Art, and Representation*, 278–85, Berkeley and Los Angeles: University of California Press.

Barthes, Roland. ([1979] 1991), 'Loving Schumann', in Roland Barthes, *The Responsibility of Forms: Critical Essays on Music, Art, and Representation*, 293–8, Berkeley and Los Angeles: University of California Press.

Barthes, Roland. ([1980] 2000), *Camera Lucida: Reflections on Photography*, London: Vintage.

Battaglia, Andy. (2018), 'At the Kitchen, Moor Mother Haunts Ghosts from the Future', *ARTnews*, 21 March. Available online: http://www.artnews.com/2018/03/21/kitchen-moor-mother-haunts-ghosts-future (accessed 27 March 2018).

Battersby, Christine. (1989), *Gender and Genius: Towards a Feminist Aesthetics*, Bloomington: Indiana University Press.

Baudrillard, Jean. ([1986] 2010), *America*, London and New York: Verso.

Baudrillard, Jean. (1991), *Seduction*, New York: St Martin's Press.

Bayton, Mavis. (1998), *Frock Rock: Women Performing Popular Music*, Oxford: Oxford University Press.

Beaumont, Matthew. (2016), *Nightwalking: A Nocturnal History of London*, London: Verso.

Beaumont-Thomas, Ben. (2017), 'Moor Mother: "We Have Yet to Truly Understand What Enslavement Means"', the *Guardian*, 20 April. Available online: https://www.theguardian.com/music/2017/apr/20/moor-mother-hip-hop-artist-camae-ayewa-black-experience-civil-rights-interview (accessed 25 April 2017).

Bell, Ilona. (2010), 'Rethinking Shakespeare's Dark Lady', in Michael Schoenfeldt (ed.), *A Companion to Shakespeare's Sonnets*, 293–313, West Sussex: John Wiley & Sons.

REFERENCES 227

Benjamin, Walter. (1969), 'The Storyteller: Reflections on the Works of Nicolai Leskov', in Walter Benjamin, *Illuminations*, 83–110, New York: Schocken Books.

Bennett, Jane. (2010), *Vibrant Matter: A Political Ecology of Things*, Durham and London: Duke University Press.

Björk. (1997), [Sound recording: CD] *Homogenic*, London: One Little Indian Records.

Björk. (2015a), [Exhibition from 8 January–7 June 2015] *Björk Retrospective*, New York: Museum of Modern Art.

Björk. (2015b), [Sound recording: CD] *Vulnicura*, London: One Little Indian Records.

Brakes, Rob. (2018), 'Anna Calvi: "There's This Place between Trying to Be a Master of Your Instrument, but Then Also Being Right on the Edge of the Cliff"', *MusicRadar*, 17 October. Available online: https://www.musicradar.com/news/anna-calvi-theres-this-place-between-trying-to-be-a-master-of-your-instrument-but-then-also-being-right-on-the-edge-of-the-cliff (accessed 14 November 2018).

Brault, Pascale-Anne and Michael Naas. (2003), 'To Reckon with the Dead: Jacques Derrida's Politics of Mourning', in Jacques Derrida (ed.), *The Work of Mourning*, 1–30, Chicago: The University of Chicago Press.

Brecht, Bertolt. (1987), *Bertolt Brecht Poems, 1913–1956*, York: Methuen.

Brendt, Logan. (2012), 'Chelsea Wolfe', *LADYGUNN*, 19 April. Available online: http://www.ladygunn.com/music/chelsea-wolfe/ (accessed 13 October 2016).

Bridle, James. (2018), *New Dark Age: Technology, Knowledge and the End of the Future*, London and New York: Verso Books.

Bronfen, Elisabeth. (1992), *Over Her Dead Body: Death, Femininity and the Aesthetic*, Manchester: Manchester University Press.

Bronfen, Elisabeth. (2013), *Night Passages: Philosophy, Literature, and Film*, New York: Columbia University Press.

Brozzoni, Vera. (2017), 'Completing the Mystery of Her Flesh: Love, Eroticism, and Identity in Björk's Videos', in Gina Arnold, Daniel Cookney, Kirsty Fairclough and Michael Goddard (eds), *Music/Video: Histories, Aesthetics, Media*, 109–120, New York: Bloomsbury.

Burton, Robert. ([1621] 2001), *The Anatomy of Melancholy*, New York: New York Review of Books.

Butler, Judith. ([1988] 2003), 'Performative Acts and Gender Constitution', in Amelia Jones (ed.), *The Feminism and Visual Culture Reader*, 392–402, London and New York: Routledge.

Butler, Judith. (1997), 'On Linguistic Vulnerability', in *Excitable Speech: A Politics of the Performative*, 1–41, London: Routledge.

Calvi, Anna. (2011), [Sound recording: CD] *Anna Calvi*, London: Domino Records.

Calvi, Anna. (2013), [Sound recording: CD] *One Breath*, London: Domino Records.

Calvi, Anna. (2018), [Sound recording: CD] *Hunter*, London: Domino Records.

Carr, Cynthia. (1993), *On Edge: Performance at the End of the Twentieth Century*, Middletown: Wesleyan University Press.

Carson, Anne. (1995), 'The Gender of Sound', in Anne Carson, *Glass, Irony and God*, 119–42, New York: New Directions.

Cave, Nick. (2000), [Sound recording: CD] *The Secret Life of the Love Song & The Flesh Made Word: Two Lectures by Nick Cave*, London: Mute Records.

Chare, Nicholas. (2007), 'The Grain of the Interview: Introducing Diamanda Galás', *parallax*, 13(1): 56–64.

Chare, Nicholas, D Ferrett and Diamanda Galás. (2007), 'Entwined Voices: An Interview with Diamanda Galás', *parallax*, 13(1): 65–73.

Chion, Michel. ([1982] 1999), *The Voice in Cinema*, New York: Columbia University Press.

Chion, Michel. ([1990] 1994), *Audio-Vision: Sound on Screen*, New York: Columbia University Press.

Citron, Marcia J. ([1993] 2000), *Gender and the Musical Canon*, Urbana and Chicago: University of Illinois Press.

Cixous, Hélène. (1976), 'The Laugh of the Medusa', *Signs: Journal of Women in Culture and Society*, 1(4): 875–93.

Cohen, Leonard. (2012), [Sound recording: CD] *Old Ideas*, Canada: Sony Music Canada Inc.

Conrad, Joseph. ([1899] 2014), *Heart of Darkness*, Open Road Media. Available online: http://ebookcentral.proquest.com/lib/falmouth-ebooks/detail.action?docID=1805200 (accessed 15 October 2019).

Cope, Julian. (2007), 'Julian Cope Presents Head Heritage | Unsung | Album of the Month | Nico - The Marble Index', *Head Heritage*, March. Available online: https://www.headheritage. co.uk/unsung/albumofthemonth/nico-the-marble-index (accessed 25 July 2017).

Cox, Christopher. (2005), 'A La Recherche d'une Musique Féminine', in Anne Hilde Neset and Lina Dzuverovic-Russell (eds), *Her Noise*, 7–13, London: Forma. Available online: http://faculty.hampshire.edu/ccox/Cox.Musique%20Feminine.pdf (accessed 17 June 2017).

Creed, Barbara. (2005), *Phallic Panic: Film, Horror and the Primal Uncanny*, Melbourne: Melbourne University Press.

Creed, Barbara. (2015), *The Monstrous-Feminine: Film, Feminism, Psychoanalysis*, London and New York: Routledge.

REFERENCES

Crenshaw, Kimberlé. (1989), 'Demarginalizing the Intersection of Race and Sex: A Black Feminist Critique of Antidiscrimination Doctrine, Feminist Theory and Antiracist Politics', *University of Chicago Legal Forum*, 1989(1): 139–67.

Culp, Andrew. (2016), *Dark Deleuze*, Minneapolis: University of Minnesota Press.

Dalton, David. (2002), 'Nico and *The Marble Index*: A Conversation with Danny Fields', *Gadfly*. Available online: http://www.rocksbackpages.com/Library/Article/nico-and-the-marble-index-a-conversation-with-danny-fields (accessed 21 July 2017).

Daly, Mary. ([1973] 1986), *Beyond God the Father: Towards a Philosophy of Women's Liberation*, London: The Women's Press Limited.

Davis, Angela Y. (1999), *Blues Legacies And Black Feminism: Gertrude 'Ma' Rainey, Bessie Smith and Billie Holiday*, New York: Vintage Books.

Davis, Angela. (2017), 'Angela Davis's, Women's March Speech: "This country's history cannot be deleted"', The *Guardian*, 22 January. Available online: https://www.theguardian.com/commentisfree/2017/jan/22/angela-davis-womens-march-speech-countrys-history-cannot-be-deleted (accessed 22 January 2017).

Deleuze, Gilles and Félix Guattari. ([1987] 2003), *A Thousand Plateaus: Capitalism and Schizophrenia*, London: Continuum.

Demers, Joanna. (2010), *Listening through the Noise: The Aesthetics of Experimental Electronic Music*, Oxford: Oxford University Press.

Derrida, Jacques. (2003), *The Work of Mourning*, Chicago: The University of Chicago Press.

Diamond, Elin. (1999), 'Mimesis, Mimicry and the "True-Real"', in Lynda Hart and Peggy Phelan (eds), *Acting Out: Feminist Performances*, 365–83, Ann Arbor: University of Michigan Press.

Diamanda Galás. (2017), [Self-titled website]. Available online: http://diamandaGalas.com/ (accessed 23 June 2017).

Dibben, Nicola. (2009), *Björk*, Sheffield: Equinox Publishing Ltd.

Diva. (2018), 'Letting Go with Art Rock Singer Songwriter Anna Calvi', August. Available online: http://www.divamag.co.uk/Diva-Magazine/Celebs/Letting-go-with-art-rock-singer-songwriter-Anna-Calvi/ (accessed 1 September 2018).

Dodds, Joseph. (2011), *Psychoanalysis and Ecology at the Edge of Chaos: Complexity Theory, Deleuze, Guattari and Psychoanalysis for a Climate in Crisis*, London and New York: Routledge.

Domino Records. (2014), 'Anna Calvi', *Dominorecordco*. Available online: http://www.dominorecordco.com/artists/anna-calvi/ (accessed 21 January 2018).

Downes, Julia (ed.). (2012), *Women Make Noise: Girl Bands from Motown to the Modern*, Twickenham: Supernova Books.

REFERENCES

Eco, Umberto. (1995), 'Ur-Fascism', *The New York Review of Books*, 22 June. Available online: https://www.pegc.us/archive/Articles/eco_ur-fascism.pdf (accessed 3 June 2018).

Ekirch, A. Roger. (2006), *At Day's Close: A History of Nighttime*, London: Phoenix.

Engh, Barbara. (1993), 'Loving It: Music and Criticism in Roland Barthes', in Ruth A. Solie (ed.), *Musicology and Difference: Gender and Sexuality in Music Scholarship*, 66–82, Berkeley and Los Angeles: University of California Press.

Engh, Barbara. (1996), 'Adorno and the Sirens: Tele-phono-graphic Bodies', in Leslie C. Dunn and Nancy A. Jones (eds), *Embodied Voices: Representing Female Vocality in Western Culture*, 120–35, Cambridge: Cambridge University Press.

Etymonline. (2019), ['Threnody' definition]. Available online: https://www.etymonline.com/word/threnody#etymonline_v_13260 (accessed 24 November 2019).

Evans, Ruth. (2003), 'The Jew, the Host and the Virgin Martyr', in Anke Bernau, Ruth Evans and Sarah Salih (eds), *Medieval Virginities*, 167–86, Cardiff: University of Wales Press.

Federici, Silvia. (2014), *Caliban and the Witch*: *Women, The Body and Primitive Accumulation*, New York: Autonomedia.

Fisher, Mark. (2014), *Ghosts of My Life: Writings on Depression, Hauntology and Lost Futures*, Winchester: Zero Books.

Flinn, Sean. (1996), 'Shrieking for Sanity: An Interview with Diamanda Galás', *Choler Magazine*, 9 November. Available online: https://cholermagazine.wordpress.com/1996/11/09/shrieking-for-sanity-an-interview-with-diamanda-Galás/ (accessed 4 October 2006).

Freud, Sigmund. ([1917] 2005), *On Murder, Mourning and Melancholia*, London: Penguin Books.

Freud, Sigmund. ([1919] 2003), *The Uncanny*, London: Penguin Classics.

Freud, Sigmund. ([1922] 2003), 'Medusa's Head', in Marjorie Garber and Nancy J. Vickers (eds), *The Medusa Reader*, 84–5, New York: Routledge.

Freud, Sigmund. ([1926] 1969), *Question of Lay Analysis*, New York: W. W. Norton & Co.

Freud, Sigmund. ([1933] 1995), *New Introductory Lectures on Psychoanalysis*, London: W. W. Norton & Co.

Galás, Diamanda. (1982), [Sound recording: LP], *The Litanies of Satan*, UK: Y Records.

Galás, Diamanda. (1991), [Sound recording: CD], *Plague Mass 1984 – End of the Epidemic*, London: Mute.

Galás, Diamanda. (1993), [Sound recording: CD], *Vena Cava*, London: Mute.

REFERENCES

Galás, Diamanda. (1996a), *The Shit of God*, London: High Risk Books.

Galás, Diamanda. (1996b), [Sound recording: CD], *Schrei X*, London: Mute.

Galás, Diamanda. (1998), [Sound recording: CD], *Malediction and Prayer*, London: Mute.

Galás, Diamanda. (2003), [Sound recording: CD], *Defixiones: Will and Testament*, London: Mute.

Galás, Diamanda. (2017), *Das Fieberspital*, Wroclaw: Grotowski Institute.

Gannon, Sharon. (2010), 'Yoga and Music', in John Zorn (ed.), *Arcana V: Musicians on Music, Magic & Mysticism: 5*, 133–51, New York: Hips Road.

Gehr, Richard. (1989), 'Mourning in America: Diamanda Galás', *Artforum International*, 27(9): 116–18.

Gill, Andy. (2007), 'Nico – Frozen Borderline 1968–1970', *Uncut*, 13 February. Available online: https://www.uncut.co.uk/reviews/album/nico-frozen-borderline-1968-1970 (accessed 28 July 2017).

Gottlieb, Joanne and Gayle Wald. (1994), 'Smells like Teen Spirit: Riot Grrrls, Revolution and Women in Independent Rock', in Andrew Ross and Tricia Rose (eds), *Microphone Fiends: Youth Music and Youth Culture*, 250–71, London: Routledge.

Gottschalk, Kurt. (2008), 'Heart of Darkness', *Signal to Noise: The Quarterly Journal of Improvised, Experimental and Unusual Music*, Spring (49): 23–7.

Hall, Kim F. (2010), 'These Bastard Signs of Fair: Literary Whiteness in Shakespeare's Sonnets', in Ania Loomba and Martin Orkin (eds), *Post-Colonial Shakespeares*, 64–83, London: Routledge.

Haraway, Donna. (1991), 'A Cyborg Manifesto', in *Simians, Cyborgs and Women*, New York: Routledge.

Harvey, Elizabeth D. (2010), 'Flesh Colors and Shakespeare's Sonnets' in Michael Schoenfeldt (ed.), *A Companion to Shakespeare's Sonnets*, 314–28, West Sussex: John Wiley & Sons.

Haslam, Dave. (2015), *Life After Dark: A History of British Nightclubs & Music Venues*, London: Simon and Schuster.

Heath, Stephen. (1977), 'Translator's Note', in Roland Barthes, *Image-Music-Text*, 7–11, London: Fontana Press.

Hegarty, Paul. (2007), *Noise/Music: A History*, New York: Continuum.

Herrington, Tony (ed.). (2015), *Epiphanies: Life-Changing Encounters With Music*, London: Strange Attractor Press.

Hester, Helen. (2018), *Xenofeminism*, Cambridge: Polity Press.

Holsinger, Bruce W. (2001), *Music, Body and Desire in Medieval Christianity*, California: Stanford University Press.

Holst-Warhaft, Gail. (2000), 'Amanes: The Legacy of the Oriental Mother', 1 September. Available online: https://www.umbc.edu/MA/index/number5/holst/holst_0.htm (accessed 25 January 2008).

REFERENCES

Homer. ([675–725], 2003), the *Odyssey*, trans. E. V. Rieu, London: Penguin.

Huang, Andrew Thomas. (2015a), [Video short] *Black Lake*, UK: Colonel Blimp/True North Productions.

Huang, Andrew Thomas. (2015b), [Video short] *Family*, UK: Colonel Blimp.

Irigaray, Luce. ([1974] 1985), *Speculum of the Other Woman*, Ithaca: Cornell University Press.

Irigaray, Luce. ([1981] 2000), 'The Sex Which Is Not One', in Shelley Saguaro (ed.), *Psychoanalysis and Woman: A Reader*, 261–7, London: Macmillan Press.

James, Robin. (2015), *Resilience & Melancholy: Pop Music, Feminism, Neoliberalism*, Winchester: Zero Books.

Jankélévitch, Vladimir. ([1961] 2003), *Music and the Ineffable*, Princeton: Princeton University Press.

Johnson, Bruce and Martin Cloonan. (2013), *Dark Side of the Tune: Popular Music and Violence*, Farnham: Ashgate Publishing.

Jones, Grace. (2008), [Sound recording: CD], 'Corporate Cannibal', London: Wall of Sound.

Joyce, Colin. (2018), 'Moor Mother and DJ Haram's Noise Band 700 Bliss Feels Like a Spa Trip', *Vice*, 23 February. Available online: https://www.vice.com/en_ca/article/d3wwjm/moor-mother-dj-haram-700-bliss-spa-700-stream-interview (accessed 26 March 2018).

Jung, Carl G. ([1962] 1995), *Memories, Dreams, Reflections*, London: Fontana Press.

Juno, Andrea and Vivien Vale (eds). (1991), 'Diamanda Galás: Interview with Andrea Juno', in *Angry Women*, San Francisco: Re/search Publishing.

Kanda, Jesse. (2015, [Video short]), *Mouth Mantra*, UK: Prettybird/True North Productions.

Kent, Nick. (2013), *The Dark Stuff: Selected Writings on Rock Music*, London: Faber & Faber.

Khanna, Ranjana. (2003), *Dark Continents: Psychoanalysis and Colonialism*, Durham and London: Duke University Press.

Kilroy, Peter and Marcel Swiboda. (2007), 'Dorsal Chances: An Interview with David Wills', *parallax*, 13(4): 4–15.

Kmt, Joy. (2015), 'Creating Worlds', in Rasheedah Phillips (ed.), *Black Quantum Futurism: Theory and Practice*, 49–54, Philadelphia: Afrofuturist Affair/House of Future Sciences Books.

Kotz, Liz. (1992), 'The Body You Want: Liz Kotz Interviews Judith Butler', *Artforum*, 31, 82–9.

Krause, Bernie. (2012), *The Great Animal Orchestra: Finding the Origins of Music in the World's Wild Places*, London: Profile Books.

REFERENCES 233

Kristeva, Julia. ([1974] 2002), 'Revolution in Poetic Language', in Kelly Oliver (ed.), *The Portable Kristeva*, 27–92, New York: Columbia University Press.

Kristeva, Julia. (1982), *Powers of Horror: An Essay on Abjection*, New York: Columbia University Press.

Kristeva, Julia. ([1989] 2002), 'Black Sun', in Kelly Oliver (ed.), *The Portable Kristeva*, 383–98, New York: Columbia University Press.

Lingel, Jessa, Daniel Sutko, Gideon Lichfield and Aram Sinnreich, (2016), 'Black Holes as a Metaphysical Silence', *International Journal of Communication*, 10: 5684–92.

Lipsitz, George. (2007), *Footsteps in the Dark: The Hidden Histories of Popular Music*, Minneapolis and London: University of Minnesota Press.

Lizhi, Xu. (2014), 'The Poetry and brief life of a Foxconn Worker: Xu Lizhi (1990-2014)', *Nao's Blog*, 29 October. Available online: http://libcom.org/blog/xulizhi-foxconn-suicide-poetry (accessed 20 May 2016).

London, Dianca. (2017), 'Chelsea Wolfe's New Album Finds Stability in Chaos', *Vice*, 15 August. Available online: https://www.vice.com/en_uk/article/gyygew/chelsea-wolfes-new-album-finds-stability-in-chaos-16-psyche (accessed 20 August 2017).

Lorca, Federico García. ([1933] 2010), *In Search of Duende*, New York: New Directions.

Lorde, Audre. ([1979] 2007), 'The Master's Tools Will Never Dismantle the Master's House', in Audre Lorde, *Sister Outsider: Essays and Speeches by Audre Lorde*, 110–13, London: Penguin.

Love, Tirhakah. (2018), 'Dismantling the Master Clock: Philadelphia's Black Quantum Futurism and Modern Afrofuturist Thought', *Red Bull Music Academy Daily*, 15 May. Available online: https://daily.redbullmusicacademy.com/2018/05/philadelphia-black-quantum-futurism (accessed 20 May 2018).

Lowe Benston, Margaret. (1988), 'Women's Voices/Men's Voices: Technology as Language', in Cheris Kramarae (ed.), *Technology and Women's Voices: Keeping in Touch*, 15–28, London and New York: Routledge.

MacCormack, Patricia. (2010), 'Becoming Vulva: Flesh, Fold, Infinity', *New Formations*, 68: 93–107.

Macnish, Robert. (1845), *The Philosophy of Sleep*, Glasgow: W. R. M'Phun. Available online: http://hdl.handle.net/2027/ucm.5325053306.

Magnússon, Haukur S. (2015), 'Björk's Folk Music', *The Reykjavik Grapevine*, 6 February. Available online: https://grapevine.is/mag/feature/2015/02/06/bjorks-folk-music/ (accessed 12 November 2016).

Marx, Leo. ([1964] 2000), *The Machine in the Garden: Technology and the Pastoral Ideal in America*, Oxford: Oxford University Press.

McClary, Susan. ([1991] 2002), *Feminine Endings: Music, Gender, and Sexuality*, Minneapolis: University Of Minnesota Press.

McIntire, Gabrielle. (2002), 'The Women Do Not Travel: Gender, Difference, and Incommensurability in Conrad's Heart of Darkness', *MFS Modern Fiction Studies*, 48(2): 257–84.

McKie, Robin. (2017), 'Edge of Darkness: Looking into the Black Hole at the Heart of the Milky Way', the *Observer*, 26 February. Available online: https://www.theguardian.com/science/2017/feb/26/black-hole-telescope-big-as-earth-event-horizon-project-sagittarius-a (accessed 5 April 2017).

Merchant, Carolyn. ([1980] 1990), *The Death of Nature: Women, Ecology and the Scientific Revolution*, New York: Bravo Ltd.

Miller-Frank, Felicia. (1995), *The Mechanical Song: Women, Voice, and the Artificial in Nineteenth-Century French Narrative*, Stanford: Stanford University Press.

Milstein, Cindy (ed.). (2017), *Rebellious Mourning: The Collective Work of Grief*, Chico and Edinburgh: AK Press.

Monbiot, George. (2019), 'The Big Polluters' Masterstroke Was to Blame the Climate Crisis on You and Me', the *Guardian*, 9 October. Available online: https://www.theguardian.com/commentisfree/2019/oct/09/polluters-climate-crisis-fossil-fuel (accessed 9 October 2019).

Moor Mother. (2016), [Sound recording: CD] *Fetish Bones*, USA: Don Giovanni Records.

Moor Mother. (2017), [Sound recording: vinyl], *The Motionless Present*, UK: Vinyl Factory.

Moor Mother. (2019), [Sound recording: CD], *Analog Fluids of Sonic Black Holes*, USA: Don Giovanni Records.

Moor Mother and Mental Jewelry. (2017), [Sound recording: CD] *Crime Waves*, USA: Don Giovanni Records.

Morrison, Toni. (1993), 'Nobel Prize Lecture', in Maria Popova (ed.), 'Toni Morrison on the Power of Language: Her Spectacular Nobel Acceptance Speech after Becoming the First African American Woman Awarded the Accolade', *Brain Pickings*. Available online: https://www.brainpickings.org/2016/12/07/toni-morrison-nobel-prize-speech/ (accessed 5 April 2018).

Morton, Timothy. (2013), 'At the Edge of the Smoking Pool of Death: Wolves in the Throne Room', *Helevete: A Journal of Black Metal Theory*, 1: 21–8.

Moten, Fred. (2003), *In the Break: The Aesthetics of the Black Radical Tradition*, Minneapolis: University of Minnesota Press.

Muessig, Carolyn. (1998), 'Prophecy and Song: Teaching and Preaching by Medieval Women', in Beverly Mayne Kienzle and Pamela J. Walker (eds), *Women Preachers and Prophets through Two Millennia of Christianity*, 146–58, Berkeley and Los Angeles: University of California Press.

REFERENCES   235

Munford, Rebecca. (2016), 'Spectral Femininity', in Avril Horner and Sue Zlosnik (eds), *Women and the Gothic: An Edinburgh Companion*, 120–34, Edinburgh: Edinburgh University Press.

Murch, Walter. (1994), 'Foreword', in Michel Chion, *Audio-Vision: Sound on Screen*, vii–xxiv, New York: Columbia University Press.

NASA. (2003), 'Interpreting the "Song" Of a Distant Black Hole', *NASA*. Available online at: https://www.nasa.gov/centers/goddard/universe/black_hole_sound.html (accessed 11 March 2017).

Neset, Anne Hilde. ([2007] 2011), 'Tangled Cartography: The Mapping of Her Noise', *Her Noise Archive*. Available online: http://hernoise.org/tangled-cartography/ (accessed 16 October 2017).

Nicholls, Tracey. (2012), *An Ethics of Improvisation: Aesthetic Possibilities for a Political Future*, Plymouth: Lexington Books.

Nico. (1968), [Sound recording: CD] *The Marble Index*, USA: Elektra Records.

Nochlin, Linda. ([1971] 2003), 'Why Have There Been No Great Women Artists?', in Amelia Jones (ed.), *The Feminism and Visual Culture Reader*, 229–33, London and New York: Routledge.

O'Brien, Lucy. (2012), *She Bop: The Definitive History of Women in Popular Music*, London: Jawbone Press.

Oldham, Will. (1999), 'Diamanda Galás', *Index Magazine*. Available online: http://www.indexmagazine.com/interviews/diamanda_Galás.shtml (accessed 4 January 2006).

Oliveros, Pauline. (2005), *Deep Listening: A Composer's Sound Practice*, Lincoln: iUniverse.

Partridge, Christopher. (2016), 'The Occult and Popular Music', in Christopher Partridge (ed.), *The Occult World*, 509–30, London and New York: Routledge.

Payne, John. (2008), 'Vengeance is Hers: a Conversation with Diamanda Galás', *Arthur Magazine*, March. Available online: https://arthurmag.com/2009/01/25/vengeance-is-hers-a-conversation-with-diamanda-Galás-by-john-payne-from-arthur-no-28march-2008/ (accessed 16 August 2008).

Pelly, Jenn. (2016), 'Moor Mother: Hardcore Poet', *Pitchfork*, 26 October. Available online: https://pitchfork.com/features/rising/9968-moor-mother-hardcore-poet/ (accessed 27 March 2017).

Petrusich, Amanda. (2016), 'Fear of the Light: Why We Need Darkness', the *Guardian*, 23 August. Available online: https://www.theguardian.com/environment/2016/aug/23/why-we-need-darkness-light-pollution-stars (accessed 25 August 2016).

Phillips, Rasheeda. (2015), 'Black Quantum Futurism: Theory and Practice', in Rasheedah Phillips (ed.), *Black Quantum Futurism: Theory and Practice*, 11–30, Philadelphia: Afrofuturist Affair/House of Future Sciences Books.

Physics of the Universe. (2009), 'Singularities – Black Holes and Wormholes – The Physics of the Universe'. Available online: https://www.physicsoftheuniverse.com/topics_blackholes_singularities.html (accessed 16 March 2018).

Piaf, Edith and Jean Noli. (1990), *My Life*, London: Penguin Books.

Pincherle, Marc. (1964), *The World of the Virtuoso*, London: Victor Gollancz.

Pinnock, Tom. (2015), 'Nico and *The Marble Index*: "She Hated the Idea of Being Beautiful"', *Uncut*, 16 October. Available online: https://www.uncut.co.uk/features/nico-and-the-marble-index-she-hated-the-idea-of-being-beautiful-71286 (accessed 21 July 2017).

Plant, Sadie. (1998), *Zeros and Ones. Digital Women and the New Technologies*, London: Harper Collins.

Plath, Sylvia. ([1961] 1981), *Collected Poems*, London: Faber and Faber.

Poe, Edgar Allan. ([1841] 2016), *A Descent into the Maelström*, CreateSpace Independent Publishing Platform.

Poizat, Michel. (1992), *The Angel's Cry: Beyond the Pleasure Principle in Opera*, Ithaca: Cornell University Press.

Pothast, Emily. (2019), 'Moor Mother', *The Wire*, July (Issue 425): 36–41.

Potts, Dianca. (2016), 'Chelsea Wolfe's Sleepless Nights Led to "Abyss"', *Village Voice*, 6 May. Available online: https://www.villagevoice.com/2016/05/06/chelsea-wolfes-sleepless-nights-led-to-abyss/ (accessed 20 May 2016).

Pratt, Susanne. (2016), '"Black-Noise": The Throb of the Anthropocene', *Helevete: A Journal of Black Metal Theory*, 3: 15–39.

Reddington, Helen. (2007), *The Lost Women of Rock Music: Female Musicians of the Punk Era*, London: Routledge.

Reed, Teresa L. (2003), *The Holy Profane: Religion in Black Popular Music*, Kentucky: The University Press of Kentucky.

Reinelt, Janelle. (1991), 'Feminist Theory and the Problem of Performance', in Sue-Ellen Case and Janelle Reinelt (eds), *The Performance of Power: Theatrical Discourse and Politics*, 49–57, Iowa: University of Iowa Press.

Reynolds, Simon. (1988), 'Loop', *Melody Maker*, 12 November. Available online: https://reynoldsretro.blogspot.com/2016/02/loop.html (accessed 6 January 2018).

Reynolds, Simon. (1989), 'Ciccone Youth: The Whitey Album (Blast First)', *Melody Maker*, 14 January. Available online: https://reynoldsretro.blogspot.com/2017/03/ciccone-youth.html (accessed 6 January 2018).

Reynolds, Simon. (1990), *Blissed Out: The Raptures of Rock*, London: Serpent's Tail.

Reynolds, Simon. (1996), 'Slipping Into Darkness', *The Wire Magazine*, June. Available online: https://www.thewire.co.uk/in-writing/essays/

REFERENCES

the-wire-300_simon-reynolds-on-the-hardcore-continuum_4_
hardstep_jump-up_techstep_1996_ (accessed 6 January 2018).

Reynolds, Simon. (2007), 'The Inner Scar', the *Guardian*, 16 March. Available online: http://reynoldsretro.blogspot.com/2007/12/nico-inner-scar-directors-cut-guardian.html (accessed 28 July 2017).

Reynolds, Simon and Joy Press. (1996), *The Sex Revolts: Gender, Rebellion, and Rock 'n' Roll*, Cambridge: Harvard University Press.

Richardson Andrews, Charlotte. (2011), 'Anna Calvi's Orchestral Manoeuvres', the *Guardian*, 13 January. Available online: https://www.theguardian.com/music/2011/jan/13/anna-calvi-classical-goth-interview (accessed 5 June 2017).

Rietveld, Hillegonda. (1998), 'Repetitive Beats: Free Parties and the Politics of Contemporary DiY Dance Culture in Britain', in George Mckay (ed.), *DiY Culture: Party & Protest in Nineties Britain*, 243–67, London: Verso.

Riley, Denise. (2005), *Impersonal Passion: Language as Affect*, Durham and London: Duke University Press.

Rivière, Joan. ([1929] 2015), 'Womanliness as Masquerade', in Russell Grigg, Dominique Hecq and Craig Smith (eds), *Female Sexuality: The Early Psychoanalytic Controversies*, 172–82, London: Karnac Books.

Roberts, Andrew. (2000), *Conrad and Masculinity*, Basingstoke: Macmillan Press.

Roberts, Christopher. (2015), 'Watch: Chelsea Wolfe – "Carrion Flowers" Video', *Under The Radar*, 24 June. Available online: http://undertheradarmag.com/news/watch_chelsea_wolfe_-_carrion_flowers_video (accessed 20 May 2016).

Rodgers, Tara. (2010), *Pink Noises: Women on Electronic Music and Sound*, Durham and London: Duke University Press.

Rodgers, Tara. (2016), 'Toward a Feminist Epistemology of Sound: Refiguring Waves in Audio-Technical Discourse', in Mary Rawlinson (ed.), *Engaging the World: Thinking After Irigaray*, 195–213, New York: SUNY Press.

Schiesari, Juliana. (1992), *The Gendering of Melancholia: Feminism, Psychoanalysis, and the Symbolics of Loss in Renaissance Literature*, Ithaca and London: Cornell University Press.

Scott, Derek B. (2003), *From the Erotic to the Demonic on Critical Musicology*, Oxford: Oxford University Press.

Self-titled. (2015), 'Chelsea Wolfe Reveals New *Abyss* Album', *self-titled*. Available online: http://www.self-titledmag.com/chelsea-wolfe-announces-new-album/ (accessed 2 January 2016).

Shadrack, Jasmine H. (2017), 'From Enslavement to Obliteration: Extreme Metal's Problem with Women', in Rhian Jones and Eli Davies (eds), *Under My Thumb: Songs That Hate Women and the Women Who Love Them*, 170–84, London: Repeater.

Shakespeare, William. ([1609] 2009), 'The Sonnets', in John Kerrigan (ed.), *The Sonnets and A Lover's Complaint*, 1–156, London: Penguin Classics.

Silva, Denis F. (2017), '1 (Life) ÷ 0 (Blackness) = ∞ – ∞ or ∞ / ∞: On Matter Beyond the Equation of Value', *e-flux*, 79. Available online: https://www.e-flux.com/journal/79/94686/1-life-0-blackness-or-on-matter-beyond-the-equation-of-value/ (accessed 2 October 2018).

Silverman, Kaja. (1988), *The Acoustic Mirror: The Female Voice in Psychoanalysis and Cinema*, Bloomington: Indiana University Press.

Smalley, Denis. (1997), 'Spectromorphology: Explaining Sound-Shapes', *Organised Sound*, 2(2): 107–26.

Smith, Mark M. (2015), 'Echo', in David Novak and Matt Sakaeeny (eds), *Keywords in Sound*, 55–64, Durham and London: Duke University Press.

Smith, Richard. (1995), *Seduced and Abandoned: Essays on Gay Men and Popular Music*, London: Cassell.

Smyth, David. (2018), 'Anna Calvi Interview: I Think My Music Has Always Been Queer', *London Evening Standard*, 15 June. Available online: https://www.standard.co.uk/go/london/music/anna-calvi-interview-i-think-my-music-has-always-been-queer-a3863851.html (accessed 20 June 2018).

Solnit, Rebecca. ([2005] 2016), *Hope in the Dark: Untold Histories of Wild Possibilities*, Edinburgh and London: Canongate Books.

Sontag, Susan. ([1975] 2013), 'Fascinating Fascism', in Susan Sontag, *Under the Sign of Saturn: Essays*, 73–108, London: Penguin.

Spiegel, Amy R. (2017), 'Moor Mother on Creating the Future You Want to See', *The Creative Independent*, 5 June. Available online: https://thecreativeindependent.com/people/moor-mother-on-creating-the-future-you-want-to-see/ (accessed 20 June 2017).

Sprenger, Jakob and Heinrich Kramer. ([1487] 2011), *Malleus Maleficarum*, Connecticut: Martino Publishing.

Stephanou, Aspasia. (2010), 'Playing Wolves And Red Riding Hoods In Black Metal', in Nicola Masciandaro (ed.), *Hideous Gnosis: Black Metal Theory Symposium 1*, 157–70, Brooklyn, New York: Glossator.

Stoever, Jennifer Lynn. (2016), *The Sonic Color Line: Race and the Cultural Politics of Listening*, New York: New York University Press.

Tanner, Grafton. (2016), *Babbling Corpse: Vaporwave And The Commodification Of Ghosts*, Winchester: Zero Books.

Thacker, Eugene. (2014), 'Sound of the Abyss', in Scott Wilson (ed.), *Melancology: Black Metal Theory and Ecology*, 182–94, Winchester: Zero Books.

The Doors. (1967), [Sound recording: CD], *The Doors*, USA: Electra.

Thompson, Marie. (2013), 'Three Screams', in Ian Biddle and Marie Thompson (eds), *Sound, Music, Affect: Theorizing Sonic Experience*, 147–62, New York: Bloomsbury.

REFERENCES 239

Thunberg, Greta. (2019), *No One Is Too Small to Make a Difference*, London: Penguin.

Till, Rupert. (2010), *Pop Cult: Religion and Popular Music*, London and New York: Continuum.

Tweddell, Ben. (2011), 'Forgotten Series: Nico – *The Marble Index* (1969)', *Something Else!*, 20 April. Available online: https://somethingelsereviews.com/2011/04/20/forgotten-series-nico-the-marble-index-1969/ (accessed 2 August 2017).

Villa, Dana R. (1999), *Politics, Philosophy, Terror: Essays on the Thought of Hannah Arendt*, Princeton: Princeton University Press.

Volcer, Juliette. (2013), *Extremely Loud: Sound as a Weapon*, New York: The New Press.

Watson, Don. (1985), 'Nico: "Watch Out, The World's Behind You"', *New Musical Express*, 3 August. Available online: https://www-rocksbackpages-com.ezproxy.falmouth.ac.uk/Library/Article/nico-watch-out-the-worlds-behind-you (accessed 27 July 2017).

Whelan, Kez. (2015), 'Chelsea Wolfe Unveils New Video For "Carrion Flowers"', *Terrorizer*, 24 June. Available online: http://www.terrorizer.com/news/video/chelsea-wolfe-unveils-new-video-for-carrion-flowers/ (accessed 5 January 2016).

Whiteley, Sheila. (2000), *Women and Popular Music: Sexuality, Identity and Subjectivity*, London and New York: Routledge.

Whiteley, Sheila. (2003), *Too Much Too Young: Popular Music, Age and Gender*, London: Routledge.

Williams, Sarah F. (2015), *Damnable Practices: Witches, Dangerous Women, and Music in Seventeenth-Century English Broadside Ballads*, Farnham: Ashgate Publishing.

Wilson, Scott. (2014), 'Introduction to Melancology', in Scott Wilson (ed.), *Melancology: Black Metal Theory and Ecology*, 5–24, Winchester: Zero Books.

Winderen, Jane. (2016), [Sound recording: CD], *The Listener*, UK: Touch Music/Fairwood Music.

Winkler, Amanda Eubanks. (2006), *O Let Us Howle Some Heavy Note: Music for Witches, the Melancholic, and the Mad on the Seventeenth-Century English Stage*, Bloomington: Indiana University Press.

Wiseman-Trowse, Nathan. (2008), *Performing Class in British Popular Music*, New York: Palgrave Macmillan.

Wolfe, Chelsea. (2011), [Sound recording: CD], *Apokalypsis*, USA: Pendu Sound.

Wolfe, Chelsea. (2015), [Sound recording: CD], *Abyss,* USA: Sargent House.

Wolfe, Chelsea. (2017), [Sound recording: CD], *Hiss Spun*, USA: Sargent House.

Wolfe, Chelsea. (2019), [Sound recording: vinyl], *Birth of Violence*, USA: Sargent House.

Woolf, Virginia. ([1915] 1981), *The Diary of Virginia Woolf*, New York: Harcourt.

Young, James. (1999), *Nico: Songs They Never Play on the Radio*, London and New York: Bloomsbury.

Young, Miriama. (2015), *Singing the Body Electric: The Human Voice and Sound Technology*, Farnham: Ashgate Publishing.

Yusoff, Kathryn. (2018), *A Billion Black Anthropocenes or None*, Minneapolis: University of Minnesota Press.

Zaretsky, Robert. (2016), 'Why Are Students Drawn to Horror?', *Times Higher Education*, 24 March. Available online: https://www.timeshighereducation.com/comment/why-are-students-drawn-to-horror (accessed 16 April 2016).

Zorn, John (ed.). (2010), *Arcana V: Musicians on Music, Magic & Mysticism: 5*, New York: Hips Road.

INDEX

'1837: Of the Refrain' (Deleuze &
    Guattari) 217–18
1984 – End of the Epidemic
    (Galás) 194

abortion legislation, biblical
    roots 5
Abyss (Wolfe) 153–4, 165, 172,
    175
abyss, the
    burden of black noise and
        a growing awareness of
        148–9
    nightmare weight of patriarchy
        and 152–5
    paradox of burden 165
    rationalizing the study of
        213–14
    reappropriation of 173–6
    of the self 110
    sonic representations 108
acousmêtre/acousmatic voice
    116–18
activism 26, 137, 205
Adler, Shelley 155
Adorno, Theodor 8, 71
African-American music,
    demonization of 9
Afrofuturism 134–7
Allsopp, Ric 153
Althusser, Louis 183
amanes 187–9
'*Amanes*: The Legacy of the
    Oriental Mother' (Holst-
    Warhaft) 188

ambient music 118–20
American dream, toxification of
    158–62
Amnesty International 179
*Analog Fluids of Sonic Black
    Holes* (Moor Mother) 133
Anatomy of Melancholy (Burton)
    170
Andalusian folk music 48
And the Ass Saw the Angel (Cave)
    118
annihilation 109, 112, 121
Anthropocene, dark sound of 147
anti-semitism 90, 206
Apocalypse Now (Coppola)
    222n3
Arendt, Hannah 205
AR Kane 119
Artaud, Antonin 177
artists, who conceptualize dark
    sound 28
assemblages, power and 181–3
*At Day's Close: A History of
    Nighttime* (Ekirch) 207
Atwood, Margaret 171
Audio-Vision: Sound on Sound
    (Chion) 114–15
Ayewa, Camae 133, 136, 139–40
    142
    see also Moor Mother

Bangs, Lester 74–6
Barney, Matthew 122
Barthes, Roland 35, 52–3, 55, 60,
    65–9

Battersby, Christine 24, 181
Baudelaire, Charles 179, 196
Baudrillard, Jean 10, 160
Beaumont, Matthew 208, 210
becoming-vulva, Calvi's guitar as 104 6
bel canto 185, 189, 195
Bell, Ilona 36
Benjamin, Walter 52
Bennett, Jane 177, 181–2
bestiality 195
A Billion Black Anthropocenes or None (Yusoff) 132
Bingen, Hildegard Von 222n1
Birth of Violence (Wolfe) 153
Björk 28
    black hole sound 111–12
    cohabitation of death and rebirth in the work of 122–3
    cultivation of maternal sexuality 131
    linking of nature and national identity 127–8
    MoMA retrospective 122
    silencing impact of throat surgery 123–4
    space and bridges in the work of 123–6
    vocal style 123
black holes
    Björk's 'Black Lake' as rebirth 126–31
    BQF sorcerer 141–3
    cosmic song 108
    creating space and bridges 123–6
    dark matter and 131–7
    discovery of inaudible sound emitted by 107–8
    Freudian dimension 113
    Moor Mother's sonic engagement with space 137–41

and Mother Earth 121–3
psychological dimensions 120
romantic responses to discovery of 107–8
in science fiction literature 120–1
and the sound of a mother 113–18
symbolic relationship with the mother 108–9
unsounding song of the mother 109–12
value 110–11
wombing sound 118–21
'Black Holes as Metaphysical Silence' (Lingel) 120
'Black Lake' (Björk) 122–3
    Björk's rationale for its length 128
    music video 126–30
    as rebirth 126–31
    trailer 127
black metal 150–1
blackness
    colonial alignment with property 132
    the concept 135
black noise 134, 147–8, 150, 158, 165
    burdening effect 148
    as mourning dirge 148–52
    Pratt's 'Black Noise' installation 147–8
black people, violence against 134
Black Quantum Futurism (BQF) 112, 133–7, 139, 141–3
    see also Moor Mother
'Black Sun' (Kristeva) 109
Bland, Sandra 139
Blissed Out: The Raptures of Rock (Reynolds) 119
blood 49, 51, 105, 140, 194–5, 201

INDEX

blues music 9–10, 47, 91–3, 103, 105, 136, 141, 186, 189
Body without Organs (BwO) 23–4
Bram Stoker's Dracula (Coppola) 223n6
Brecht, Bertolt 145–6
Bridle, James 29
Bronfen, Elizabeth 11, 13, 167
de Brossard, Sebastian 178
Burton, Robert 170
Butler, Judith 24–5, 54, 193

Cale, John 72–3, 75
Calvi, Anna 28, 87
   cinematic approach to music making 100–101
   creation of erotic tension 102–3
   guitar technique and effects 103–5
   iconography 102
   performance persona 101
   subversion of blues rock phallocentricism 101–2, 105–6
   vocal style 102–3
Camera Lucida (Barthes) 64–5
capitalist networks, infrasound as the vibrations of 149
Carr, Cynthia 190
'Carrion Flowers' (Wolfe) 155, 159–61
Carson, Anne 84
castration anxiety 113–14, 170
Cave, Nick 34, 118
Chion, Michel 114–17
Ciccone Youth 119
cinema
   gendered relationship of sight and sound in 117
   sound and the maternal 114–15
Citron, Marcia J. 24, 181
Cixous, Hélène 15–16, 23, 87, 119

Claudius, Matthias 67
climate change/crisis 28, 146–7, 205, 216
Cloonan, Martin 8
coal industry 147–8
Cocteau Twins 119
Cohen, Leonard 31–2
colonialism
   and the conceptualization of dark sound 27
   and demonization discourse 88–90
   and the female body 99
   impact in Iceland 132
   and journeys to the dark 16
   relationship with psychoanalysis 14
   and whiteness 41, 132
   and witchcraft 156
coloratura 22, 197, 199–200
Community Future Labs, North Philadelphia 136
Conrad, Joseph 16, 115
   see also *Heart of Darkness*
Cope, Julian 76
corporations, problematic treatment of people, animals and resources 161
'Cosmic Slop' (700 Bliss) 133
Cox, Christopher 23
Creed, Barbara 113, 121
Crenshaw, Kimberlé W. 25
Culp, Andrew 215
cult leader, the rock god as 8

Daly, Mary 4–5
the dark
   endurance of association between women and 11
   journeys into 11–16
'dark ages' 76, 214
'dark continent'
   Africa as 14

of female sexuality 13–16, 20, 37, 84
Dark Deleuze (Culp) 215
dark feminine
  Galás's sound 180, 187, 193, 203
  as haunted/haunting apparition 153
  importance of movement and journey 12
  in the music lover's discourse 58
  Nico's sound 81
  occult power 152
  paradoxical weight 173
  Piaf's sound 52
  relationship with light 219
  suppressed powers 216
  and troubled heteronormative male desire 63
  witches' embodiment of the burden 155, 158, 164–5
  Wolfe's sound 151–3, 155, 158, 164–5, 172–4
  see also dark lady
darkfemphonosophy 3
dark forces 29, 206, 208, 218
dark lady in love-sick poetry
  black sound 42–7
  characteristics and temporality 35
  contagious nature of darkness 31–3
  dark singing presence 50–2
  dark sound and the singer's body 47–50
  as musician 42–4, 47
  and the recurring deployment of 'blackness' 39–42
  in Shakespeare's sonnets 34–46
'Darkness' (Cohen) 31–3
darkness
  before the creation of the world 2

of the Fall 3
feminized (*see also* dark feminine) 5, 39
historical and cultural association between women and 11–12
threat to and need for 206–12
Dark Side of the Tune (Johnson & Cloonan) 8
dark sound
  canon that privileges masculinity 27–8
  the concept 3
  gendered dimension, ramifications 11
dark sound artists 28, 212
'dark studies', Zaretsky on the fascination with 212–14
dark times
  alternatives to singing about 145–8
  the concept 145
dark white voice 53
Das Fieberspital (Galás) 183
Davis, Angela 91–2, 206
Davos 215
death
  cohabitation with rebirth in Björk's work 122
  cult of 30
  dark voice of 67–70, 80
  death-bearing activity of humanity 147–8
  the death-bearing woman 109–11
  death drive 12, 54, 95, 149, 175
  death fantasies 150–1
  death metal 151
  duende's association with 48–52
  and Eve's fall 3–4
  ineffability and 58–9
  lamenting 187–90

INDEX

in music lover's discourse about Nico 70, 71–5, 78–9
obsession with 99
relationship between femininity and 167–8
romanticization of 119
sleep as a temporary state of 154
'sterilizing inexplicability' 62
threshold/boundary between life and 172–3, 180
witchcraft and 89, 157, 165
'Death and the Maiden' (Schubert) 67–8
'Death-Bearing Woman' (Kristeva) 109
Death Valley 160
De Civitate Dei (Augustine) 155
deep listening 124, 126, 132, 137
Defixiones: Will and Testament (Galás) 183, 188, 216
defloration, ancient theories of effect on the female voice 84
degradation, Bakhtin's understanding of 121–2
Deleuze, Gilles & Félix Guattari 5, 23, 104, 181, 217–18
Demers, Joanna 72
the demonic
mothers and 94–100
see also openness to the demonic
demonic possession, the sounds of 90–4
demonization, function of 88
Derrida, Jacques 168–9
'A Descent into the Maelström' (Poe) 85
desire
blues music and 92–3
and death drive 150, 169
end of 66–70
and loss 65–6

as malady in Shakespeare's sonnets 34–46
of the music lover 71
new forms of being and 106
primacy of phallic desire 105
queered 102–3, 105–6
regulation of female sexuality and 83, 87, 98, 112
relationship with light 59
relationship with the mother 94–5, 97–100, 113, 115, 117, 131, 175
relationship with witchcraft 89
struggle between revulsion and 6–11
troubled heteronormative male desire 63
white female body as object of 80
'The Devil' (Calvi) 87, 104
the Devil, as regulating technology 87–90
'Devil's music' 9
Devil's tritone 7
Dibben, Nicola 127–8
Dictionnaire de Musique (Brossard) 178
'die-ins' 172
DJ Haram 133
Dodds, Joseph 175
'Don't Explain' (Holiday) 46
A Door and a Sigh (Henry) 223n8
drone 72–3, 79, 95, 119–20
The Duchess of Malfi (Webster) 174–5
duende 47–52

Eastman, Max 155
Eco, Umberto 29–30
'eco-activism' 150
ecocide 146, 150, 164–5, 175, 205
eco-fascism 175
ecology
etymology 121

246 INDEX

melancholy and 150–1
relationship between mourning
and 149
écriture féminine 23, 119
'Edge of Darkness: Looking into
the Black Hole at the Heart
of the Milky Way' (the
Guardian) 113
Edith of Wilton 91
effeminacy, the risk of carried by
music 6, 10
ego 12, 96, 149–51, 184
Ekirch, A Roger 207, 210
electric guitar
Calvi and the becoming-vulva
of the 100–106
phallocentricism 105
electronic music 23, 136
'The End' (The Doors) 95–100
Engh, Barbara 64–5, 85
Enlightenment, the 11, 76, 133,
155, 209–210, 212–15
Eno, Brian 118, 120
*Epiphanies: Life Changing
Encounters with Music* 59
Erickson, Roky 166–7
Evangelicalism 91
Evans, Ruth 90
Eve 3–6, 157

Fabian, Andrew 107
'the Fall' 3–6
'Family' (Björk), 'moving album
cover' 124–6
Farewell Anatolia (Soteriou) 189
fascism 8, 29–30
'Fear of the Light: Why We Need
Darkness' (Petrusich) 206–7
Federici, Silvia 88–9, 156
female bodies
colonial psychology in the
understanding of 99
as dark portals to other worlds
98

sexualization and demonization
of 87–90
similitude between openings of
the earth and 124–5, 131
theft of 5–6
female composers, squeezing out
of 26–7
female genitals
Freud's contention 94
symbolism 14
female sexuality
connection between the voice
and 84
dark continent analogy 13–16,
20, 37, 84
demonized 87–90, 90–4, 105
historical suspicion of 40
regulation and control of 83,
87, 98, 112
relationship of music with 60
vocal pitch and 84
witches' connection with 157
female voice, fetishization 84–5
feminine darkness *see* dark
feminine
Feminine Endings (McClary) 24, 191
feminine music, in search of 23–30
feminine mythologies, signalling
the dangers of music and
sound through 9–10
femininity, spectral 172
feminism 3, 33, 192, 206
Fetish Bones (Moor Mother) 133,
139, 141
Fever Ray 28
First World War 216
Fischer-Dieskau, Dietrich 56
FKA Twigs 28
flamenco 48, 103, 105
folk music 24, 52, 76, 105
*Footsteps in the Dark: The
Hidden Histories of Popular
Music* (Lipsitz) 27
'Founding Fathers' 213–14

INDEX 247

Foxconn 163
fracking 207
Freud, Sigmund 12–15, 67, 84, 94,
    113, 120–1, 149, 155, 170
'Frozen Warnings' (Nico) 71, 73–5
Fuseli, Henry 154

Galás, Diamanda 28
    career span 183
    death laments 188–90
    describes her work and vocal
        technique 183, 185–7,
        200
    early performances 179
    extreme sound 180
    influences 186
    mandatory technique 184–90
    suffering and horror in the
        work of 183
    vocal range 190, 197–202
    vocal studies 185
    witch-cyborg mutations 190–7
    see also virtuosity
Gannon, Sharon 125
Gender and Genius (Battersby) 24
Gender and the Musical Canon
    (Citron) 24
gender binary 2
gendered relations, relationship
    with the myth of the Fall of
    Adam and Eve 4–5
gender identity, Butler on 24–5
*The Gendering of Melancholia:
    Feminism, Psychoanalysis,
    and the Symbolics of Loss
    in Renaissance Literature*
    (Schiesari) 33
'Gender of Sound' (Carson) 84
Genesis, first book of 1
geno-song 56, 68
gentrification, activism against
    137
'Glen of *Freischütz*' (Wolf) 68
Globokar, Vinko 179

glossolalia 90–1
God
    alienation from 168
    in the first book of Genesis 1–4
    Galás's relationship to the idea
        of 194–6
    ineffability 57, 63
    relationship with light 207
    relationship with music 91
    relationship with virtuosity
        178–9
    unification with 49, 90
'going dark' 208, 211
Gordon, Kim 28
grain, Barthes's concept of a voice
    with 44, 47, 52, 55–6, 68–9
Greenfield, Elizabeth Taylor 79
Gregorian chant 76
Gretchen at the Spinning Wheel
    (Schubert) 66
grief
    Björk's performance of 126–9
    devaluation of women's 171
    paradoxes 165
    suppressed unsoundings of
        109–10, 112, 122
    vocal expression of 187–8, 195
    Wolfe's articulation of 158, 165
    women's association with 34
guitar, role of in androcentric
    mastery 93–4
gypsy jazz 105

Haeny, John 80
Hall, Kim 40
Hampton, Mary 28
The Handmaid's Tale (Atwood)
    171
Haraway, Donna 22, 191
Harder, Susan 207
Harpies 85, 194
Harvey, Elizabeth 46–7
Harvey, PJ 28
Haslam, Dave 27

INDEX

Hausswolff, Anna Von 28
Hayden, Bridget 28
Heart of Darkness (Conrad)
    racist effects 20
    representation of women in
    16–19
heavy metal 9, 164, 165
Hegarty, Paul 54
Heidegger, Martin 210
Hensler, Jenni 156
'Her Noise' website 25–6
Herrmann, Bernard 101
Hildegard of Bingen 76
Hiss Spun (Wolfe) 152, 172, 175
Holiday, Billie 46–7
Holst-Warhaft, Gail 188
Homer 9
Homogenic (Björk) 127
homophobia 179, 214
Hope in the Dark (Solnit) 206
Huang, Andrew Thomas 122
Hunter (Calvi) 100, 106
Hurt, Mississippi John 91
hydrophone recordings 146–7
hysteria 21–2, 61, 84–6, 99, 187,
    200

Iceland 123–4, 126–8, 132
incest 195
incubi 154–5
industrialization 148, 150, 158–9,
    167
ineffability 54, 57–9, 62, 196
    Jankélévitch's embrace of 56–7,
    60, 62–3
infrasound 107–8, 121, 147–9
intersectional feminism 25, 206
intersectionality 25–6
'Intravenal Song' (Galás) 201
Irigaray, Luce 24, 86, 99, 104,
    112, 170–1
'Iron Moon' (Wolfe) 162–4
'Irreversible Entanglements'
    (Moor Mother) 136

Islamophobia 206
'I Swallowed a Moon Made of
    Iron' (Lizhi) 163–4

James, Robyn 215
Jankélévitch, Vladimir 53, 55,
    60–2
jazz 10, 136
    gypsy jazz 105
Jefferson, Blind Lemon 91
Johnson, Bruce 8
Johnson, Robert 91
Jones, Grace 28
jouissance
    the high voice and 197–8
    the scream in terms of 21
    vocal grain and 56
    'wombing' sound and 119
Jung, Carl 118, 154
Junko 28

Kent, Nick 27
Khanna, Ranjana 14–16
Kitt, Eartha 28
Klein, Melanie 175
Kmt, Joy 142
knowledge, correspondence
    between light and 11, 14
Kramer, Heinrich 89, 155
Kraus, Sharron 28
Krause, Bernie 2
Kristeva, Julia 21, 23, 47, 64, 100,
    108–10, 114, 195

La Niña de Los Peines 47, 49–50
'A La Recherche d'une Musique
    Féminine' (Cox) 23
'The Last Graveyard' (Lizhi) 164
'The Laugh of the Medusa'
    (Cixous) 15, 87
Les Fleurs du Mal (Baudelaire)
    179
Leviticus 195
lieder 64–9, 76–7, 217

INDEX

*Life after Dark: A History of
British Nightclubs & Music
Venues* (Haslam) 27
light
    correspondence between
        knowledge and 11, 14
    white patriarchal occupation
        of 14
light pollution 206–7
Lind, Jenny 79
Lingel, Jessa 113, 120
Lingua Ignota 28
Lipsitz, George 27
The Listener (Winderen) 147
Litanies of Satan (Galás) 179
Lizhi, Xu 163–4
longing 35, 95
Loop 119
Lorca, Federico García 47, 49–50
love-sick poetry, dark lady in *see*
    dark lady in love-sick poetry
the love song, secret life lecture 34
'Love Won't Be Leaving' (Calvi)
    100
'Loving Schumann' (Barthes) 64
Lynch, David 101

Macbeth (Shakespeare) 78
MacCormack, Patricia 104
madness
    Björk's performance of 123
    constructed associations
        between music femininity,
        sexuality and 199
    operatic 191
    and the 'wandering womb' 85
    Wolfe's performance of 156,
        166
Malediction and Prayer (Galás)
    201
male-dominated music canons,
    challenges to 26
Malleus Maleficarum (*The
    Hammer of Witches*)

(Sprenger & Kramer) 89,
    155
The Marble Index (Nico) 59,
    70–1, 73–6, 78, 80
Marx, Leo 159
Masai Mara, Kenya, Krause's
    trip 2
masquerade 10–11, 24
mastery 93, 178, 180–1, 184, 186
matricide
    psychic 109
    of psychoanalysis 111
'Maw' (Wolfe) 166
McClary, Susan 21–2, 24, 85,
    97–8, 181, 191, 199
McIntire, Gabrielle 16
McKenna, Natasha 139
Medusa 14, 62–3, 70, 194
melancholy/melancholia
    comparison with a black hole
        109–10
    ecology and 150–1
    female 114, 158, 169–70, 172
    Freud's work 170
    male privileging 32–4, 171
    relationship with mourning
        149, 151, 173
    womb-based 110
'melancology' 150
melted glaciers, mourning
    ceremonies 172
Memories, Dreams, Reflections
    (Jung) 154
Memphis Minnie 91
Men in Dark Times (Arendt) 205
menstrual bleeding 140
Mental Jewelry 133
'Mer' (Wolfe) 167
Milky Way 50, 113, 207
Miller Frank, Felicia 157–8
misogyny
    in the enforced hiding of
        women 140
    female somnambulism and 209

and the grudge against music 61
internalized 15
pathological nature 61
patriarchy and 214, 219
Mohawk, Frazier 80
moiroloyia/moiroloyistres 187–9
Monbiot, George 222n1
Moor Mother 28, 107
  black hole sound 111–12,
    131–7
  DIY aesthetic 136–7
  linking of practice and
    performances to black holes
    134
  re-appropriation of the witch
    141–3
  sonic engagement with space
    137–41
  see also Black Quantum
    Futurism (BQF)
morality 140, 145, 178, 196, 203,
  207
Morricone, Ennio 101
Morrison, Jim 95–9
Morrison, Toni 54
Moten, Fred 43, 46–7
mother, luminous shadow of
  64–6
Mother Earth, black holes and
  121–3
mother's genitals
  as entrance to the former home
    121
  familiarity of 94
  symbolism 14
The Motionless Present (Moor
  Mother) 133
mourning
  as act of resistance 172
  burden of mourning dirge
    148–52
  politics of 168–9
  role of the female voice 187–8

song for machinic bodies
  162–5
'Mouth Mantra' (Björk) 123
Munford, Rebecca 172
Murch, Walter 114–16
Muse/Muses 48–9, 61–2, 70
music
  dark power of 6–11
  Dionysian propensity to
    channel disruption and
    dissonance 7
  Puritan grudge against 61
musical genius, presentation of as
  male preserve 24
Music and the Ineffable
  (Jankélévitch) 56
music cultures and history,
  marginalization of women
  12, 24, 26–7
music lover's discourse
  about Nico 70
  Barthes 55–6, 59, 63–9
  the concept 55
  dark voice of Death 67–70, 80
  the disconnected dark white
    voice 66–70
  epiphanies on music's
    transformative power
    59–63
  gendered perspective 58
  the hyper-white voice and its
    dark other 76–9
  ice queens 78
  Jankélévitch 56–9
  Nico's cryogenic beauty 71–5
  Nico's mythology 59
  preoccupation with limitations
    of language 53–5
  and the shadow of the mother
    64–6
  white sonic identity 79–81
'Music of the Spheres' 7
mysticism 107, 142, 167, 220

INDEX

narcissism 66, 169–70, 176
Narcissus 67
NASA 107
nature
  disrespect of by corporations
    161
  inaudible frequencies of 148
  sublime phenomena of 157–8
Nazi ideology, Nico's work and 77
Neset, Anne Hilde 26
*New Dark Age: Technology
  and the End of the Future*
  (Bridle) 29
Nicholls, Tracey 138
Nico 28, 59
  cryogenic beauty 71–5
  impermeable iciness 78
  lover's discourse around
    mythology of 59
  reported racism 77
  timing issues 76
  voice 72–3
'The Nightmare' (Fuseli) 154–5
'Night of the Vampire' (Erickson)
  166
Night Passages (Bronfen) 11
*Nightwalking: A Nocturnal History
  of London Chaucer to
  Dickens* (Beaumont) 208–9
nihilism 151
Nochlin, Linda 24
Noli, Jean 51
nostalgia 66, 98, 175, 188, 211
'N'shima' (Xenakis) 179

Odyssey, the (Homer) 9–10
Oedipal perspectives
  black holes 113
  'The End' (The Doors) 95–100
  Oedipus myth 96–7
Old Ideas (Cohen) 31
*O Let Us Howle Some Heavy
  Note* (Winkler) 173–4

Oliveros, Pauline 26, 126
Once upon a Time in the West
  (Leone) 101
openness to the demonic
  Calvi and the becoming
    vulva of the electric guitar
    100–106
  construction of women's voices
    in Western discourses 83–7
  the Devil as technology of
    control 87–90
  mothers and the demonic
    94–100
  sounds of possession 90–4
optimism, tools of 212–16
'Orders from the Dead' (Galás)
  189
original sin 4–5
Otherness 15

paganism 9, 76
Panzéra, Charles 52, 56
Partridge, Christopher 7
patriarchy
  examining with the 'master's
    tools' 215
  and the marginalization of
    women 12
  and misogyny 214, 219
  nightmare weight of 152–5
  unravelling the power of 184,
    204
  virtuosity and 178–9
  and the widow's relationship
    with mourning 169
  the witch as terrorist against
    190
penis envy 13–14
Pentecostalism 91
Petrusich, Amanda 206
phallocentricism 15, 20, 87, 104–5
Pharmakon 28
phenosong 56, 68

252 INDEX

Phillips, Rasheedah 133, 135, 142
Piaf, Edith 28
Pincherle, Marc 178
Plague Mass (Galás) 183, 195, 199
Planned Parenthood 172
Plath, Sylvia 167–8
'Platoon II' (Ciccone Youth) 119
'Playing Wolves and Red Riding Hoods in Black Metal' (Stephanou) 151
Poe, Edgar Allan 85
Pop Cult: Religion and Popular Music (Till) 9
popular music consumers, behavioural types 8
populism, the rise of 213
power, Galás's darkening of virtuosity through engagement with 180–4
Powers of Horror (Kristeva) 195
Pratt, Susanne 147–9, 165
Press, Joy 78, 118, 190
psychoanalysis
    as colonial discipline 14
    links with witch-hunting discourses 95
    and the lost connection with the mother 170
    matricides and silencing of 111
Pythagoras 7

quotas 25

Rabelais, François 121
racism 77, 139–41, 176, 179, 206, 214
Rainy, Ma 92
rebellious mourning 172
rebirth, Björk's 'Black Lake' as 126–31
recordings of the dark 146–7
Reed, Lou 72

Reed, Teresa 91
Reinelt, Janelle 21
reproductive rights 172
'Rethinking Shakespeare's Dark Lady' (Bell) 36–7
Reynolds, Simon 76, 78, 118–19, 190
rhizome, Deleuze and Guattari's notion of 181
Riley, Denise 201
Rivière, Joan 24
Roberts, Andrew 20
rock 9, 23, 26, 103, 151, 165
rock and roll 10
Rodgers, Tara 22
Rolling Stones 118
'The Romantic Song' (Barthes) 69

'Saint of the Pit' (Galás) 190
sanctified motherhood, romanticization of the masculine notion 21
Sant, Gus Van 101
Satanism 9, 150, 196
Savages 28
Schiesari, Juliana 33, 171
Schopenhauer, Arthur 108
Schrei X (Galás) 183, 199–200
Schubert, Franz 55, 65, 67
Schumann, Robert 64–5
scold's bridle 86
Sedgwick, Eve Kosofsky 20
sexism in the music industry 25
sexual violence 139, 152
Shadrack, Jasmine 151
Shah, Nadine 28
Shepard tone, Eve's fall as 6
'The Sights and Sounds of the Passage' (Ayewa) 139
Silva, Denis F. 134
Silverman, Kaja 117
Simone, Nina 28
singing in dark times

INDEX

burden of mourning dirge
148–52
echoes of witches and widows
165–73
femmeheavy sound 173–6
mourning song for machinic
bodies 162–5
patriarchy's effects and 152–5
performing/inhabiting the
witch 155–8
and the toxification of the
American dream 158–62
see also Wolfe, Chelsea
Sinnreich, Aram 113
Siouxsie Sioux 28
Sirens 9–11, 61–3, 85, 191–2, 194,
216
slaveship punk 135
slave ships, conditions on 139–40
slave trade 88–9, 132, 138, 159
Smith, Mark M. 173
Smith, Patti 28
social media 26, 29, 210–11
Solnit, Rebecca 206
Sontag, Susan 77
Soteriou, Dido 189
sound waves, feminized 22
Spanish civil war 48
'spectral femininity' 172
Sprenger, Jakob 89, 155
Stanley, Matt 207
state violence 206
Stephanou, Aspasia 151
Stoever, Jennifer Lynn 79
supernatural, Freud's intended
medicalization 155
'Swing Low, Sweet Chariot'
(Galás) 199
'Synth Altar' (Moor Mother) 134

'Tangled Cartography' (Neset) 26
Tanner, Grafton 211
Taxi Driver (Scorsese) 101

technologies of control, role of the
Devil 87–90
technology, use of in Wolfe's music
159, 162
Temple, Paula 28
temporality 1, 35, 42, 76, 146,
209
Thacker, Eugene 108
theft of the girl's body 5–6
'These Bastard Signs of Fair:
Literary Whiteness in
Shakespeare's Sonnets'
(Hall) 40–1
'This Sex Which Is Not One'
(Irigaray) 86–7
Thompson, Marie 85, 199
threnody 72
Thunberg, Greta 215
Till, Rupert 9
Torre, Manuel 47
torture 38, 87–9, 156, 164, 174,
183, 188–9
'Towards a Feminist Epistemology
of Sound' (Rodgers)
22
Tutti, Cosey Fanni 28

Uldalen, Henrik Aarrestad
154
the uncanny
female genitals and 94
primal 121
types of 94–5
the unconscious 12–14, 47, 86–7,
118, 120
underwater insects, recording the
sound of 147
Un Jour Comme Un Autre
(Globokar) 179
unsounding mothers, black hole
song of 107–43
'Ur-Fascism' (Eco) 29–30
'uterine darkness' 114, 116

the vagina, black holes'
    association with 113
'vagina dentata' theory 113
veiling 10–11
Velvet Underground, the 72, 78
Vena Cava (Galás) 183
vessel
    the body as 91
    wombs and women as 94
'violations of nature' 195
violence against women, aesthetic
    representation of 151
virgin martyr narratives 90–1
virtuosity
    Calvi's appropriation of male-
        reserved guitar virtuoso
        position 101
    darkening of through
        engagement with power
        180–4
    definition and etymology
        177–8
    evolution of the discourse
        178–9
    and the exclusion of women
        181
    and mandatory technique
        184–90
    morality's relationship with
        178
    necessity for performing the
        abject 202–4
    technically articulate vocal
        range 197–202
    see also Galás, Diamanda
The Voice in Cinema (Chion) 116
Voltaire 213
Vulnicura (Björk) 122

'wandering womb' 84–6
wave metaphors, Rodgers's
    analysis 22
Webster, John 174

Whiteley, Sheila 97
whiteness
    colonial alignment with
        freedom 132
    inaudible sonic markers of
        79–81
'Why Are Students Drawn to
    Horror?' (Zaretsky) 212–13
'Why Have There Been No Great
    Female Artists?' (Nochlin)
    24
'Widow' (Plath) 167–8, 172
'Wild Women with Steak Knives'
    (Galás) 183, 191–3
Winderen, Jana 147–8
Winkler, Amanda 173–4
The Wire magazine 59
Wiseman-Trowse, Nathan 118
witchcraft 88–9, 157–8, 164–5,
    167
    connection with nature 158
    and the persecution of the
        female body 88–9
    treatise on 89
    and Wolfe's work 152
witches
    connection with female
        sexuality 157
    echoes of widows and 165–73
    and the historical legacy of
        persecution and torture 156
    performing/inhabiting the
        witch 155–8
    witch-cyborg mutations in
        Galás's work 190–7
Wolfe, Chelsea
    interest in Jung 154
    musical style 149
    technology, articulation of
        sound through 150
Wolves in the Throne Room 150
woman, place in the hierarchical
    chain of beings on earth 2

womb, sound of the 114–15
'wombing', the concept 119
women-only festivals 25
Women's March 205–6, 213
Wong Kar Wai 101
Woolf, Virginia 205, 216–17
The World of the Virtuoso
 (Pincherle) 178

Xenakis, Iannis 179

Yusoff, Kathryn 132

Zaretsky, Robert 212–13
Zorn, John 220n1

Lightning Source UK Ltd.
Milton Keynes UK
UKHW020759021221
394960UK00007B/294